AN

EXALTATION

OF

AN
EXALTATION
OF

SOUPS

THE SOUL-SATISFYING STORY OF SOUP,
AS TOLD IN MORE THAN 100 RECIPES

PATRICIA SOLLEY

THREE RIVERS PRESS • NEW YORK

Published by Three Rivers Press, New York, New York. Member of the Crown Publishing Group, a division of Random House, Inc.
www.crownpublishing.com

Many of the recipes in this work have previously appeared on the author's website: www.soupsong.com.

THREE RIVERS PRESS and the Tugboat design are registered trademarks of Random House, Inc.

Printed in the United States of America

DESIGN BY LAUREN DONG

Library of Congress Cataloging-in-Publication Data

Solley, Patricia.
    An exaltation of soups : the soul-satisfying story of soup, as told in more than 100 recipes / Patricia Solley. — 1st ed.
        p. cm.
    Includes index.
    1. Soups.   2. Cookery, International.   I. Title.
    TX757 .S63 2004
    641.8'13 — dc22   2004012691

ISBN 1-4000-5035-9

10 9 8 7 6 5 4 3 2 1

First Edition

To Mother and Dad

Contents

CHAPTER 20   KWANZAA   338

AN
EXALTATION
OF

INTRODUCTION

To my mind, when you talk about soup, you're talking about so much more than a mostly liquid way of filling your stomach.

Consider the story of Prime Minister Indira Gandhi at dinner in Japan with Prime Minister Zenko Suzuki. Mrs. Gandhi was served a clear soup in a dark bowl painted inside with pictures of the bamboo tree. Only a few vegetables and a single pigeon egg were floated in the broth, leaving the bowl's design visible. Mr. Suzuki asked her what she thought of the presentation. Instantly Mrs. Gandhi replied: "To my eyes, it [the egg] is a full moon shining over a dark forest on a clear night." Prime Minister Suzuki sat up straight, completely amazed at her spontaneous and accurate reply.

I like this story a lot because it captures in one fell swoop all the layers of purpose held in a bowl of soup: its edibility, yes, but also its intrinsic beauty, its identification with specific cultures, its universality, and its resonance on the most basic levels.

After all, what is the broth but salt and water—the sea, the source of all life? What are the ingredients in the soup but fauna and flora that man, oh so painfully and over millennia, domesticated, tamed, made his own, and sacrificed as food for his own survival? The soup served by Suzuki was quintessentially Japanese, symbolizing that country's cultural aesthetic and Buddhist values, and at the same time universal, so that it could evoke Mrs. Gandhi's intuitive reaction.

Look at a bowl of soup and see the evolution of foods created in remote locations over thousands and thousands of years, made into recipes passed from hand to hand, transported on the backs of Indian, Asian, and Arab traders, Roman soldiers, and European explorers, all the way to your supermarket.

Eat a bowl of soup and savor mouthfuls of human resolve since Neolithic times to bring warmth, health, and richness into the lives of their family members, their tribe, their community, their culture.

Consider a bowl of soup from any culture, and think how it came to reflect that specific people, their times of celebration, their passages of life, their most intimate life experiences.

That's what *An Exaltation of Soups* is all about. In these pages are the stories and recipes of both soups and soup traditions that most profoundly connect people all over the world. I began the collection many years ago out of sheer love of food and, yes, sheer love of research, too. An initial batch of interesting soup recipes evolved into a loose-leaf cookbook on top of my refrigerator, and this grew thick with notes and glosses as I stumbled over stories and histories and quotes that illustrated the soups and their ingredients. Over time, this raggy book seemed to take on a life of its own, naturally shaping itself into storied recipes that gave insight into the cultures from which they sprang. And when I translated it in 1997 into an ordered website at www.soupsong.com, the floodgates opened: readers from around the world commented on, corrected, refined, and authenticated my materials. It's been a long, rewarding journey for me, really an exaltation of good food, good friends, warmth, and insight — an exaltation of soup. I hope you find in this book the long-lost recipe of the soup your great-great-grandmother used to make to celebrate a family wedding, and I hope you find a wealth of other recipes that will inspire you to share warmth, food, and fellowship with all the people in your life.

PART I

SOUP

BASICS

"AMAZING SOUP"

Amazing soup! (how sweet the taste!)
That fill'd a wretch like me!
I once did hunger, now am sate;
Did thirst, am now replete.

'Twas soup that filled my heart with pain
And soup that pain reliev'd;
How precious did that soup appear,
When I was lost and grieved.

Thro' many sauces, salads and sweets,
I have already bent;
'Tis soup that gratified my need,
And soup that does content.

The Lord has promis'd broth to me,
His word my hope secures;
He will my consommé provide,
As long as life endures.

Yes, when this meat and bone shall fail,
And mortal life shall cease;
I shall possess, within the veil,
Some vichysoisse and peace.

This earth shall soon dissolve like snow,
The sun forbear to shine;
But borscht, which call'd me here below,
Will be for ever mine.

—JERRY NEWMAN, *contemporary Canadian poet and novelist*

1

THE ORIGINS AND HISTORY
OF SOUP

STONE AGE PEOPLE created soup before they had a pot to cook it in, a bowl to serve it in, or a gourd to drink it from.

In fact, it's not completely clear who first stumbled onto the concept of soup — anthropologists disagree, depending on their interpretation of existing artifacts. Some say it was one of the *Homo sapiens* gang, sometime after 80,000 B.C.E. — either the Neanderthals or the Cro-Magnons who ultimately did those poor Neanderthals in. Others argue for a later generation — Neolithic man, around 10,000 B.C.E.

I kind of like the Neanderthal theory. It was a particularly tough and dangerous world back then. These hunter-gatherers were stuck in the last blast of an Ice Age that killed off much of their food and many species. It was every man for himself as the Neanderthals ran fearfully from — and ran hungrily after — woolly mammoths, saber-toothed tigers, wolves, and other hominids. And yet Neanderthal skeletons have been found in France with teeth worn down below gum level — and deeply crippled skeletons have been found, too. This means that some older or sickly prehistoric men and women were kept alive only through the compassion of their communities and the brilliance of someone who could create hot and soupy food alternatives to incredibly cold indigestible plants and tough meat.

I try to put myself under the toque of that Stone Age Julia Child. I imagine him or her using bark to dip and carry water . . . putting food in the water and noticing it soften or swell . . . marking how plants and berries, meat and marrow chunks would infuse the

HERODOTUS ON SCYTHIANS BOILING SOUP IN ANIMAL SKINS, CIRCA 440 B.C.E.

If they do not happen to possess a cauldron, they make the animal's paunch hold the flesh, and pouring in at the same time a little water, lay the bones under and light them. The bones burn beautifully; and the paunch easily contains all the flesh when it is stript from the bones, so that by this plan your ox is made to boil himself, and other victims also to do the like.

—HERODOTUS, *fifth-century B.C.E. Greek historian,* BOOK IV, THE HISTORIES

water with color and flavor. I imagine him or her getting the idea of warming the broth from the warm mother's milk that kept little Neanderthal babies happy.

Soup! It's an unbelievable achievement—a matter of thought overreaching what was technologically possible at the time. In the words of anthropologist Sally McBrearty: "The earliest *Homo sapiens* probably had the cognitive capability to invent Sputnik . . . but didn't yet have the history of invention or a need for those things." But soup? Yes, he needed soup. He needed soup, so he imagined soup. He imagined soup, and he brought it into being, despite his lack of pots to cook it in.

In fact, soup turned out to be a transforming concept that changed early man's relationship to nature, increased his life choices, and created completely new needs and desires. One eon he's a vegetarian in the garden of Eden, the next he's scavenging or hunting raw flesh and sucking bone marrow . . . then, almost suddenly, he's figured out an unbelievably complex process with tools to produce a hot meal. It's a gastronomic miracle, and it's art: multiple colors, multiple textures, multiple flavors—something created by man that had never existed before in the history of the world.

But how on earth could early man in 10,000 B.C.E., at the latest, have boiled things . . . without the pottery that he finally created in 6000 B.C.E. and the cauldrons that followed in 3600 B.C.E.?

HOW CAN YOU MAKE SOUP WITHOUT POTS?

I propose two theories.

First, prehistoric man might have boiled animals in their skins. He could have flayed his prey, suspending the skin on forked sticks, filling the bag with water and food, and lighting a fire underneath. The skin would not catch fire because it would be cooked by the boiling water on the inside (but don't try this trick at home). In fact, this technique has been used by many cultures in recorded history, from Scythians in the fifth century B.C.E. to Irish and Scots in the sixteenth century.

Second, our ancestors might have used the "hot stone" method. First you dig a hole or find one, and fill it with water. Then you build a fire close by and heat stones in it. Then, one by one, and v-e-r-y carefully, you transfer the stones to the water until it boils. And it will. Stones can be heated to a temperature of 1,300 degrees Fahrenheit in a well-laid hearth. How do I know that? Because in 1954, archeologist Michael J. O'Kelly proved it in experiments with his students at primeval Irish sites: "They used the hearths to heat stones, used a dampened wooden shovel to dump them in the water, brought the water to a boil, and simmered a 10-pound leg of mutton for 3 hours 40 minutes by adding stones every few minutes.... Then they ate the results: 'excellently cooked and most tasty.' "*

What Went into the Earliest Soups?

After those first catch-as-catch-can soups of wild plants and animals, and after vast fields of grain sprang up in Europe and Asia, it turned out to be grains and beans — early man's first agricultural triumphs in Neolithic times — that went into soup. By 7000 B.C.E., Emmer wheat had been domesticated in Turkey, and barley, millet, and beans in Greece. By 5000 B.C.E., rice was being cultivated in China. These were the stuff of early soups. And, of course, these remain our most revered modern comfort foods. Read on.

Grains cooked in broth continue to be lovingly prepared in most cultures: porridges and gruels from ground wheat; couscous soups and farina soups; barley soups and *tsampas;* oatmeal soups and rice congee. Imagine the astonished look on ancient man's face when he first witnessed the miracle of chemistry — when heating

*M. J. O'Kelly, "Excavations and Experiments in Early Irish Cooking-Places," *Journal of the Royal Society of Antiquities in Ireland* (1954), 84, 105–55.

"THE TOLLUND MAN"

... Some day I will go to
    Aarhus
To see his peat-brown head,
The mild pods of his eye-lids,
His pointed skin cap.

In the flat country near by
Where they dug him out,
His last gruel of winter seeds
Caked in his stomach. ...

Out here in Jutland
In the old man-killing
    parishes
I will feel lost,
Unhappy and at home.

—SEAMUS HEANEY, contemporary
Irish poet

caused these cereal grains to release starch granules into the broth and make it thick.

Bean/pea soup was in vogue long before Esau sold his birthright for it (that biblical "mess of pottage" was lentil soup), and it is an established part of every cuisine in the world without exception—every one! From *feijoada* in Brazil, to *huku ne dovi* in Zimbabwe, to *misoshiru* in Japan, and everything in between.

And then there's the ancient variation of ground wheat made into a bread that turns so hard without today's modern preservatives that it can be made edible again only by pouring boiling broth over it. I know this bread from the years I spent living in Morocco: that marvelous freshly baked *kisra*—a thick Frisbee of chewy bread—would turn to stone in twenty-four hours. This is called "sop" when dunked in hot liquid and is the origin of our words soup, *soupe, sup, sopa, soppe, zuppe, shorba, çorbasi.* This combination is the basis of Portuguese *sopa secos* and *asordas;* Arabic *shorbas;* Spanish garlic soup; French panades, onion soup, and *garbure;* Italian *aquacotta;* Danish *ollebrod,* Estonian *leivasupp,* and French *l'aïgo boulido.* You'll find an Egyptian *fatta* soup on page 248 whose very name means to break crisped pita bread into food.

So there you have it. This part of our everyday cuisine, this soup that we take so much for granted, began life as a miracle of intellection, kept humankind alive through extremes of privation over the ages, and now serves to bind our common humanity, nurse our ills, and mark life's passages.

When I ponder soup, I think of ancient Tollund Man, dug out of a Danish peat bog in the 1950s and perfectly preserved. He'd been ritually sacrificed to the gods—strangled—but first given a fine last meal, still intact in his stomach. What was it? You know what it was: it was soup. A thick soup of grain and weed seeds ground in a hand mill and boiled.

PROVERBIALLY SOUP

IN THE SOUP

"Oh, you are SO full of soup!"

"No, not at all. Alas, after what I did last night, with all the best intentions, I'm actually in the soup."

"Ah, and crying in your soup, no doubt. What happened?"

"The usual: too many cooks spoiled the broth."

"Oh right, it's always so easy to blame others for your own mistakes: the chicken always blames the soup pot for its tragic end."

"I protest! You aren't seeing both sides. Remember, the bowl cannot be warmer than the soup."

"Protest away, but I still say that whatever is put in the soup kettle comes out on the spoon."

"You are so hard-hearted. And yet, I admit that it's been hard eating all this bad soup with a big spoon."

"Well, you know what they say, 'a spoon does not know the taste of soup, nor a learned fool the taste of wisdom.' "

"Ouch, give me a break, doll. And yet I've learned my lesson: He who once burns his mouth, always blows the soup."

Phew. Ten soup proverbs from as many different countries. Proverbs sure are funny things. You wouldn't believe the ink exhausted by scholars of proverbs (yes, they do exist and are called paremiologists) just trying to define the damn things:

"Old gems of generationally tested wisdom"

"The smallest genre of verbal folklore"

"The wit of one; the wisdom of many"

"A condensed allegory"

"The edged tools of speech"

Paremiologically speaking, here's my favorite, from Bartlett Jere Whiting's *The Nature of the Proverb:* "A proverb is an expression which, owing its birth to the people, testifies to its origin in form and phrase. It expresses what is apparently a fundamental truth— that is, a truism—in homely language, often adorned, however, with alliterations and rhyme. It is usually short, but need not be; it is usually true, but need not be. Some proverbs have both a literal meaning and a figurative meaning, either of which makes perfect sense; but more often they have but one of the two."

In short, there's a lot of soup in them thar proverbs and a lot of proverbs about soup, and I think there's good reason why.

Let me take you back in the history of the world. It wasn't always like it is now, people hunched in front of computers munching on take-out pizzas and creating high-tech proverbs about "garbage in, garbage out." Stay with me here.

Once upon a time, people came home to a hearth and a cooking pot and made conversation in flickering firelight about the events of the day. Young people would speak up naively or impatiently, "I can't *believe* the corn hasn't started sprouting!" Older folks would philosophically gaze into the simmering dinner, thinking about the unsprouting corn and their own hunger, and opine, "A watched pot never boils." Bingo, proverb.

It's nice to think about, isn't it—that time of apparently slower natural rhythms? When was the last time you gathered things from the garden, built a fire, brought water to a boil, and, hungry and expectant, thought about how these processes spoke to the larger questions that tug at the heartstrings of mankind? There is something beautiful about rituals building metaphors for life and finding room for reflection.

As Mr. Whiting said, though, some proverbs are just talking about that liquid stuff in a bowl, pure and simple:

"Eat soup first and eat it last, and live till a hundred years
    be passed." (FRANCE)

"To make a good soup, the pot must only simmer or
    'smile.'" (FRANCE)

"A good soup attracts seats." (GHANA)

"A house without soup is an unlucky house." (RUSSIA)

"Of soup and love, the first is best." (SPAIN)

"Troubles are easier to take with soup than without."
    (YIDDISH)

"Good broth will resurrect the dead." (SOUTH AMERICA)

"Broth to a cook is voice to a singer." (CHINA)

Other proverbs are still about soup pure and simple, but they imply other things, too:

> "A soup that tastes good by licking must taste better by eating." (AFRICAN ANNANG TRIBE)

> "Plenty fish or meat does not spoil the soup." (GHANA)

> "Cheap meat never makes good soup." (AZERBAIJAN)

> "If there are two cooks in one house, the soup is either too salty or too cold." (IRAN)

> "The best soup is made of old meat." (FRANCE)

> "Ye who buy cheap meat will regret when you taste its broth." (SYRIA)

> "One cannot make soup out of beauty." (ESTONIA)

> "Too many peas spoil the soup." (UNITED STATES)

> "He who stirs the soup pot eats first." (UNITED STATES)

> "If they can't eat the soup, they can spit in it." (HAITI)

> "The more eggs, the thicker the soup." (BRAZIL)

> "Soup is cooked hotter than it's eaten." (GERMANY)

And then there are those proverbs that, with a leap of imagination, use the image of soup to express a truth that really has nothing to do with soup at all:

> "A rat's droppings can spoil a whole cauldron of soup." (CHINA)

> "The chicken in the coop has grain, but the soup pot is near; the wild crane has none, but its world is vast." (CHINA)

> "The disobedient chicken obeys in a pot of soup." (BENIN)

> "It is only the bones that rattle in the pot." (LEBANON)

"If a man makes soup of his tears, ask him not for broth." (AFRICA)

"Between the hand and mouth, the soup is lost." (ITALY)

"The broth is cooking, and now we have to act as one." (BEDOUIN)

"When it rains soup, the poor man has no spoon." (SWEDEN)

"Better no spoon than no soup." (GERMANY)

"Boil stones in butter and the broth will be good." (SCOTLAND)

"In your neighbor's soup, there is always one fatty morsel." (IRAN)

"From all the fish in the pot, you can only make one soup." (MADAGASCAR)

And remember the "lesson learned" (GERMANY) about the burned mouth blowing soup in the opening story? Here are more of the same:

"One who has been burned by the soup begins to blow on the yogurt." (SAUDI ARABIA)

"Having learned his lesson with hot soup, he blows cold fish salad." (JAPAN)

"Who has been scalded with hot soup blows on cold water." (RUSSIA)

"He who burnt himself with soup blows also in the sour milk." (ROMANIA)

So, all around the world, everyday language for a variety of circumstances is peppered with proverbs, and often these proverbs refer to food . . . and soup. Is it any wonder, then, that food — and soup in particular — is a major operative in the conventional wisdom of proverbs, the very recipes of culture?

3

SOUP REFLECTIONS

SOUP AS HUMOR

Well, dinner would have been splendid if the wine had been as cold as the soup, the beef as rare as the service, the brandy as old as the fish, and the maid as willing as the Duchess.

—WINSTON CHURCHILL, *twentieth-century British statesman*

It looks like a tortoiseshell cat having a fit in a bowl of tomato soup.

—MARK TWAIN, *nineteenth-century American humorist, about a J. M. W. Turner landscape painting*

Sex is like eating a meal. Sometimes you just want a bowl of soup, and other times you want the three-course meal.

—ELIZABETH HUSS, *contemporary American sex therapist*

Marriage is the meal where soup is better than the dessert.

—AUSTIN O'MALLEY, *early-twentieth-century American medical writer*

*Memories are like mulligatawny soup in a cheap restaurant.
It's best not to stir them.*

—P. G. WODEHOUSE, *twentieth-century English humorist*

SOUP AS A CAUSE OF PLEASURE AND GOODNESS

*Whenever I sit with a bowl of soup before me, listening to the
murmur that penetrates like the distant song of an insect, lost
in contemplation of the flavors to come, I feel as if I were
being drawn into a trance.*

—JUNICHIRO TANIZAKI, *twentieth-century Japanese novelist,*
In Praise of Shadows

*I'm now painting with all the élan of a Marseillais eating soup,
which won't surprise you when I tell you I'm painting large
sunflowers.*

—VINCENT VAN GOGH, *nineteenth-century Dutch artist,*
writing to his brother Theo in 1888

*Do you have a kinder, more adaptable friend in the food
world than soup? Who soothes you when you are ill? Who refuses to leave you when you are impoverished and stretches its
resources to give you a hearty sustenance and cheer? Who
warms you in the winter and cools you in the summer? Yet
who also is capable of doing honor to your richest table and
impressing your most demanding guests? . . . Soup does its
loyal best, no matter what undignified conditions are imposed
upon it. You don't catch steak hanging around when you're
poor and sick, do you?*

—MISS MANNERS (JUDITH MARTIN), *contemporary American
etiquette columnist*

What I love about cooking is that after a hard day, there is something comforting about the fact that if you melt butter and add flour and then hot stock, it will get thick! It's a sure thing! It's a sure thing in a world where nothing is sure; it has a mathematical certainty in a world where those of us who long for some kind of certainty are forced to settle for cross-word puzzles.

—NORA EPHRON, *contemporary American food writer*

SOUP AS A MEANS OF SURVIVAL

An army travels on its stomach. Soup makes the soldier.

—NAPOLÉON BONAPARTE, *nineteenth-century French emperor*

When we were growing up, we were so poor that our heritage was the only thing we had. Mama would say, "Kids, pour more water in the soup. Better days are coming."

—ASHLEY JUDD, *contemporary American actress*

When I see a shipwreck, I like to know what caused the disaster . . . [I learned] nothing but the glow that wrapped her face when the soup came. That's the story.

—O. HENRY (WILLIAM SYDNEY PORTER), *nineteenth-century American short story writer, about bringing a homeless woman home to dinner*

SOUPS AS AN AID IN ECONOMY

Of Soups: no good housewife has any pretensions to rational economy who boils animal food without converting the broth into some sort of soup.

—MARGARET HUNTINGDON HOOKER,
The Gentlewoman's Housewifery, *1896*

SOUP ETIQUETTE

It is usual to commence with soup, which never refuse. . . . When all are seated, send a plate of soup to every one. Do not ask anyone if they will be helped, as everyone takes it, of course.

—AN AMERICAN LADY, True Politeness, *1853*

Good manners: The noise you don't make when you're eating soup.

—BENNETT CERF, *twentieth-century American humorist*

In taking soup, it is necessary to avoid lifting too much in the spoon, or filling the mouth so full as to stop the breath.

—ST. JOHN THE BAPTIST DE LA SALLE, *French educator,*
The Rules of Christian Manners and Civility, *1695*

Gentlemen do not take soup at luncheon.

—LORD CURZON, *nineteenth-century British statesman*

Never blow your soup if it is too hot, but wait until it cools. Never raise your plate to your lips, but eat it with a spoon.

—C. B. HARTLEY, The Gentlemen's Book of Etiquette, *1873*

I discovered that dinners follow the order of creation — fish first, then entrées, then joints, lastly the apple as dessert. The soup is chaos.

—SYLVIA TOWNSEND WARNER, *twentieth-century English writer*

SOUP PHILOSOPHY

What an awful thing life is. It's like soup with lots of hairs floating on the surface. You have to eat it nevertheless.

—GUSTAVE FLAUBERT, *nineteenth-century French writer*

Food probably has a very great influence on the condition of men. . . . Who knows if a well-prepared soup was not responsible for the pneumatic pump or a poor one for a war?

—G. C. LICHTENBERG, *eighteenth-century German physicist/ philosopher,* Aphorism 14

A first-rate soup is more creative than a second rate painting.

—ABRAHAM MASLOW, *twentieth-century American psychologist*

I believe I once considerably scandalized her by declaring that clear soup was a more important factor in life than a clear conscience.

—SAKI (H. H. MUNRO), The Blind Spot, *1914*

There are two types of people in this world: shlemiehls and shlimazls. A shlemiehl is the person who always spills soup, and a shlimazl is the person he spills it on. I'm the shlemiehl and you're the shlimazl.

—JEWISH BERNSTEIN *talking to archconservative Archie Bunker on the 1970s U.S. sitcom* All in the Family

An idealist is one who, on noticing that a rose smells better than a cabbage, concludes that it will also make better soup.

—H. L. MENCKEN, *American journalist/critic,* Chrestomathy, *1949*

Soup and fish explain half the emotions of life.

—SYDNEY SMITH, *nineteenth-century English clergyman and wit*

Whoever tells a lie cannot be pure in heart — and only the pure in heart can make good soup.

—LUDWIG VAN BEETHOVEN, *German composer, in a letter to Mme. Streicher in 1817*

4

STOCKS AND FOUNDATIONS

HOMEMADE STOCKS MAKE a difference. And it's nice to use up those vegetable scraps, those chicken backs, those choking fish bones that drive the kids crazy, by boiling them. The smell of roasting veal, beef, even lamb bones is divine, and when these are simmered into broth with fragrant roots and herbs, they fill the house with memories of meals and shared times that make the most chaotic household feel the comfort of easier, slower days.

But professional soup bases, bouillon cubes, bags of powdered stock, concentrates, and canned stocks work, too—and produce wonderful soups that are well flavored and belie hours of kitchen work that never took place. No one would quarrel with the results. I swear.

I will give you the choice throughout this book whenever possible, although some traditional recipes insist on being started from scratch. By all means, when you are pressed for time, take the excellent shortcuts that are offered on the shelves of your local market. But when you've got the time and the place and are in the mood, I hope you'll dig into the recipes below to get back in touch with your primordial self. Please note that you may halve or double these stock recipes according to your needs and achieve the same quality result.

A COUPLE OF CAUTIONS ON COMMERCIAL STOCK PREPARATIONS

• Because canned and cube stocks are usually saltier than homemade stocks, be sure to taste your soup before you season it—and reduce salt additions accordingly.

• As a matter of interest to weight watchers, canned chicken broth has twice as many calories as canned beef broth.

A FEW DEFINITIONS

• *Stock* is the liquid extracted from foods slowly cooked in water and/or wine and used as a foundation for soup and other things. In olden days, it was the "never-ending" broth that was kept going year-round in the back of farmhouse fires, cooked in large iron kettles, with little bits of this and little bits of that meat and vegetable scraps added just about every day.

• *Broth* is an English term for the liquid extracted from meat cooked slowly with water, which is then concentrated and used either as a foundation for soup or as a simple soup itself (pretty much like the French *bouillon* and the Italian *brodo*).

• *Consommé* is a double-strength stock "finished" into a clear soup.

• *Double consommé* is a consommé that has been clarified (see page 31 for instructions). When the stock is boiled down further, it becomes, progressively, a *flavoring*, an *essence*, and a *glaze*.

TIP: If you freeze stock in ice cube trays, you can pop the cubes into plastic bags and use as much or as little as you want at any time.

COOLING STOCK

Always cool stock uncovered. If you cover it, you'll delay the cooling process and end up with cloudy stock.

FISH STOCK

Makes 8 cups

> *2 medium onions, chopped*
> *2 carrots, trimmed, scrubbed, and chopped*
> *2 celery stalks with leaves, chopped*
> *8 to 10 cups cold water*
> *Twist of lemon peel*
> *Salt and white pepper to taste*
> *1 bay leaf*
> *2 to 3 pounds of fish trimmings, heads, and bones, even shrimp shells*
> *Up to 1 cup white wine (optional)*

TO PREPARE

Prep the ingredients as directed in the recipe list.

TO COOK

1. In a large soup pot, bring all the ingredients to a boil over medium heat, skimming as necessary. Partially cover and cook over medium heat for 20 to 30 minutes.

2. Strain the stock, discarding the solids. If you're not going to use the stock immediately, cool it down quickly, uncovered, and then either refrigerate it or freeze it for later use.

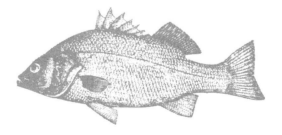

VEGETABLE STOCK
Makes 8 cups

> *5 carrots, trimmed, scrubbed, and chopped*
> *2 celery stalks with leaves, chopped*
> *2 medium onions, chopped*
> *1 garlic head, unpeeled and cut in half widthwise*
> *Potato peelings (wash potatoes before peeling)*
> *1 turnip, peeled and sliced*
> *Any wilted veggies in the fridge, chopped, avoiding ones that are*
> *   strongly flavored (like cabbage) or strongly colored (like beets)*
> *1 bay leaf*
> *Handful of fresh parsley*
> *1 teaspoon each salt and peppercorns, plus additional salt to taste*
> *12 cups (3 quarts) water*

To Prepare
Prep the ingredients as directed in the recipe list.

To Cook
1. In a large soup pot, bring all the ingredients to a boil over medium high heat, then reduce the heat to low and cook gently, uncovered, for 45 minutes to 1 hour.

2. Strain the stock, discarding the solids. Season with salt. If you're not going to use the stock immediately, cool it down quickly, uncovered, and then either refrigerate it or freeze it for later use.

Note: If you want darker broth, brown the vegetables in 2 tablespoons of oil for 10 to 15 minutes over medium heat, then add the water and herbs and bring to a boil, scraping up any dark bits from the bottom of the pan. Cook over medium heat for 45 minutes, uncovered, then strain, discarding the solids.

Note: If you want more fragrance and complexity in the stock, add any combination of fresh tomatoes, fennel, mushrooms, or other aromatic vegetables to the browning process, then cook and strain as above.

CHICKEN STOCK

Makes 8 cups

> 4 to 5 pounds chicken parts — backs, wings, necks, feet (with the nails clipped off)
> 2 medium onions, peeled and chopped
> 2 garlic cloves, crushed
> 1 carrot, trimmed and scrubbed
> 2 tablespoons fresh parsley
> 2 bay leaves
> 2 teaspoons salt
> 1 teaspoon white peppercorns
> 12 cups (3 quarts) cold water

TO PREPARE

Prep the ingredients as directed in the recipe list.

TO COOK

1. Place all the ingredients in a large soup pot and pour in the water — the water should cover them by a minimum of 2 inches. Bring to a boil slowly over medium heat, then reduce the heat to low and simmer, covered, for 2 hours.

2. Remove the cover and simmer for at least another hour.

3. Strain the stock, discarding the solids. If you're not going to use the stock immediately, cool it down quickly, uncovered, and then either refrigerate it or freeze it for later use, leaving the chicken fat on top to seal for freshness.

NOTE: For an entirely different "essence" of chicken, see the recipe for Chicken Soup with Ginger or Sesame Oil, on page 37.

VEAL STOCK

Makes 8 cups

> 4 pounds veal knuckles, or 3 pounds veal knuckles and 1
>   pound boneless beef
> 16 cups (4 quarts) cold water
> 8 white peppercorns
> 1 bay leaf
> 1 teaspoon dried thyme
> 6 whole cloves
> 6 stems fresh parsley
> 1 medium onion, chopped
> 3 celery stalks with leaves, chopped
> 1 carrot, trimmed, scrubbed, and chopped

TO PREPARE

Prep the ingredients as directed in the recipe list.

TO COOK

1. In a large soup pot, bring all the ingredients to a boil over medium heat, then reduce the heat to low and simmer, uncovered, for 2½ to 3 hours, or until the stock is reduced by half.

2. Strain the stock, discarding the solids. If you're not going to use the stock immediately, cool it down quickly, uncovered, and then either refrigerate it or freeze it for later use.

BEEF STOCK

Makes 8 cups

> *4 pounds beef bones, cracked by a butcher so the goodness of*
>   *the marrow can be easily extracted*
> *2 pounds beef soup bones*
> *Any leftover beef or beef fat*
> *12 cups (3 quarts) cold water*
> *2 carrots, trimmed and scrubbed*
> *4 medium onions, quartered*
> *Handful of fresh parsley sprigs*
> *1 parsnip, scrubbed and trimmed*
> *2 garlic cloves, crushed*
> *2 bay leaves*
> *1½ teaspoons salt*
> *1 teaspoon black peppercorns*

TO PREPARE

Prep the ingredients as directed in the recipe list.

TO COOK

1. In a 450°F. oven, roast the bones and any meat in a large roasting pan for 1 hour. Put all the bones in a large soup pot, then pour 1 cup water into the roasting pan and scrape up any browned bits, then pour that liquid into the pot.

2. Add the remaining ingredients, then fill the pot with the remaining water, so it is at least 2 inches over the ingredients. Bring to a simmer slowly over medium heat, skimming as needed. Don't let the stock come to a hard boil or it will cloud.

3. Cover and let simmer for 2 hours, then remove the cover and simmer for at least 2 more hours, skimming and adding water as needed.

4. Strain the stock, discarding the solids and rescuing any meat bits for another use. If you're not going to use the stock immediately, cool it down quickly, uncovered, and then either refrigerate it or freeze it for later use, leaving the fat on top to seal the stock for freshness.

HUNGARIAN SMOKED MEAT STOCK

Makes 8 cups

THIS STOCK IS a classic base for traditional Hungarian and other central European soups, and it is marvelous to use as a smoky, aromatic addition to any recipe for plain bean or pea soups.

> *10 ounces smoked ham shank or smoked ribs*
> *8 cups (2 quarts) cold water*

TO PREPARE

In advance of cooking: soak the smoked meat in cold water for at least 2 hours, changing the water several times to remove impurities.

TO COOK

1. Place the meat in a soup pot and cover with the cold water. Bring to a boil over medium heat, then reduce the heat to low and simmer for at least 30 minutes. Turn off the heat and let the meat cool in the stock.

2. Strain the stock, discarding the solids. If you're not going to use the stock immediately, cool it down quickly, uncovered, and then either refrigerate it or freeze it for later use. Cut the meat off the bones for soup or another use, discarding the bones.

WHAT ON EARTH IS *DASHI*?

Like nothing else in the world, that's what. It's a heady combination of bonito (*katsuobushi*) fish and dried kelp, but not just fresh bonito and kelp, mind you. Oh, no: the bonito is caught, filleted, simmered, dry-smoked for some two weeks in fragrant wooden chambers, dried in the sun, and cured with mold for six weeks—at which point it looks just like chunks of wood and is ready to go. Likewise, the kelp (or *konbu*, chock full of natural, non-headachy monosodium glutamate) is harvested from *konbu* boats with long forked poles, then spread out on shore to dry—first in the sun, then in drying chambers, at which point they are folded, bundled, and sent to market. All the soup maker needs to do is shave pieces of the bonito block with a carpenter's plane (honest! that, or buy it already shaved), wipe down the *konbu*, briefly simmer one after the other in the same water, voilà: perfect *dashi*, truly the *fond de cuisine* of Japanese kitchens.

JAPANESE SOUP STOCK
DASHI
Makes 8 cups

> 8-inch square of konbu (*dried kelp*), *sponged clean and cut
>   into a* $1/2$-*inch fringe*
> $10^{1/2}$ *cups* ($2^{1/2}$ *quarts*) *cold water*
> 1 *cup* katsuobushi (*dried bonito*), *flaked*

TO PREPARE
Prep the ingredients as directed in the recipe list.

TO COOK
1. Place the kelp and cold water in a soup pot and bring just to a boil over medium heat. Remove the kelp (you can reserve it for one more stock-making session).

2. Return the broth to a boil over medium heat, stir in the bonito, and immediately remove from the heat. Let it sit for 2 to 3 minutes, then strain (also reserving the bonito for one more round) and use as needed. The stock will keep for a few days in the refrigerator.

TIP: Many Asian markets sell *dashi* stock granules (*hon-dashi*).

CONCENTRATED STOCKS

Stock is heavy, it spills, it spoils, it's cumbersome to store, and it's not easy to carry around if you're on the road. Thus the evolution of today's bouillon cubes and soup bases. But the history of concentrated stocks is ancient, "portable soup" being a mainstay of nomadic cultures nearly a thousand years earlier. A fourteenth-century Italian chronicler, in fact, described how, in medieval times, the Magyar warriors who swept into Europe on horseback from the Urals made their instant soup: they'd boil heavily salted beef in huge kettles until it fell off the bone, then cut it into small pieces, dry it in the sun or in an oven, grind it to a powder, and carry it in bags so that, on a campaign, all they had to do was boil up some water to make a proper soup. A recipe from the eighteenth century follows on the next page.

THE HISTORY OF CONCENTRATED STOCK

It's downright romantic. Count Rumford (1753–1814), an American-born physicist, inventor, and all-around dashing character, is credited with popularizing "portable soup" while in the service of the Duke of Bavaria. Using the highest technology of the time, he mass-produced a fully nutritious, solidified stock of bones, inexpensive meat by-products, and other ingredients; fed the Duke's army with it; then transferred his findings to the private sector—effectively inventing the concept of municipal soup kitchens. The sensation this concentrate caused is captured in the 1773 journals of Scotsman James Boswell, best known as literary groupie to Samuel Johnson: "A page of my Journal is like a cake of portable soup. A little may be diffused into a considerable portion."

—*Journal of a Tour to the Hebrides, September 13, 1773*

"PORTABLE" SOUP

To make a Veal Glue, or Cake Soup to be carried in the Pocket, take a Leg of Veal, strip it of the Skin and the Fat, then take all the muscular or fleshy Parts from the Bones; boil this Flesh gently in such a Quantity of Water, and so long a Time, till the Liquor will make a strong Jelly when it is cold: This you may try by taking out a small Spoonful now and then, and letting it cool.

Here it is to be supposed, that though it will jelly presently in small Quantities, yet all the Juice of the Meat may not be extracted; however, when you find it very strong, strain the Liquor through a Sieve, and let it settle; then provide a large Stew-pan, with Water, and some China Cups, or glazed Earthenware; fill these Cups with Jelly taken clear from the Settling, and set them in a Stew-pan of Water, and let the Water boil gently till the Jelly becomes as thick as Glue; after which, let them stand to cool, and then turn out the Glue upon a piece of new Flannel, which will draw out the Moisture; turn them once in six or eight Hours, and put them upon a fresh Flannel, and so continue to do till they are quite dry, and keep it in a dry warm Place: This will harden so much, that it will be stiff and hard as Glue in a little Time, and may be carried in the Pocket without Inconvenience.

You are to use this by boiling about a Pint of Water, and pouring it upon a Piece of the Glue or Cake, about the Bigness of a small walnut, and stirring it with a Spoon till the cake dissolves, which will make a very strong good Broth. As for the seasoning part, every one may add Pepper and Salt as they like it, for there must be nothing of that Kind put among the Veal when you make the Glue, for any Thing of that sort would make it moldy.... So may a Dish of good Soup be made without Trouble, only allowing the Proportion of Cake Gravy answering to the abovelaid Direction: Or if Gravy be wanted for Sauce, double the Quantity may be used that is prescribed for Broth or Soup.

—*The Lady's Companion, 1753*

CLARIFYING STOCK

Nothing is more elegant than a crystal-clear hot broth or cold jellied stock that shows off the design of an exquisite porcelain bowl, such as the jellied consommé recipe on page 100. Clarified stock, in fact, is the very soul of soups served in classic French cuisine—and it is easy to accomplish, if time-consuming.

> *Homemade stock at room temperature (if your stock is hot, cool it down with ice cubes)*
> *1 egg white, slightly beaten, and 1 crumpled eggshell per 4 cups of stock*

TO PREPARE

Prep the ingredients as directed in the recipe list.

TO COOK

1. Pour the stock into a large soup pot and stir in the egg whites and eggshells. Put the pot over very low heat and very slowly, without stirring, bring the mixture just to a simmer. As the sediments coagulate with the egg whites, a thick scum will rise to the surface of the liquid. Don't succumb to the temptation of skimming the pot. Just push the scum aside so you can keep an eye on the simmer of the stock—anything close to a boil will disturb the clarifying process.

2. Simmer for 10 to 15 minutes, then carefully remove the pot from the heat and let stand for anywhere from 10 minutes to 1 hour.

3. When you are ready to collect the stock, just push the scum aside and ladle the stock through a sieve lined with several layers of cheesecloth that have been dipped in hot water and wrung out.

4. If you're not going to use the stock immediately, cool it down quickly, uncovered, and then either refrigerate it or freeze it for later use.

ENRICO CARUSO SINGS FOR HIS SOUP

In a newspaper interview, the world-famous operatic tenor Enrico Caruso recounted the following story about his life at age twenty-one in 1894: "I went into the artillery and my major wanted to know who was that fellow who was singing all the time. . . . One great day he took me to a friend, a wealthy amateur musician, who listened to me and taught me the tenor roles in *Cavalleria Rusticana* and *Carmen*. One day I did not sing at all. The major sent for me. 'Why did you not sing today, Caruso?' 'I cannot sing on greasy soup.' Next day, my soup was strong and there was no grease on it."

SOUP TALES FROM VERSAILLES

The French king Louis XIV, the Sun King, was known to eat four bowls of clear soup with both lunch and dinner, commissioning his chefs to create a consommé so clear it would reflect his royal image. Alas, some seventy years after his death, this same clear consommé was the last thing his granddaughter-in-law Marie Antoinette could choke down before she was led to her destiny with Monsieur le Guillotine on October 16, 1793.

PART II

OF

PASSAGE

"THE MEANING OF SOUP"

The meaning of soup has been lost.
Life moves slowly, with a warm, oozing tread,
It smells like river mud, like cows and slow earth.
The woman under a man knows that smell.

An odor as nourishing as good soup,
A nutritious weeping, a few patient days
(Here is where we eat, drink, breathe, and make love.)

Must I explain? Is there anyone who doesn't know this?
Life is a heavy humus, sweet and black.
It has the heat of the loins and insists on shedding tears.

It is the dammed up river of the woman we love,
The ripe fruit of exhausted hours,
And a job, a house, an impulse, a routine.

Because all of us live and life is just like that.
It is not love, or happiness, or ideas, or the future.
It is just a hot, thick, dirty soup.

—Gabriel Celaya, *twentieth-century Spanish poet*

5

TO CELEBRATE AND RECOVER FROM GIVING BIRTH

How but in custom and in ceremony
Are innocence and beauty born?

—WILLIAM BUTLER YEATS, *twentieth-century Irish poet,*
from "A Prayer for My Daughter," 1919

ONCE UPON A TIME, a baby is born. Any baby. Hallelujah! No matter how dire the time or circumstances, it's inevitably a time of joy . . . and also a time of ritually sustaining mother and child with gentle foods, to bring them into health and strength.

Bid a strong ghost stand at the head
That my Michael may sleep sound,
Nor cry, nor turn in the bed
'Till his morning meal come round;
And may departing twilight keep
All dread afar till morning's back,
That his mother may not lack
Her fill of sleep.

—WILLIAM BUTLER YEATS,
"A Prayer for My Son," 1928

In times past, of course, "prenatal care" and postpartum nutrition were largely in the hands of women—family members, maids, and midwives. Moms-to-be "ate for two" when food was plenty, and made do when it wasn't, but customarily they got preferential treatment in expectation of the value a healthy baby would eventually bring to the family.

Most soups for new mothers are meant to be served the first weeks after delivery—the critical time when these women need to regain their strength and produce rich breast milk . . . and lots of it.

Not surprisingly, these soups look a lot like traditional soups for the sick and convalescent: lots of meat, lots of digestible things, soft and bland but packed with protein. It is good advice to this day to feed new mothers this way, like so much folk wisdom and so many traditions that have stood the test of millennia.

The recipes that follow, with the exception of *Gee tong*, are offered in small "at home" portions, meant to be prepared quickly and served immediately, though they could easily be doubled to serve family members and guests. *Gee tong*, of course, is specifically designed to be reheated for the new mom and to last a week.

CHINA

CHICKEN SOUP WITH GINGER OR SESAME OIL

GEE TONG

Serves a new mother for 1 week, or 6 to 8

SINCE ANCIENT TIMES until today—and no matter in what province of China—a daily dose of chicken soup for one month is prescribed for new mothers. Why chicken soup? Because it is yang—and new mothers, like the chronically fatigued, need to be warmed up, bucked up, and have their blood loss replenished. In eastern provinces, this soup is flavored with ginger; in southern provinces, it's given a shot of sesame oil. It is prepared by the "double boiling method," which makes the soup a kind of essence. It doesn't at all taste—or look—like "regular" chicken stock, that's for sure. This is truly the champagne of chicken elixirs: pale gold in color, pure in taste.

> *1 whole chicken, 3 to 3½ pounds, or 4 pounds chicken backs*
> *and wings, fat removed, washed in cold water, drained,*
> *and cut through the bones into about 12 pieces*
> *½ pound chicken feet, nails removed*
> *8 cups (2 quarts) boiling water*
> *3 cups sliced green onions, green parts only (in 2-inch lengths)*
> *6 whole peppercorns*
> *10 slices fresh ginger, the size of a quarter, smashed with the*
> *flat side of a knife, or 2 teaspoons toasted sesame oil, plus*
> *more to taste*
> *1 teaspoon salt, or to taste*

TO PREPARE

1. In a large soup pot, bring at least 8 cups of water to a rolling boil. Drop in the chicken pieces and blanch them for 1 minute after the water returns to a boil. Drain the chicken, discarding the water, then rinse the chicken in cold water and drain again.

THE ONE-MONTH CHICKEN-SOUP ANNIVERSARY

According to Chinese tradition, once a baby reaches one month of age, baby and mother are deemed "recovered" from the birthing process and they are presented to the world. Guests bring a red egg for baby, to symbolize good luck, and ginger (yang) for mom, to keep warding off evil spirits and balancing her yin. And what are party guests served for refreshments? A potent "whiskey" soup, bursting with rare ingredients—and chicken.

LI PO CELEBRATES
CHILDREN AND CHICKEN
SOUP

*Here in the mountains in
autumn-tide
Of new-brewed wine and
yellow chick fattened on
grain,
I call the boy to boil the fowl
and pour the white wine,
While my children, playing
noisily about, tug me by
the sleeve.
I sing and imbibe the bland
ecstasy of the cup;
I rise and dance in the tangled beams of the setting
sun.*

*—LI PO, eighth-century T'ang
dynasty poet and Taoist bon
vivant*

2. Prep the remaining ingredients as directed in the recipe list.

TO COOK

1. Heat the oven to 425°F. Bring a large kettle of water to a boil.

2. Place the chicken pieces and feet, 8 cups of boiling water, green onions, peppercorns, and either the ginger pieces or sesame oil in a Dutch oven. Seal the top with heavy-duty aluminum foil, then cover with a heavy lid.

3. Place the pot into a deep baking pan, then fill the baking pan with enough boiling water to reach about 2 inches up the side of the Dutch oven.

4. Bake for 2 to 3 hours, adding boiling water to the baking pan as necessary to keep the oven filled with steam.

5. Remove the Dutch oven from the water bath, unseal it, and skim the top of the broth to remove any impurities and fat. Strain the soup through a colander, then through a sieve that has been lined with moistened cheesecloth. Reserve any meaty chicken pieces. Stir the salt into the broth.

TO SERVE

Ladle the soup into a serving bowl. At this point, if you are making the southern variation, you can whisk in a few more drops of sesame oil, if your new mother likes it. Then add a piece of the chicken meat and serve. For the rest of the week, reheat the broth and chicken pieces in a sealed pot in a 375°F. oven for 10 to 15 minutes, or until piping hot — this will keep the broth clear.

France

"BOILED WATER" GARLIC SOUP
PROVENÇAL L'AÏGO BOULIDO
Serves 4

REPUTEDLY A FRENCH elixir for convalescents and birthing mothers — and a godsend for those with hangovers — this delicate soup is almost unexplainably comforting. It's very soft, and the fragrances of the herbed broth and fruity olive oil help the tender bread sop and cheese slip right down to comfort a tight stomach. It's also traditionally part of *Le gros souper,* the meatless meal in Provence taken on Christmas eve before Midnight Mass.

> *Thin slices of day-old French bread, 1 to 3 per person,*
> *   depending on size (they should fill the bottom surface of the*
> *   soup plate you are using)*
> *4 tablespoons olive oil*
> *4 cups (1 quart) water*
> *Salt to taste*
> *24 garlic cloves, sliced lengthwise (tradition says to remove*
> *   any green sprouts from the garlic centers, but I don't think*
> *   it's worth the trouble. Today's green sprouts aren't bitter as*
> *   they were in days past)*
> *2 bay leaves*
> *1 sprig sage (if you use dried sage, tie 1 teaspoon of it in a*
> *   cheesecloth bag so you can easily remove it from the broth)*
> *Grated Gruyère cheese, for garnish*

TO PREPARE
1. Brush the bread slices with olive oil and toast in a 350°F. oven until dry, about 10 minutes. Set aside.
2. Prep the remaining ingredients as directed in the recipe list.

TO COOK
1. In a large saucepan, combine the water, salt, garlic, bay

"THE YOUNG MOTHER"

The young mother, in the cheeks of the little child she is holding, breathes in her own purest substance. She presses him to her so that he shall remain always herself. She embraces the being she has made. She forgets and rejoices at having given herself, since she has retrieved and found herself again in the tender contact of the intoxicating freshness of his flesh. And vainly those beautiful hands squeeze the fruit she has formed, she feels herself pure, through and through, and like a virgin fulfilled. . . .

She is not sure whether the center of the universe is in her heart or in this little heart that is beating in her arms and that, in its turn, brings all things to life.

—PAUL VALERY, twentieth-century French poet-philosopher

HEADY GARLIC

The English poet Thomas Nash, in *The Unfortunate Traveller* (1594), describes garlic as making "a man winke, drinke and stinke." Alèxander Dumas *père,* in his *Le Grand Dictionnaire de Cuisine,* remarks, "Everybody knows the odor garlic except the one who has eaten it and wonders why everybody turns away from him." These truisms have been updated in a New York City saying that goes: "A nickel will get you on the subway, but garlic will get you a seat."

leaves, and sage. Bring to a boil over high heat, reduce the heat to medium low, cover, and cook for 20 minutes or until the garlic is very soft.

2. Remove the bay leaves and sage sprig, and puree the soup in a blender. Pour it back into the pan, cover, and let steep until you are ready to serve it, at least 10 minutes.

TO SERVE

Heat your soup plates in the oven for a few minutes, then layer their bottoms with the toasted bread slices. Sprinkle the toast with the cheese, then with any remaining olive oil. Reheat the soup to a boil, ladle it over the toast, and serve immediately.

JAPAN

CABBAGE AND CLAM MISO SOUP
KYABETSU TO ASARI NO MISOSHIRU
Serves 4

REPUTED TO PRODUCE good breast milk after the birth of a child, this soup is both hearty and delicate, with many layers of flavor delivered in every spoonful. It can be served at any meal. *Shiru-mono* — a classic thick miso soup — is a traditional breakfast food in Japan served with rice and salted pickles; it is also served with three-dish meals at lunch and dinner, often ending the meal with rice and salt pickled vegetables. This recipe was generously given to me by Yukari Odegawa, my dear friend in Kamioka who introduced me to the pleasures of both Japanese food and Kabuki theater. The soup is fragrant and tasty, the earthiness of miso setting off the sea saltiness of the clams and the fiber of the greens. It's so pleasant to eat with chopsticks, bit by bit, then drink the broth directly from the bowl.

> *4 cups Japanese Soup Stock (dashi; page 28)*
> *4 Napa cabbage leaves, or hakusai, stems removed, leaves cut into 1-inch pieces*
> *3 tablespoons red (aka) miso*
> *8 small hard-shell clams (ideally, asari clams), removed from their shells and washed in salty water (leave them in the water until you're ready to cook them)*

TO PREPARE

1. Prep the ingredients as directed in the recipe list. Make the *dashi* broth as explained on page 28 or dilute *hon-dashi* stock granules in 4 cups broth.

2. Heat the serving bowls, in the oven if they are porcelain, or by filling them with hot water if they're lacquer.

GAZING INTO THE HEART OF MISO SOUP

I was once invited to a tea ceremony where miso was served. And when I saw the muddy, claylike color, quiet in a black lacquer bowl beneath the faint light of a candle, this soup that I usually take without a second thought seemed somehow to acquire a real depth, and to become infinitely more appetizing as well.

—JUNICHIRO TANIZAKI, *twentieth-century Japanese novelist*

TO COOK

1. In a large saucepan, heat the *dashi* over medium heat to a slow boil. Stir in the cabbage and cook, covered, for 5 minutes.

2. Pour about ½ cup of the hot liquid into a small bowl and whisk the miso into it to soften.

3. Add the clams to the hot soup and let cook a minute, uncovered. Strain the miso mixture into the pan and take the pan off the heat immediately.

TO SERVE

Ladle the soup into the heated bowls, placing two clams in each, and serve immediately. It's nice to have lids for the bowls so your new mother can be delighted by both the beauty of the presentation and the fragrance of the soup when she uncovers the bowl.

WHAT ON EARTH IS MISO?

Miso is a fermented soybean paste that actually comes in different varieties, each with its own aroma and flavor, color, and texture. But all types of miso are made the same way: by smashing boiled soybeans and letting them ferment in cedar vats with either wheat, barley, or rice that has been cultured with yeast mold. The miso "matures" for months—even up to three years. Red miso is made with barley and is savory and good for winter soups. Rice-mold misos (*shiromiso*) are yellow and white, relatively light and sweet. The third type of miso is made with bean *koji* and is dark and thick. Miso can last up to a year, refrigerated.

Miso soups evolved in the twelfth century when, with the rise of the powerful Shogun in Kamakura, epicurean Buddhist monks lost their powerful Imperial protectors in Kyoto and forsook their fancy ways. New "common man" Buddhist sects, led by Honen and Nichiren, preached the virtues of a simple diet and discouraged harming any living thing, including fish. These monks encouraged people to eat simple vegetable meals: rice (or barley/millet), salt-pickled vegetables, and miso soup, the last made with a seaweed-only broth.

Korea

CLEAR SEAWEED SOUP
Malgun miyok kuk
Serves 4, or 1 mom in the course of a day

This nutritious soup is prescribed for a new mother three or four times a day for twenty-one straight days! It can be simple — a beef and kelp soup seasoned lightly with garlic, soy sauce, and green onion — or it can be rich and complex, made with chicken stock, chicken, tofu, and sesame oil, as more of a celebration dish that can also traditionally commemorate a child's birthday. *Malgun miyok kuk* is a pretty soup — thick with beef and meaty seaweed, fragrant with sesame and oil, all in a light but rich-tasting broth.

> *1 ounce dried brown* miyok (wakame) *seaweed*
> *½ pound boneless beef shoulder or flank steak, thinly sliced,*
>   *then cut into thick strips 2 inches long*
> *2 garlic cloves, minced*
> *2 tablespoons soy sauce*
> *1 teaspoon toasted sesame oil*
> *1 teaspoon peanut oil*
> *2 green onions, cut lengthwise, then into 2-inch lengths,*
>   *including white and some green*
> *4 cups (1 quart) water*
> *Cooked white rice (optional)*
> *1 green onion, minced, for garnish*

Tip: partially frozen meat is very easy to slice.

To Prepare

1. Soak the seaweed in warm water for 30 minutes.
2. Prep the remaining ingredients as directed in the recipe list, to include making the rice if you plan to serve it.

The Samshinsang

In ancient times, after first bathing a newborn, a new Korean mother would make a *samshinsang* — an altar for the three divine Shaman beings — in a corner of her room, close to her head, and make offerings of white rice and *malgun miyok kuk* on it. This showed respect and gratitude to the three gods who so strongly influenced fertility in the family, not to mention the health of the fetus from conception to birth.

Proverbially not in the Scheme of Things

When Koreans talk about doing something impossible, they say, "Ask a woman to give birth to a child she has not conceived."

MARVELOUS MIYOK

Miyok is considered to act as a powerful blood cleanser and bone strengthener. This seaweed is abundant off all sides of Korea's peninsula, and so has always been available even to the poorest families. When my Korean grocer helped me sort through his aisle-long display of seaweeds to find it, he couldn't disguise his curiosity. "You know how to make it?" he asked me with an amused look. "Tell me," I said. "Wash it," he said. "Cut it and put it to soak. Get good beef. Not pork, only beef! Cook with sesame and garlic. I don't know if you'll like!" "Do *you* like it?" I asked. He blew his lips impatiently: "Of course," he said. "All Koreans like it."

3. Mix the beef strips with the garlic, soy sauce, and sesame oil and let marinate until the seaweed is ready to be cooked.

4. When the seaweed has rehydrated, scrub it under running water, rinse, drain, lay it flat, and use scissors to cut it into 2-inch squares, discarding the hard center stalks.

TO COOK

In a large saucepan, heat the peanut oil over high heat, then fry the beef mixture and green onions for a minute, letting the beef brown on all sides. Stir in the drained seaweed pieces, followed by the water, and bring to a boil over high heat (it will foam a bit). Reduce the heat to low, cover, and simmer for 30 minutes.

TO SERVE

Ladle the soup into the new mother's bowl and sprinkle with minced green onion. The soup can be reheated for subsequent servings during the day or, if you are serving it to others, ladled evenly among four bowls, sprinkled with minced green onion, and served with white rice on the side.

PUERTO RICO

SPICED CHICKEN NOODLE SOUP
SOPA DE FIDEOS Y POLLO
Serves 4

THIS *SOPA* IS comforting to look at—a study of creams and whites, nothing jarring—thick and rich, intensely chicken, and so nicely tasty that you just want to follow one spoonful with the next one until the whole bowl is gone. Not only is the dish used to strengthen new mothers and heal the sick, it is also one of the first solid foods given to Puerto Rican babies.

> *1 pound boneless raw chicken, cut into bite-size pieces*
> Adobo *seasoning to taste (page 46)*
> *4 cups (1 quart) Chicken Stock (page 24)*
> *¼ cup* recaíto *(page 46)*
> *2 tablespoons short-grain white rice*
> *1¼ cups peeled and diced potatoes*
> *1 cup angel hair pasta broken into short lengths*
> *2 sprigs fresh cilantro*
> *Salt and white pepper to taste*

TO PREPARE

1. Prep the ingredients as directed in the recipe list, and make the *adobo* and *recaíto*, if necessary.

2. Sprinkle the *adobo* on the chicken and let marinate for a few minutes.

TO COOK

1. Bring the stock, *recaíto*, and seasoned chicken bits slowly to a boil in a large saucepan over medium heat. Stir in the rice, potatoes, pasta, and cilantro sprigs, and bring back to a boil, then reduce the heat to low, cover, and let simmer until the rice is tender, about 20 minutes.

PUERTO RICAN SOUP TRADITIONS

Puerto Rico was discovered by Christopher Columbus on his second voyage to the New World. It's no surprise, then, that its cuisine is a combination of *cocina criolla*—native cookery—plus all the influences brought from the Old World by African slaves, Europeans, and even Chinese (who were shipped in as plantation labor after slavery was abolished). Soup was often the main meal in slave or indentured-servant days, as workers would pool all their available food bits in the morning in one *caldero* and cook them over a coal fire until lunch break, at which point they'd sit down and serve it out. Soup is commonly served as the first course of dinner in Puerto Rico, followed by rice, beans, and a meat dish.

CAN'T FIND PUERTO RICAN
SEASONINGS AT YOUR
LOCAL GROCERY? THEY'RE
EASY TO MAKE.

ADOBO: mix 1 tablespoon garlic powder, 1 tablespoon
onion powder, 1 tablespoon
oregano powder, and $\frac{1}{2}$ tablespoon each salt and
white pepper. Makes $\frac{1}{4}$ cup.

RECAÍTO: puree in a blender
$\frac{1}{4}$ diced onion, 1 garlic clove,
$\frac{1}{2}$ small sweet green pepper,
1 tablespoon chopped
cilantro, and 2 recao leaves
(or substitute 1 more tablespoon fresh cilantro as this
herb is like cilantro but
stronger in flavor). Makes $\frac{1}{2}$
cup.

2. Remove the cilantro sprigs, and season with the salt and white pepper.

TO SERVE

Ladle the soup into bowls and serve immediately.

6

To Celebrate Religious Confirmation

ONCE UPON A TIME, feasts were traditionally served by families to celebrate a child's confirmation of baptism and entry into the life of the church—and such celebrations often included soup. In today's hectic world, alas, these elaborate feasts have largely gone by the wayside. *Klarsuppe*, however, remains an exception. And no wonder. This Danish meatball and dumpling soup is a honey: very tasty, very pretty, and with a great contrast of textures, taking advantage of the sweet baby vegetables of spring, the time when thirteen-year-olds are traditionally welcomed into the Danish church.

The recipe on the following page, adapted from Beatrice Ojakangas's *Scandinavian Feasts*, is designed to feed a small party, but it can easily be doubled or halved to accommodate your guest list.

DENMARK

MEATBALL AND DUMPLING SOUP
KLARSUPPE
Serves 8

IMAGINE A SOUP plate brimming with a pure, clear beef broth, then mentally fill it with buttery dumplings and tiny meatballs, accented by bits of carrots and sweet baby peas. It may look complicated to make, but in fact it isn't. You just need to make the dumplings and meatballs a bit in advance, then it's a snap to assemble at the last minute . . . like, if you're rushing in from church after witnessing the confirmation of your thirteen-year-old daughter.

FOR THE MEATBALLS
½ pound pork filet, trimmed of fat and partially frozen for easy grinding (other meats are also fine)
½ cup finely chopped onion
1 teaspoon salt
¼ teaspoon pepper
¼ teaspoon ground allspice
3 tablespoons all-purpose flour
3 tablespoons milk
1 egg white, lightly beaten (save the yolk for the dumplings)

FOR THE DUMPLINGS
½ cup (1 stick) butter
1 cup water
1 teaspoon salt
1 cup all-purpose flour
2 eggs plus the leftover egg yolk

FOR THE SOUP
8 cups (2 quarts) Beef Stock (page 26)
½ cup peeled and diced carrots (about the size of the baby peas)

¹/₂ cup baby peas
Chopped fresh chervil (or tarragon or parsley), for garnish

To Prepare

For the meatballs

1. Grind the meat in a food processor until finely cut (you can also ask your butcher to grind the meat, or you can cut it by hand). Put it into a bowl, stir in the onion, and season with salt, pepper, and allspice.

2. In a small cup, beat the flour and milk together, then stir into the meat. Finally, mix in the egg white. Let sit for at least 30 minutes.

3. When you are ready to cook the meatballs, bring 2 inches of water to a boil in a large, wide pot over medium-high heat. Season liberally with salt.

4. With a teaspoon, shape and drop 40 small meatballs into the boiling water and let cook for 4 to 5 minutes. Strain with a perforated spoon, let drain in a sieve until dry, then store in the refrigerator until needed.

For the dumplings

1. In a small saucepan, bring the butter, water, and salt to a boil over medium-high heat. Pour in the flour all at once and stir hard with a wooden spoon, until the mass is smooth and forms a ball that peels off the sides of the pot. Remove from the heat and let cool for 10 minutes.

2. Bring 2 inches of water in a large, wide pot to a boil over medium-high heat and season well with salt.

3. After the dumpling dough has cooled, beat in the eggs and egg yolk, one at a time, until the dough is satiny.

4. When the water is at a medium boil, use two small spoons to make and drop 40 dumplings into the water.

5. When you have finished dropping the dumplings into the water and the water again begins to boil, pour about ¼ cup of cold water into the pot to stop the boiling. When it comes to a strong

FRETTY CHERVIL

Originally a native of western Asia, chervil was first cultivated in Syria, according to Pliny the Elder, where its roots and leaves were eaten raw and also cooked as a vegetable. It got its name in Greece, from *chaerophyllon,* "herb of rejoicing." And it was spread far and wide by the Romans, who planted it near all their many camps throughout the Roman Empire to use as a flavoring herb. John Parkinson says about it in his 1629 *Paradisus:* "Sweet Chervil or Sweet Cis is so like in taste unto Anis seede that it much delighteth the taste among other herbs in a sallet." The English poet Gerard Manley Hopkins, in frustration with God, begs Him to water *his* roots the way He lavishes water on "fretty chervil."

boil again, pour in another bit of cold water. And, again, for the third time, pour in cold water when it returns to strong boil. At this point, the dumplings should be firm and completely cooked. Lift them out of the water with a perforated spoon and let them drain in a sieve. When they are completely drained, you may store them in the refrigerator until needed.

6. When you are ready to finalize the soup, take the dumplings and meatballs out of the refrigerator and put them in a warm spot. They should be room temperature when you are ready to assemble the soup.

TO COOK

Bring the stock to a boil over medium-high heat in a large soup pot and stir in the carrots. Cook for 5 minutes, then add the baby peas. Cook for 5 more minutes.

TO SERVE

Set out the soup bowls and arrange five meatballs and five dumplings in each. When the soup is ready, ladle some into each of the bowls and top with chopped chervil. Serve immediately.

7

To Celebrate Marriage . . . and Recover from the Rigors of the Honeymoon

ONCE UPON A TIME, there were no June brides, nor May ones either, at least in the Northern Hemisphere. Why? Because in agrarian societies there was work to be done then, planting and cultivating the fields. Back in ancient Roman times, Ovid noted, *"Mense malum Maio nubvero vulgus ait,"* or, "Common folk say 'tis ill to wed in May." Then, again, in medieval times, it was thought that "they that wive between sickle and scythe, shall never thrive."

Weddings back then were for fall and winter, after the harvest was in — which is likely why hot wedding soups became traditional fare in many cultures. Baby, it was cold outside . . . and dark. Granaries were full; animals were back in the barn. Bachelors and maids alike turned their thoughts toward domestic comforts. In China, marriage was thought best at the first new moon of the year. In ancient Greece and Italy, it was winter or late autumn. In Japan, the best times were the tenth, eleventh, and twelfth lunar months. In England and Germany, it was at the harvest moon, and in Scotland and Ireland, "Marry when the year is new,/Always loving, always true."

These old customs are hardly remembered in today's age of industrialized agriculture and global agritrade. June weddings now seem more natural, often following school graduations and signaling the beginning of the work life. But traditional wedding soups continue to be brought steaming to the table, no matter what the temperature outside.

RIDDLE ME THIS

QUESTION: What fastens two
people together but
touches only one?

ANSWER: A wedding ring

The recipes that follow are offered in portions for six to eight people, to suit a small wedding party. They can, however, be doubled — or halved — as appropriate.

CHINA

RED BEAN AND LOTUS SEED SOUP
HUNG DAU LIN JEE TONG
Serves 6 to 8

THIS SWEET SOUP sends the bride and groom off to a sweet life — with the lotus seeds standing for the many babies the marriage will produce. The custom was perhaps most memorably enacted in Chinese film director Ang Lee's charming and hilarious movie *Hsi Yen,* or *The Wedding Banquet,* where dutiful son Wai-Tung Gao, anxious to conceal his long-term relationship with Andrew from his parents, arranges a marriage of convenience in New York City with one of his female tenants, adorable Wei-Wei, who needs a green card. Mom and Dad arrive in ecstasy from Taiwan for the wedding and a two-week stay. Wai-Tung and Wei-Wei's modest marriage plans almost immediately go stratospheric, ending in a completely over-the-top wedding and banquet.

> *8 cups (2 quarts) cold water*
> *14-ounce package small red beans, washed to remove grit and*
>   *drained*
> *1½-ounce package lotus seeds, washed and drained*
> *1 piece dried tangerine skin, soaked in hot water 10 minutes*
>   *until soft*
> *¾ cup brown sugar*

TO PREPARE
Prep the ingredients as directed in the recipe list.

TO COOK

1. In a large pot, combine the water, red beans, lotus seeds, and tangerine skin. Bring to a boil over high heat, then reduce the heat to low and simmer, partially covered, for about 1½ hours, or until the beans are tender (when you blow on them, the skins will burst).

2. Stir in the brown sugar and let simmer for another minute to let the flavors blend.

TO SERVE

Remove the tangerine skin, then pour the soup into a heated tureen and bring to the table, to be ladled into exquisite little cups.

"LADY NIGHT SONG OF AUTUMN"

She opens her window
To the autumn moon's light.
She puts out the candle
And slips off her silken shirt.

Softly she smiles
Within the curtains of her
*   bed.*
She raises her body —
An orchid fragrance spreads.

—ANONYMOUS, *from China's Six Dynasties Period*, A.D. 300–600

THE SOUP RITUAL IN ANG LEE'S *HSI YEN*

MRS. GAO: "Sister Mao, please get the lotus soup."
[Wai-Tung and Wei-Wei bow three times to the parents and are handed an envelope.]
WAI-TUNG: "Thank you, Ma."
WEI-WEI: "Thank you."
MRS. GAO: "We're turning Wai-Tung over to you."
MR. GAO: "And you, Wai-Tung, must care well for Wei-Wei."
WAI-TUNG: "I will."
MR. GAO: "Here's a soup for a quick first son."
WAI-TUNG: "Wei-Wei, kneel for the soup."
MRS. GAO: "Have some lotus soup; a son will come quickly."
WEI-WEI: "Come on, Wai-Tung, kneel down and have some soup with me."
WAI-TUNG: "Having a son is a female thing."
MRS. GAO: "She can't give birth without your help, right?"
[Mrs. Gao feeds Wei-Wei the soup, blowing on each spoonful. Wei-Wei bursts into tears and is led out of the room.]

It's a miracle: by the end of the movie, Wei-Wei has conceived and Wai-Tung and Andrew can't wait to become the proud fathers. It's precisely what wedding soup is all about.

FRANCE

BRETON WEDDING SOUP
SOUPE DE MARIAGE BRETAGNE
Serves 6 to 8

I FOUND THE inspiration for this recipe in the town of Guimiliau—
actually for sale as a book about Breton cooking, in the Ossuary, or
former bone house, of Guimiliau's parish close. Maybe it's a sad
statement about the preemption of old holy places for tourism, yet
a think piece, too. Recipe books served up in the place where food
and life end physically suggests that the bone house still has the
power to feed the spiritual life of the village. And the milk soup?
Delicious—sweet and garlicky.

> *6 to 8 slices stale bread*
> *3 tablespoons butter*
> *4 large onions, very thinly sliced*
> *2 garlic cloves, very thinly sliced*
> *10 cups milk*
> *Salt to taste (preferably* sel de mer, *with its tang of the sea)*
> *White pepper to taste*

TO PREPARE

Toast the bread in a 350° F. oven for 10 to 15 minutes, until dry
and crisp. Prep the remaining ingredients as directed in the recipe
list.

TO COOK

1. Melt the butter in a large soup pot and brown it over
medium heat. Add the onions and cook until they are browned.
Add the garlic and stir until well browned.

2. Pour in the milk, salt, and pepper. Bring to a boil over
medium-high heat, then reduce the heat to low and simmer, uncovered, until the onions are tender, 10 to 15 minutes.

TO SERVE

Arrange the toasted bread in six or eight bowls, depending on the number of guests, and ladle the soup into each, serving immediately.

NOTE: Ironically, *soupe au lait*, or "milk soup," is an expression in France for someone who is short-tempered and boils over easily. Uh, oh.

BRETON MARRIAGE CUSTOMS

According to Pierre-Jakez Helias, in *The Horse of Pride: Life in a Breton Village*, "Custom still required that the newlyweds not be left to themselves until the evening of the third day. The first night was dedicated to the Virgin; the second, to Saint Joseph. And then came the 'milk soup' ceremony, which was both symbolic and rather spicy. The recipe for that soup varied from one region to another and depended on the young people's imaginations, but it always included a string of garlic cloves. The milk in the soup proclaimed that the couple's life together would be pleasant; the garlic warned them to expect many disappointments. The younger guests would generally bring it to husband and wife at the banquet table, heartily singing the song of their ancestors—a sad ballad that was meant to make any bride of good stock weep with one eye and laugh with the other. Then the bombardists and bagpipers would strike up another milk-soup tune that was livelier and well known for its tendency to 'dry away the tears,' prompting all the people at the tables to loudly rejoice."

BRETON "JOHNNIES"

This honeymoon soup is also called *"la soupe de Johnny,"* dating from the nineteenth century, when Breton onion sellers, or Johnnies, braved the rough waters of the English Channel to sell their wares from door to door in England. They could be spotted from a distance throughout England and into Scotland, wearing black berets and riding bicycles slung with strings of fat onions from the fertile Breton fields that are still producing delicious onions today.

FRANCE

BRETON HONEYMOON SOUP
SOUPE À L'OIGNON "JOHNNY"
Serves 6 to 8

HERE IS A superb soup that goes to the heart of robust country humor. No sooner do the Breton bride and groom drink their sobering wedding soup (see page 54) than they are escorted by well-wishers straight to the bedroom. Leaving the couple some privacy, the well-wishers return to the kitchen and prepare this soup. Once it is ready—and it takes only about an hour to make—these "friends" carry it back to the bedroom and burst in on the couple, singing, *"L'apportons-nous la soupe, la soupe? L'apportons-nous la soupe à l'oignon?"* or "May we bring the soup, the soup? May we bring the onion soup?"

> 8 cups (2 quarts) water
> Salt to taste
> 1½ pounds big onions (about 4), quartered
> 2 medium potatoes, peeled and quartered
> 2 tablespoons tapioca
> 1 egg yolk
> ½ cup heavy cream
> 2 tablespoons butter

TO PREPARE
Prep the ingredients as directed in the recipe list.

TO COOK
1. Bring the water to a boil in a large soup pot over high heat, then add the salt, onions, and potatoes. When the water returns to a boil, reduce the heat to low and simmer, partially covered, for 30 minutes.

Sprinkle in the tapioca and boil gently, uncovered, for 10 more minutes.

2. Puree the soup, solids first, and return to the pot. Taste for seasoning.

3. To finish the soup, whisk the egg yolk into the cream, lighten with ½ cup of the hot pureed soup, then stir into the pot and simmer for a few minutes to thicken.

To Serve

Stir the butter into the soup as an enrichment, then ladle the soup into bowls and carry it to the lucky couple . . . and serve the rest to the other members of the party.

Riddle Me This

QUESTION: What am I? I'm a strange creature, for I satisfy women, a service to the neighbors! No one suffers at my hands except for my slayer. I grow very tall, erect in a bed. I'm hairy underneath. From time to time a beautiful girl, the brave daughter of some churl, dares to hold me, grips my russet skin, robs me of my head and puts me in the pantry. At once that girl with plaited hair who has confined me remembers our meeting. Her eye moistens.

Mercy! Can't guess? Here's another one with the same answer:

QUESTION: Quick; quite mum; I die notwithstanding. I lived once, I live again. Everybody lifts me, grips me, and chops off my head, bites my bare body, violates me. I never bite a man unless he bites me; there are many men who bite me.

Puzzled? These are riddles #25 and #65 from the Old English *Exeter Book*, made public by Leofric, first Bishop of Exeter in 1072.

ANSWER: An onion.

GUATEMALA

LAMB SOUP WITH TAMALES
CALDO DE CARNERO
Serves 6 to 8

THIS SIMPLE SOUP reflects the hardscrabble life of Indian farmers, who grow lots of potatoes but for whom meat of any kind is a great luxury. A meat soup, reserved for weddings and other high festivals, should not be complicated by vegetables and seasonings, but rather savored in small portions for its own pure meatiness. The small tamales, though, serve as rich corny dumplings and make this a very special soup indeed.

FOR THE SOUP
> *3 pounds boneless lamb, cut into bite-size cubes*
> *2 large onions, cut into cubes*
> *8 cups (2 quarts) cold water*
> *2 teaspoons salt, or to taste*

FOR 40 SMALL CORN FLOUR TAMALES (*TAMALITOS PACHES*)
> *4 cups masa harina (instant cornmeal mix for making*
> *tortillas)*
> *4 cups (1 quart) cold water*
> *2 teaspoons salt*
> *½ cup corn oil*
> Mashan (*palm*) *leaves or—and I recommend this—forty*
> *6-inch squares of aluminum foil (a modern convenience*
> *that is so easy to use that you'll actually make the tamales*
> *instead of just thinking about it)*

TO PREPARE
1. For the soup, cube the lamb and the onions.
2. For the tamales, mix the masa, water, salt, and corn oil into a paste. For each tamale, spoon a heaping tablespoon of the paste

onto a 6-inch square of aluminum foil (or *mashan* leaves, if you have them). Match opposite edges of the square and double-fold it to seal, then twist each end tightly a couple of times so you end up with what looks like a fat saltwater taffy or firecracker party favor. Continue until you use up all the paste.

To Cook

1. In a large soup pot, combine the lamb, onions, and water. Bring to a boil over medium heat, then reduce the heat to low and simmer, covered, until the lamb is tender, about 1½ hours. Do not skim the foam, as it should remain to intensify the meatiness of the soup. Season with the salt.

2. Bring about 2 cups of water to a boil over medium-high heat in a large pot and add the tamale packets. Reduce the heat to low, cover tightly with a lid, and steam the tamales for 1 hour.

To Serve

Ladle the soup into bowls. Hand around the tamales, inviting your guests to untwist them and pop them into their soup bowls to eat like dumplings.

Riddle Me This

Question: What kind of ear cannot hear?

Answer: Corn

"IN PRAISE OF BOUILLON"

*Shine oh eyes, drool oh
mouth with joy: the delicious
bouillon is ladled up, served
right in front of you.
Look, how golden yellow it
is, glistening, and how nose-
titillating its smell is! What a
taste! Ambrosia!
Surely it has its own soul —
this is what you really need —
Do you divine — tell me — its
marrowbone, its aromatic
vegetables, and its spicy soul
of ginger that cures all ills? —
Believe me, this is the only
thing to live for, this is the
direct line to salvation, otherwise you are a bitter toothless
dog, barking at the world —
not transported beyond by
this heavenly morsel of
heavenly ham.*

—BERDA JÓZSEF (1902-1966), "the
vagabond poet of Budapest sa-
lons," also known as the "Saint
Francis of Hungarian poetry," the
"Sacrificer of Well-Laid Tables,"
the "Patron Saint of Poke Pud-
dings," and the "Exarch of Geese"

HUNGARY

CHICKEN SOUP WITH "SNAIL" PASTA
TYÚKHÚSLEVES
Serves 6 to 8

ORDINARILY MADE IN huge quantities for a typical country wedding feast, this soup is very rich but pure — a strong broth with special homemade pasta in the shape of little snails, traditionally made
by the friends of the bride. The soup is always served as the first
course of the feast after the wedding, and is followed by the cooks
being invited to dance at a "snail stomping." Because making the
"snails" requires laboriously rolling the pasta dough around a stick
on a ribbed board, I have substituted either small shell pasta or
gemelli pasta. I brought some "snails" — *csiga tészta* — back home
from a trip to Eger, though, and they are adorable. I don't think
anything could be sweeter than to begin wedded bliss with a white
soup plate full of crystalline chicken broth that is stuffed with these
funny ribbed coils.

> *4 pounds chicken, cut into pieces*
> *A few chicken feet, with their nails clipped off (optional)*
> *1 tablespoon salt*
> *1 teaspoon black peppercorns*
> *12 cups (3 quarts) cold water*
> *2 carrots, trimmed, scrubbed, and chopped*
> *2 parsley roots, trimmed, scrubbed, and chopped (or 1 parsnip)*
> *1 small celery root, peeled and chopped (or chopped celery)*
> *1 kohlrabi, trimmed, scrubbed, and chopped (can also use
>   cabbage or turnip)*
> *2 garlic cloves*
> *1 small onion*
> *1 cup small shell pasta or gemelli pasta*

TO PREPARE
Prep the ingredients as directed in the recipe list.

To Cook

1. Place the chicken pieces in a high-sided soup pot and sprinkle with the salt and peppercorns. Pour the cold water on top. Bring to a boil over medium heat, then reduce the heat to low and simmer, uncovered, for 30 minutes, not removing or stirring in the scum.

2. Add the vegetables, but don't stir them. Return the broth briefly to a boil over high heat, then reduce the heat again, partially cover, and simmer for another hour. Take the soup off the heat and let sit for 10 minutes.

3. Carefully ladle the soup through a strainer lined with moistened cheesecloth into a clean pot. You do not want to cloud the soup by pouring it through the strainer. Discard the solids. Cool down to room temperature, uncovered, if you plan to refrigerate before serving, to avoid clouding the broth.

4. In a separate large pot, bring at least 8 cups of water to a boil. Add a tablespoon of salt and pour in the pasta. Cook until tender. Drain and reserve.

To Serve

Reheat the broth to a boil and taste it to make sure it is well seasoned. Stir in the cooked pasta, and let the flavors mix for a minute or two. Take the pot out to the table and ladle the soup into bowls.

"EVER THUS AND AS YOU WERE"

In this classic Hungarian folktale, a poor but clever soldier, discharged from the army, seeks his fortune from his commander-in-chief, the King. The King, as kings are wont to do, gives him an impossible task: "You can be my coachman," he says, "if you hitch up my horses, drive them to the Royal forest, fill their cart with timber, and drive back by sundown." It turns out, of course, that the horses are old, skinny, and at death's door. Even so, that soldier gives it his best shot. Just at the point of failure, he does a favor for a poor old man in the forest—and is repaid a thousand times over when the old man gives him two magic commands to use. "Just say, 'Ever thus' to someone," the old man says, "and he or she will do what you want at lightning speed and without stopping. Then, just say, 'As you were,' and that poor soul will finally be able to stop." The soldier puts these commands to good purpose, and not just to get those horses back to the King to secure the coachman job. No, he almost immediately sets his sights on the youngest daughter of the King, a beautiful princess if there ever was one. Alas, she is to be married the next day.

Disconsolate, he wanders through the dazzling halls of the castle until he comes to the banquet room. There are the Princess and her bridegroom eating *tyúkhúsleves*—chicken soup with snail pasta. He sneaks up behind them and whispers, "Ever thus!" Instantly they begin eating at top speed, bowl after bowl, growing so fat they can hardly sit in their chairs. The Queen looks over and says, "Mercy, aren't you ashamed of yourselves, you pigs?" and she just keeps on and on talking about how much they are eating.

So the soldier leans over in mid-sentence and says, "Ever thus!" Oh my, now the Queen can't *stop* talking and her voice gets louder and louder and louder until the King finally comes over to shut her up . . . but suddenly he hiccups, maybe from the flagon of *tokaj* wine he's just drunk. "Ever thus!" whispers the soldier—and now the King can't *stop* hiccuping. The place is in an uproar, with people running about, plates and dishes crashing and smashing, the King hiccuping, the Queen gabbling, the bridegroom and the adorable Princess shoveling in the *tyúkhúsleves* as fast as they can—what a mess!

"Help!—*hic!*—soldier! Help us—*hic!*" the King cries. "Help—*hic!*—and I'll give you—*hic!*—half my kingdom!"

"It's not your kingdom I want," says the soldier, "it's your daughter."

"Princess—*hic!*—what do you say?"

"Oh yes," she wails, "if only I could stop eating." As the soldier and the King shake hands to seal the deal, the soldier says, "As you were!" Ahhh, the hiccups stop. "As you were!" to the Queen. Ahh, the words die on her lips. "As you were!" to the Princess and the hapless bridegroom. That bridegroom slinks away, leaving a trail of chicken soup behind him.

The Princess and the soldier are married before you could say, "Good King Mattias." "Oh," says she, "I liked you the minute I clapped eyes on you."

"Are you happy?" he asks.

"Yes," she says sweetly.

"Ever thus!" says the soldier. And since he hasn't yet said, "As you were!" to her, it's a fact that they lived happily ever after.

ITALY

WEDDING SOUP WITH MEATBALLS
ZUPPA MARITATA
Serves 6 to 8

ZUPPA MARITATA is one of the most requested soups on my web-site, *www.soupsong.com*, a wedding soup from Abruzzo that features the meatballs traditional to that part of Italy. It's a pretty soup, and very substantial with all those meatballs. The torn escarole floats on the broth, enriched by the meat and molten cheese. This dish is flavorful yet subtle, something to throw a bouquet about. For nonbridal occasions, it can be a proper meal for four persons.

FOR THE MEATBALLS
½ pound ground veal
½ pound ground sirloin beef
1 egg, slightly beaten
½ cup fresh bread crumbs
¼ cup minced fresh parsley
½ cup finely grated Romano cheese
Pinch of nutmeg
Salt and pepper to taste

FOR THE SOUP
8 cups (2 quarts) Chicken Stock (page 24)
2 cups washed and torn escarole, in little pieces
¼ cup freshly grated Romano cheese, or more to serve

TO PREPARE

1. An hour ahead, mix the veal, beef, egg, bread crumbs, parsley, grated cheese, nutmeg, salt, and pepper until the paste is uniform, but be careful not to overwork it. Form the paste into small meatballs (about the size of oversized marbles)—about 50 of them—arrange them on a baking sheet, and cook them in a 350°F. oven for about 30 minutes. They should still be tender and not too

---

DANTE WOOS HIS BEATRICE

Within my Lady's eyes abideth Love,
Hence where she looks all things must needs grow kind,
And when she passeth all men glance behind,
And those she greeteth such fond raptures prove
That from each downcast face the colour fades
And every fault repentance doth inspire:
Before her flee presumptuousness and ire;
Help me to do her honour, gentle maids!
The heart which heareth her when she doth speak
Becometh, through her virtue, pure and meek,
Hence praise to who beholds her first is due;
The vision of her softly smiling face
In neither speech nor memory hath place,
It is a miracle so sweet and new.

—DANTE ALIGHIERI, *fourteenth-century Italian poet*

ITALIAN WEDDING SOUP AT THE U.S. MASTERS

Not just for newlyweds! Bernhard Langer, a German golf pro, ordered this soup in 1993, his prerogative as reigning U.S. Masters champion, to be served at the traditional Champion's Dinner at the Augusta National Golf Club on the eve of the tournament. This menu-selecting tradition was begun in 1952 by Ben Hogan.

brown. Drain off the fat, then transfer to paper towels to drain the fat completely.

2. Prep the remaining ingredients as directed in the recipe list.

TO COOK

Bring the chicken stock to a boil in a large soup pot over medium-high heat. Add the escarole, cover, and boil for 5 minutes. Add the meatballs, reduce the heat to low, and bring back to a simmer. Let the soup simmer, covered, for a few minutes, then stir in the grated cheese.

TO SERVE

Ladle the soup into bowls, evenly distributing the meatballs among them, and serve immediately, sprinkling with more cheese, if you like. Pass more grated cheese on the side for your guests to help themselves.

EGG AND WINE HONEYMOON SOUP
GINESTRATA
Serves 2

THIS RICH NORTHERN Italian soup goes all the way back to medieval times in Tuscany, when families would humorously prepare it
to revive the flagging spirits of the bride and groom the morning
after their wedding. Like a thin, savory *zabaglione*, it is sweet enough
to pump up the newlyweds, mellow enough to restore their perspec-
tive, and so highly nutritious that they won't miss a night's loss of
sleep. That said, it's also a suggestive way to start a romantic cold
supper with the one you love . . . or any supper, for that matter. This
recipe may be multiplied to serve four . . . or even eight if you'd like
to try an unusual dinner-party course.

> *3 egg yolks*
> *¼ cup dry Marsala wine*
> *1½ cups heated chicken stock, without a scrap of fat in it*
> *Pinch of cinnamon*
> *2 tablespoons unsalted butter, softened*
> *¼ teaspoon sugar mixed with a pinch of nutmeg, for garnish*

TO PREPARE
Prep the ingredients as directed in the recipe list. Warm the
serving bowls.

TO COOK
1. Bring water to a simmer over medium heat in the bottom of
a double boiler.

2. In the top pan of the double boiler, off the heat, beat the egg
yolks with a whisk until they are thick and light yellow in color.
Then, bit by bit, whip in the Marsala, chicken broth, and cinnamon.

3. Fit the soup pot over the simmering water (not in it) and
cook over medium heat, whisking constantly with a whisk, as you
add the butter, spoonful by spoonful, very slowly.

CINNAMON DROPS AT AN ELOPEMENT

*And still she slept an azure-
lidded sleep,
In blanched linen, smooth,
and lavender'd,
While he from forth the closet
brought a heap
Of candied apple, quince, and
plum, and gourd;
And lucent syrops, tint with
cinnamon . . .*

—JOHN KEATS, *nineteenth-century
English poet, from his Italianate
"The Eve of Saint Agnes," in which
Porphyro stages an exotic vision
in fair Madeline's bedroom in
hopes of eloping with her*

4. When the soup starts to thicken — it will coat the spoon, but never get very thick — remove it from the heat.

TO SERVE

Ladle the soup into warmed, elegant bowls and sprinkle with the sugar and nutmeg mixture.

Japan

FRESH CLAM SOUP
HAMAGURI NO SUMASHI-JIRU
Serves 8

THIS DELICATE SOUP is served at Shinto wedding feasts precisely to symbolize the union of the happy couple through the paired valves of the clam. It is also typically served on March 3 every year for Girl's Day, when Japanese people pray for the wealth and happiness of their daughters and set up special *hina* dolls to celebrate the occasion. I recommend you find and use soup bowls with lids — ideally lacquer — for serving this soup. Why? Because the presentation is dramatic in beauty and fragrance when each person removes the lid, gazes into the soup, and inhales the lemony brine aroma. It's delicious, too — light and stimulating.

16 small hard-shell clams (asari, if possible)
2 thick green onions (called negi *in Japanese), green part only, cut into eight 1½-inch pieces on the diagonal*
8 pieces fresh lemon or lime peel (Japanese yuzu, *if you can get it), cut into 2 × ¾-inch rectangles that are scraped of all white pith*
8 cups Japanese Soup Stock (dashi; page 28)
1 tablespoon saké
¼ teaspoon soy sauce, or to taste

TO PREPARE

1. Two hours ahead, start the clams soaking in cold salt water. Then scrub, rinse, and drain the clams.

2. Prep the green onions as directed in the recipe list.

3. Cut deep notches in the top and bottom long sides of the lemon or lime rectangles, so each piece looks like a capital N, then cross the legs of the N over each other to make a triangle shape known as the "pine needle cut." Set the pieces aside.

"WHAT A LITTLE GIRL HAD ON HER MIND"

What a little girl had on her mind was:
Why do the shoulders of other men's wives
give off so strong a smell like magnolia;
or like gardenias?
What is it,
that faint veil of mist,
over the shoulders of other men's wives?
She wanted to have one,
that wonderful thing
even the prettiest virgin cannot have.

The little girl grew up.
She became a wife and then a mother.
One day she suddenly realized;
the tenderness
that gathers over the shoulders of wives,
is only fatigue
from loving others day after day.

—IBARAGI NORIKO,
twentieth-century Japanese poet

WHAT IS JAPANESE SOY SAUCE?

It's extraordinary. Today called *shōyu*, soy sauce started out as a revolution against the ancient *uoshōyu* (made of fermented fish, like today's Southeast Asian fish sauces *nuoc mam* and *nam pla*). When the Japanese embraced Buddhism and adopted vegetarianism as a way of life, they turned away from fish and looked to plant-based seasonings, the Chinese soybean in particular. Then they proceeded to take soy sauce to a whole new level.

Tamari shōyu was developed by A.D. 775. It's rich and thick, a product made exclusively from fermenting soybeans. Today's *shōyu* wasn't perfected until the seventeenth century. It is made from steamed soybeans mixed with parched and cracked wheat grains, then cultured for three days with the same mold used to make miso and *dashi*. This mash is then added to salted water and stored in cedar barrels for at least two summers, the longer the better. Finally, it is strained and pressed, pasteurized, and bottled. Of course, many of today's soy sauces are made with shortcuts taken, with proportional cuts in quality. If you can find *Kanro shōyu*, though, grab it: it's a handmade sauce produced only in the city of Yanai and is known for its *umami*, the "tastiness factor" in Japanese cooking that is reputed to be beyond sweet, sour, salty, and bitter.

4. Heat the serving bowls and their lids in the oven or, if they are lacquer, by filling them with hot water.

TO COOK

In a wide soup pot, bring the *dashi* to a boil over medium-high heat, then add the clams in a single layer, cover, and cook until the clams just open, about 3 minutes. Remove the pot from the heat and reserve the broth. Take out the clams and remove the clam meat from the shells, being careful to end up with eight shells whose halves are still joined together.

TO SERVE

1. Place one double shell in each of the eight warmed Japanese soup bowls, filling each side of each shell with clam meat, then covering the bowls with their lids.

2. Reheat the broth, adding the saké and a few drops of soy sauce, then ladle it over the clams, being careful not to stir up any sand that might still be in the bottom of the pot. Arrange the green onion pieces and the citrus peel in each bowl and cover the bowls with lids.

3. Serve immediately, allowing each person to remove the lid, regard the soup, and inhale its fragrance.

Morocco

WEDDING LAMB SOUP WITH RICE AND BEANS

Harira

Serves 6 to 8

FROM THE GULISTAN

Whose wife is tender, wise, and true,
In fact, Beloved, just like you,
Although he merits no such thing
Will live, as I do, like a King.

—SAADI,
thirteenth-century Persian poet

THIS SPECIAL WEDDING version of the rich, lemony *harira* that traditionally breaks the fast during Ramadan (see page 288) uses rice as a symbolic ingredient and dispenses with the eggs used to thicken traditional *harira* recipes. It's wonderful, as all *hariras* are, and a great start to both an extravagant banquet and wedded bliss.

> 1¹⁄₂ cups dried chickpeas, or two 15-ounce cans chickpeas, drained and rinsed
> 3 tablespoons olive oil
> 1 pound boneless lamb, cubed into bite-size pieces
> 2 medium onions, chopped
> 1 large red pepper, seeded and chopped (hot or sweet, as you prefer)
> 1 teaspoon cinnamon
> 1 teaspoon freshly ground black pepper
> 1 cup chopped fresh cilantro
> ¹⁄₂ cup chopped fresh parsley
> 2 pounds ripe or canned tomatoes, chopped, juice reserved
> 1 cup red lentils, washed and picked through for stones
> 10 cups (2¹⁄₂ quarts) water
> ¹⁄₂ cup rice
> Salt to taste
> Cinnamon and lemon slices, for garnish

TO PREPARE

1. The night before, soak the dried chickpeas overnight in lots of water. The next morning, drain and husk the chickpeas by rubbing them between your palms.

2. Prep the remaining ingredients as directed in the recipe list.

Cilantro/Coriander—the Twofer Herb

This member of the parsley family is now in the produce sections of most supermarkets, but I'd never seen nor heard of it in 1983, when I first set foot in the souks of Morocco and found it everywhere, called "Moroccan parsley." Love at first bite. Native to southern Europe, cilantro has been cultivated for thousands of years by many, many cultures—for its seeds (often called *coriander*, from the Greek *koris*, or "bed bug," because of the buggy smell of the seeds when they're still green) and for its leaves (often called *cilantro*, its Spanish name). In ancient Egypt, the seeds were bruised to mix with bread. Romans prescribed the leaves, freshly chopped, for invalids and brought the plant with them to England. There, in Tudor times, the seeds were part of a highly spiced wedding drink called Hippocras—perhaps for their reputed aphrodisiac effect—and, indeed, if consumed in large quantities, coriander acts as a narcotic. What else does it do? It combats flatulence, and women throughout the Arab world chew the seeds to ease labor pains.

To Cook

1. Heat the oil over low heat in a large soup pot, then add the lamb, onions, red pepper, cinnamon, black pepper, ½ cup of the cilantro, and the parsley. Cook, stirring, over medium-low heat for 5 minutes.

2. Add the tomatoes, turn the heat to medium, and continue cooking for another 15 minutes.

3. Stir in the lentils, chickpeas (unless you're using canned chickpeas), reserved juice from the tomatoes, and the water, then bring to a boil over high heat. Reduce the heat to low and simmer, partially covered, for 1½ hours.

4. Add the rice and cook another 30 minutes. If you're using canned chickpeas, add them now.

5. Stir in the remaining ½ cup of cilantro and the salt. Let simmer for another 5 minutes.

To Serve

Ladle the soup into festive pottery bowls and sprinkle with cinnamon, pinching the grains between your thumb and forefinger to get a fine dusting. Serve lemon slices on the side—or you may pass around tiny bowls of fresh lemon juice with tiny spoons on the side. My family was served *harira* with bowls of lemon juice at a dinner hosted by a friend remotely connected to the Moroccan royal family, and I watched my lemon-loving young daughter across the low-slung table methodically spoon some 30 spoonfuls into her soup until she'd delicately emptied the entire bowl.

TURKEY

BRIDE SOUP
Ezo Gelin çorbası
Serves 6 to 8

THIS RICH TURKISH SOUP is attributed to an astonishingly beautiful girl born in 1909 in the village of Dokuzyol, located on ancient caravan routes in Turkey's Barak plain. Ezo had red cheeks and black hair and was adored by camel riders who stopped by her house for water. Her story ends badly, though; her first marriage to a villager was unhappy and she was permitted to forsake him on grounds of maltreatment. Her second marriage took her to Syria and a mother-in-law who couldn't be pleased — and for whom, it is said, she haplessly created this soup. Ezo died of tuberculosis in Syria in 1952, but in the interim had become a legend in her native land in both folk song and film. Her name lives on in this very popular, oniony, and stick-to-the-ribs soup, which is now traditionally fed to new brides right before their wedding to sustain them for what lies ahead.

> 6 tablespoons (¾ stick) butter
> 3 medium onions, finely chopped
> 2 teaspoons paprika
> 1½ cups red lentils, washed and picked over
> ¾ cup fine-grain bulgur wheat
> 10 cups (2½ quarts) Vegetable or Beef Stock (pages 23 and 26)
> 3 tablespoons tomato paste
> ¼ teaspoon cayenne pepper or red pepper flakes
> 2 tablespoons dried mint leaves
> Lemon slices and fresh small mint leaves or parsley, for
>   garnish

TO PREPARE
   Prep the ingredients as directed on the recipe list.

NASRETTIN HOCA AT A WEDDING PARTY

One day, Nasrettin Hoca was invited to a wedding. He arrived in his shabby, everyday clothing, and no one seemed to take any notice of him. He didn't like this a bit, and slipped out unnoticed. When he returned, he was wearing his best robe and his fine fur coat. At once people greeted him and showered him with compliments. He was given the best seat at the table and urged to eat the tastiest morsels. Smiling, he dipped the sleeve of his fur coat into the soup and said, "Here, help yourself, dear fur coat." Everyone was amazed and asked what he was doing. "Why, I was just inviting my coat to enjoy this excellent soup since it seems to command so much respect. A few minutes ago, without my fur coat, I wasn't even noticed, so I think it is the one that deserves the honor of feasting."

—NASRETTIN, *also known as Nasrudin and Yehá, is a fabled folklore figure throughout the Islamic world, but is specially claimed by Turkey, that says this real-life holy man was born in the village of Ak Shehir (Eskishehr) in the fifteenth century.*

TO COOK

1. Heat the butter over low heat in a large soup pot and sauté the onions until they are golden, about 15 minutes. Stir in the paprika, then the lentils and bulgur to coat them in the butter.

2. Add the stock, tomato paste, and cayenne; bring to a boil over medium-high heat, then reduce the heat to low and simmer until the bulgur is soft and creamy, about 1 hour.

3. Crumble the mint between your palms into the soup. Stir the soup and remove it from the heat. Let the soup rest for 10 minutes, covered.

TO SERVE

Ladle the soup into bowls and garnish each portion with a lemon slice and one or two mint leaves.

SPICY BEEF WEDDING SOUP
Dugun çorbası
Serves 6 to 8

In the old days, wedding celebrations in Turkey lasted forty days and forty nights. Today, they have been compressed to three at the most, with lots of gift giving and henna painting, but many are just overnight celebrations at a local hotel. Even so, *Dugun çorbasi* continues to mark the celebration. This hearty soup is traditionally served after the ceremony, beginning the banquet.

> *½ cup (1 stick) butter*
> *2 pounds boneless lamb or beef, finely diced or ground*
>   *(mutton is traditional, but lamb is really much better)*
> *2 carrots, peeled and finely chopped*
> *2 medium onions, finely chopped*
> *8 cups (2 quarts) Beef Stock (page 26)*
> *4 egg yolks*
> *1 lemon, juiced*

> Garnish
>   *Bread for 32 small croutons*
>   *2 tablespoons butter*
>   *1 tablespoon paprika*
>   *Cayenne pepper to taste*
>   *Ground cinnamon*

To Prepare
Prep the ingredients as directed in the recipe list. Also, cut 32 cubes of bread and make them into croutons for the garnish by toasting them in a 350°F. oven until they are dry and crisp, 5 to 10 minutes.

To Cook
1. Melt the butter over low heat in a large soup pot, then add the meat, carrots, and onions and sauté for 10 minutes. Gradually

---

A "Humorous" Turkish Song

*Your father, O beautiful one!
Has so often screamed and shouted,
And lowered the price of your dowry,
And said, "My daughters are beautiful!"*

stir in the stock, scraping up any bits stuck on the bottom of the pan. Bring to a boil over high heat, then reduce the heat to low and simmer, partially covered, for 1 hour.

2. Remove the soup from the heat. Beat the egg yolks in a small bowl, then beat the lemon juice into them and slowly stir into the soup. Cover the soup and let it rest while you finalize the soup garnishes.

3. In a small skillet, heat the butter and quickly sauté the paprika and cayenne in it. Take off the heat immediately.

TO SERVE

Ladle the soup into bowls. Then, swirl scant teaspoons of the paprika seasoning equally into the individual bowls. Top each portion with croutons and a dusting of cinnamon.

NASRETTIN HOCA AND THE WEDDING SOUP

On his way to preach at a mountain village, Nasrettin Hoca, the Turkish sage, was lost in an unexpected snowstorm. The next morning, the villagers found him half frozen under an oak tree, some distance from the village inn. When he came to himself, he thanked them for saving his life. "I kept myself warm by watching the glow of the inn's light," he told them. The villagers were delighted that they had saved Hoca's life, and they asked him for a show of appreciation. He agreed and said he would prepare a feast for them. The next night, all the villagers showed up at the inn and sang and danced in happy expectation of the feast that was being prepared for them. Time passed and Hoca continued to rush back and forth between the dining room and the kitchen, but still no food appeared. Finally the villagers lost patience and insisted that he hurry and serve them as they were becoming very hungry. "A festive occasion like this calls for a wedding soup," he answered.

"Come and see how it is being prepared." In the kitchen they found a huge cauldron hanging from the ceiling with a tiny candle underneath.

"You don't expect this candle to cook the soup, do you," they shouted with annoyance.

"Why not?" Hoca answered. "If the glow of the inn's light can keep a poor soul in the forest warmed up, surely a candle can cook a cauldron of wedding soup."

—For another Nasrettin story, and a little history about this fifteenth-century Sufi Master, see page 72.

8

To Honor the Dead

O NCE UPON A TIME, ancient man conceived of death as the beginning of a journey to another world. Not extinction, mind you, but a passage. Thus was the life of the spirit born. And no matter how advanced the civilization, like dynasties in Egypt and China, or rudimentary, like Germanic, Turkic, and Amerind tribes, all sent their leaders off on this journey with food to sustain them. Sometimes the food was real; sometimes pictures of it were drawn at the place of burial.

With the rise of monotheistic religions, though, earthly food traditions began to move out of the caskets and onto the tables of the mourners. Why soup? Because it stretched meager food supplies. It was the ideal food in times when community mourning was common, when people didn't have much food, and when soup could make that food go a long way ... and warm people's bellies besides, either before or after the graveyard ceremony.

The traditional recipes that follow make a generous number of portions to feed the guests who mourn with you. All, however, are excellent soups in their own right and are easy to double for larger gatherings or halve for small family dinners.

"DEATH IS SITTING AT THE FOOT OF MY BED"

*My bed is unmade: sheets on
    the floor
and blankets ready to fly out
    the door.
Ms. Death announces she'll
    make up the bed.
I beg her not to bother: just
    leave it like that.
She insists and replies that
    our date's for tonight,
Snuggles down and adds that
    she's in love and in the
    mood.
I answer that I've made a
    promise, on the level,
not to two-time life. She says
    go to the Devil.
Ms. Death is sitting at the
    foot of my bed.
This wretched Lady Death
    has got the hots for me
and wants to suck me drier
    than a fig plucked off a
    tree.
Now she wants to lie down
    for a minute by my side
just to sleep a little, I need not
    be afraid.
From respect, I don't suggest
    her reputation's not so
    good.
Ms. Death is sitting at the
    foot of my bed.*

—ÓSCAR HAHN, *twentieth-century Mexican poet*

75

FRANCE

SAFFRON SOUP
PÉRIGOURDINE LE MOURTAÏROL
Serves 6 to 8

IN PÉRIGORD, FRANCE, this bread soup is traditionally served after funerals. Heavy with saffron, thick, and hearty, it certainly goes back to medieval times. Too bad it's so closely associated with death: it's a wonderful—and beautiful—soup, maybe worth resurrecting, say, for occasions when you need a ceremonial dish to put something officially behind you.

> *1 loaf stale French bread, cut into thin slices*
> *1 cup diced cooked chicken*
> *2 carrots, peeled and sliced into thin rounds*
> *8 cups (2 quarts) rich Chicken Stock (page 24)*
> *1/4 teaspoon saffron, ground or crushed to a powder*

TO PREPARE

Prep the ingredients as directed in the recipe list. Preheat the oven to 400°F.

TO COOK

1. Make one layer of bread slices in the bottom of a deep casserole, sprinkle with chicken pieces and carrot rounds, then continue to layer the bread-chicken-carrots until all the ingredients are used, ending with bread on top. Don't layer to the top of the pot or the soup will splash in the oven.

2. Heat the chicken stock in a saucepan over medium heat. In a small cup, mix the crushed saffron with several tablespoons of the hot broth and let it steep for about 5 minutes, for the saffron color and flavor to be completely released. It will be a dark orange liquid. Stir this into the rest of the stock, then ladle over the casserole. When the top layer of bread slices begins to float, gently add about another cup of broth.

3. Put the casserole, uncovered, in the oven and reduce the heat to 350°F.

4. Check back in about 1 hour; most of the liquid will be absorbed and a gratin will have formed on the top.

TO SERVE

Ladle the soup into flat soup plates and serve immediately.

"OBLIVION"

Vast black slumber falls deep
On my life which expires—
All hopes, go to sleep,
Go to sleep, all desires.

I see nothing; Night fills
Me; remembrances fail
Of past good and past ills.
O the poor sorry tale!

I a cradle in gloom
That a hand seems to brush
In the depths of a tomb:
Silence, hush! . . .

—PAUL VERLAINE, *nineteenth-century French "decadent" poet*

SOUP AT THE WAKE

In Leon Uris's *Trinity,* his novel about Ireland before the Easter Rising of 1916, "Grandfar" Kilty Larkin dies in the first page of the book and his proper wake begins in the next chapter, with the food, tobacco, whiskey, Banshee stories, and keening described in glorious and wide-eyed detail.

"Kilty Larkin looked ever so grand laid out in the best room. . . . They knelt, intoned a quick prayer and drifted to the fringes of the room. Brigid had filled dozens of small clay pipes with tobacco which had supernatural qualities at times like this, and offered them about with a plate of snuff to hasten Kilty's journey and resurrection. Three lambs had been slaughtered and an immense stew boiled in the great pot and a dozen loaves of fadge, a potato bread, browned on the baking boards. . . ."

IRELAND

COTTAGE BROTH FOR THE WAKE

Serves 6 to 8

SO THICK WITH vegetables and barley, and so rich with lamb shank meat and broth — it's enough to bring the dead back to life, or at the very least sustain the mourners through their long evening of smoking, drinking, and telling stories.

FOR THE BROTH
   2 pounds lamb shanks
   8 cups (2 quarts) cold water
   1 medium onion, quartered
   2 celery stalks with leaves, chopped into big pieces
   2 carrots, scrubbed and chopped into big pieces
   2 bay leaves
   ½ teaspoon black peppercorns
   2 teaspoons salt

FOR THE SOUP
   ¼ cup barley
   3 tablespoons butter
   2 leeks, washed and sliced well into the green
   1 medium onion, diced
   3 carrots, peeled and diced
   2 celery stalks with leaves, diced
   2 medium turnips, peeled and diced
   1 cup finely shredded cabbage
   1 teaspoon dried thyme
   Salt and pepper to taste

To Prepare

1. The day before, prepare the broth and meat. Roast the lamb shanks in a 400° F. oven until well browned, then place in a pot with the cold water, onion, celery, carrots, bay leaves, peppercorns, and salt. Bring to a boil over medium heat, then reduce the heat to low, cover, and simmer for 3 hours, until the meat is very tender.

2. Remove the meat from the broth. Strain the broth, discarding the solids; let cool, then refrigerate. Cut the fat and tissues away from the meat, then cut the meat into small pieces and reserve in the refrigerator until you are ready to make the soup.

3. Also the day before, put the barley in plenty of water to soak overnight.

4. The next day, prep the remaining ingredients as directed in the recipe list.

To Cook

1. Heat the butter in a large soup pot over medium heat and stir in the leeks, onion, carrots, celery, and turnips. Cook over medium heat, stirring occasionally, while the vegetables sweeten, about 5 minutes. Stir in the cabbage and cook for 5 more minutes, until the vegetables are tender.

2. Meanwhile, remove the fat from the soup stock and discard or save for another purpose. Pour the stock into the vegetables, adding enough water to make 8 cups. Drain the barley and stir into the soup. Add the reserved lamb and also the thyme, crumbling it between your palms. Stir well, bring the soup to a boil over medium-high heat, then reduce the heat to low, cover, and let simmer for another hour, until the barley is tender. Season with salt and pepper.

To Serve

Ladle the soup into bowls and serve with hot potato bread, cheeses, tobacco, and lots of liquor . . . and get ready to talk of the Banshee.

"The Ballad of Father O'Hart"

Good Father John O'Hart
In penal days rode out
To a shoneen who had free lands
And his own snipe and trout.

In trust took he John's lands;
Sleiveens were all his race;
And he gave them as dowers to his daughters,
And they married beyond their place.

But Father John went up,
And Father John went down;
And he wore small holes in his shoes,
And he wore large holes in his gown.

All loved him, only the shoneen,
Whom the devils have by the hair,
From the wives, and the cats, and the children,
To the birds in the white of the air.

The birds, for he opened their cages
As he went up and down;
And he said with a smile, 'Have peace now';
And he went his way with a frown.

But if when anyone died
Came keeners hoarser than rooks,
He bade them give over their keening;
For he was a man of books.

And these were the works of John,
When, weeping score by score,
People came into Coloney;
For he'd died at ninety-four.

There was no human keening;
The birds from Knocknarea
And the world round Knocknashee
Came keening in that day.

The young birds and old birds
Came flying, heavy and sad;
Keening in from Tiraragh,
Keening from Ballinafad;

Keening from Inishmurrah,
Nor stayed for bite or sup;
This way were all reproved
Who dig old customs up.

—William Butler Yeats, *twentieth-century Irish poet*

PHILIPPINES

CRYSTAL NOODLE AND CHICKEN SOUP

SONTANGHON

Serves 6 to 8

ACCORDING TO GILDA Cordero-Fernando, in *Philippine Food and Life,* after a death "the corpse was kept in the house for three days, and these were the days of feasting. The widow was supposed to cook her grief away in a river of *sotanghon* or *bami. . . .*" And well she might. This is a dramatic and unusual soup—a bloodred broth stuffed with big chunks of chicken flesh and a mass of clear yellow noodles. Sound gory-looking? It is—along the lines of some Francis Bacon portraits I've seen that look like they're missing their skin. But this soup is also fragrant, savory, tart, overstuffed, and just flat-out delicious—it will take your breath away. And did I tell you those long noodles are slippery? Serve with forks or chopsticks as well as spoons. Many thanks to dear friend Art Meyer for tracking down this tradition.

> 8 cups (2 quarts) cold water
> Lard or chicken fat for frying
> 4 to 5 pounds chicken, cut up (with liver and gizzard)
> 1 cup chopped green onions, white and green parts
> Salt and pepper to taste
> 2 tablespoons peanut oil
> 15 garlic cloves, sliced
> 1 medium onion, diced
> 2 hot chile peppers (or to taste), seeded and finely diced
> 2 teaspoons annatto (achiote) powder (pulverize the seeds with a hammer or pestle if you can't find powder)
> 6 ounces (about 2 cups) cellophane noodles (bean threads)
> 1 tablespoon patis (or nuoc mam/nam pla) fish sauce, or more to taste

GARNISH

8 garlic cloves, sliced
Diagonal slices of green onion
1 calamansi (a very acidic hybrid of the mandarin orange and
     kumquat) or lime

TO PREPARE

1. You might consider making the broth the day before (steps 1 to 3) and refrigerating it. It makes it so easy to finalize the soup — just minutes to remove the congealed fat from the broth, sauté the giblets and seasonings, cook the noodles, and toss together with the chicken pieces.

2. Prep the ingredients as directed in the recipe list to include the garnish: frying the garlic slices in a little peanut oil until crisp, then draining on paper towels; thinly slicing the green onion; and slicing wedges of calamansi or lime.

TO COOK

1. Pour the cold water into a large soup pot and keep handy.

2. Melt the fat in a large skillet over medium-high heat. Brown the chicken parts in the fat and add them to the cold water in the soup pot. Begin heating the soup over medium heat, then toss in the green onions, salt, and pepper, and bring to a slow boil. Reduce the heat and simmer until the chicken is tender and falling off the bone. Depending on the age and toughness of the chicken, this could take as long as 2 hours.

3. Strain the soup, removing the chicken and discarding the vegetable solids. Return the broth to the pot, skimming any fat. Let the chicken cool, uncovered, then shred and reserve, discarding the skin and bones. (You may refrigerate the broth at this point.) Cut the liver and gizzard into small pieces and reserve them apart from the chicken.

4. Heat the peanut oil in a skillet over medium heat and fry the garlic for 1 minute. Toss in the onion and sauté until transparent, then add the liver and gizzard pieces, the diced chiles, and the an-

natto powder and sauté, stirring constantly, for 2 minutes. Remove from the heat and set aside.

5. Bring the broth in the soup pot back to a low boil over medium heat and add the noodles, simmering them for 5 minutes. Add the shredded chicken, the sautéed vegetables from the skillet (washing the skillet with the broth to get every scrap of seasoning into the soup), and the fish sauce. Simmer for 5 more minutes. Taste for seasoning, adding more fish sauce as needed.

To Serve

Ladle the soup into bowls, evenly distributing the noodles, and garnish each portion with crispy garlic, green onion slices, and a slice of calamansi or lime.

"Suns Have Gone"

Beneath the arcade of flame trees,
My love walks alone,
A frail creature from whose eyes
The twelfth sun has gone.

As she goes by feeling her way
With a swaying bamboo cane,
A panel of kindly faces wears
A long tender look of pain.

Sitting on a familiar stone,
Where she held hands with me,
Tears of lost desires flow down
The stony bone of her memory.

Beneath the deflowered trees,
My love still walks alone,
A gray woman in whose enfeebled eyes
Suns have brightly shone.

—Oscar de Zuñiga, *twentieth-century Filipino poet*

PART III

SOUPS OF PURPOSE

"THE FURY OF RAINSTORMS"

The rain drums down like red ants,
each bouncing off my window
These ants are in great pain
and they cry out as they hit,
as if their little legs were only
stitched on and their heads pasted.
And oh they bring to mind the grave,
so humble, so willing to be beat upon
with its awful lettering and
the body lying underneath
without an umbrella.

Depression is boring, I think,
and I would do better to make
some soup and light up the cave.

—ANNE SEXTON, *1974*

9

To Lose Weight

ONCE UPON A TIME, soup was primarily prescribed to *stimulate* the appetite, not depress it.

Oh, right. Mmmm. But those were the days when even the leisure classes got a fair amount of exercise (no cars), didn't eat snacks (no refrigeration; mouth-buckling preservatives), and had little concept of "empty calories." It was also a time when ideal feminine beauty was on the plump side, manly torsos were comfortable, and fleshiness was a sign of affluence and position in a poor, thin world. Not so anymore. And ain't it great that soup—early on a way to stretch tough and meager ingredients, later a way to tickle dainty taste buds—now, in its soulful adaptability, is one of the most reliable ways around to shed those unwanted pounds.

How so?

For a bunch of reasons, all working together to shrink our burgeoning waistlines.

1. Eating soup at the start of a meal fills the stomach, which signals the brain to curtail appetite. A ten-week study involving ten thousand students at the University of Pennsylvania in the late seventies gave proof to this commonsense observation. Imagine: ten thousand contrary adolescents agreed that when they started a meal with soup, they got full fast and ate less.

2. Eating soup fools the body's natural sensors into thinking more calories have been consumed than actually have. Dr. Elizabeth Bell, at the University of Pennsylvania, conducted a study in 1999 to determine "if the effect of increasing the water content of food can enhance the effect of that food on satiety, therefore reducing subsequent calorie intake." That is to say, one day, her cadre of twenty-four women began lunch with a 270-calorie chicken-and-rice casserole; the next day, they started with that same casserole plus they drank a 10-ounce glass of water with it; on the third day, they started with the casserole and water mixed, heated, and served as a soup. After each round, researchers measured exactly how much the women ate during the rest of the meal. Hands-down victory was for the soup: instead of chowing down for 300+ calories at the open buffet, as they had the first two days, the soup eaters daintily pushed their plates away after 200 calories.

3. Eating soup is a low-calorie way of satisfying a person's need for a certain **volume of food.** Nutrition researcher Barbara Rolls conducted studies in the late 1990s that show people eat the same weight of food day after day, pretty much no matter what. So you can eat that weight in hamburgers or in tuna fish sandwiches or in candy bars . . . or you can eat that weight in soup. Now then, if you regularly choose those nice low-calorie soups—say, every day at lunch—you're going to lose weight. Just that many fewer calories to burn.

4. Eating soup on a regular basis helps you lose weight because it changes your eating patterns. In 1979, Dr. Henry Jordan, behavioral weight-control specialist, made some five hundred volunteers eat soup for lunch every day for ten weeks. His findings? Soup eaters consumed fewer calories and lost an average of 20 percent of their excess body weight. Why? Because soup is complicated to eat—it takes time and motor skills to consume, so you tend to eat less.

Consider: You have to sit down to eat it. You have eat it with a utensil, and you can shovel in only so much of it per spoonful. You can't gulp it down because it's hot. If you put it in a big bowl, you're fooled into thinking you're eating a big portion. Then, because it comes as a complex package of stuff—different textures, shapes, and tastes all together and all at once—you have to work it around in your mouth, take time to process it. Not to mention worrying about slurping and slopping it all over the place.

Compare eating a 500-calorie bowl of Vietnamese *phó,* which takes a good 30 minutes of concentrated pleasure to get down, not to mention taking time to wipe the sweat off your forehead, with going to a McDonald's take-out window so you can wolf down that 560-calorie Big Mac and super-size fries while you've still got the blinker on to pull out of the parking lot.

So, SOUP IS a very good thing for dieters—a sure thing, if you eat it regularly and avoid the *crèmes* and the *beurres*—and infinitely interesting and satisfying no matter how often you eat it, whether it's cool *tarator,* spicy *laksa,* rich *sopa de camarão,* or hearty borshch.

But yes, yes. I hear what you're thinking. What about that seven-day cabbage soup diet that is specially designed to make the pounds fall off? In fact, I like it and believe that soup works *within carefully drawn limits*—that is, if you want to drop a few pounds fast, rediscover your waist, or most especially, kick-start a longer weight-loss campaign. But remember: it's for seven days only and you should stop immediately if you feel weak or sick.

THE CABBAGE SOUP DIET

WONDERFULLY PURE, a "vat" of this stuff lasts about a week, depending on how much you eat each day. Eat as much of the soup as you like, as often as you like. Here's what else you can eat along with the soup, and when:

DAY 1: All fruits except bananas.

DAY 2: All vegetables, raw or cooked. This includes baked potatoes with a *little* butter.

DAY 3: Fruits and vegetables, but no potatoes or bananas.

DAY 4: Bananas and skim milk — eat as many as 8 bananas and drink as many as 8 glasses of skim milk. You may substitute nonfat yogurt for the milk and flavor it with vanilla or mashed bananas.

DAY 5: Beef, skinless chicken, and/or fish — as much as 20 ounces total. You can also eat 6 tomatoes. And you must drink 8 glasses of water. Don't forget at least 1 bowl of soup.

DAY 6: Beef, skinless chicken, or fish and vegetables. Drink 8 glasses of water and eat at least 1 bowl of soup.

DAY 7: Brown rice, vegetables, and unsweetened fruit juice.

1 head green cabbage, finely shredded or chopped
2 large onions, chopped
16 to 28 ounces canned tomatoes, chopped, with juices
2 green bell peppers, seeded and chopped
4 celery stalks with leaves, chopped
6 carrots, peeled and sliced
½ pound green beans, stem ends snapped, sliced on the
  diagonal
Black pepper to taste
Chopped fresh herbs, such as parsley, sage, dill, cilantro, or
  thyme

GARNISH
Balsamic vinegar or lemon or lime juice
Minced fresh herbs
Chopped green onions

TO PREPARE

Prep the ingredients as directed in the recipe list.

TO COOK

Put all the vegetables in a big soup pot and cover with water. Bring to a boil over high heat, then reduce the heat to medium and boil gently for 10 minutes. Cover, reduce the heat to low, and simmer until all the vegetables are soft. Stir in the black pepper and chopped herbs.

TO SERVE

This soup can be served hot or cold. It can be pureed or partially pureed to vary textures. It can be seasoned differently for variety, with balsamic vinegar, lemon or lime juice, different fresh herbs, or chopped green onions.

STARVING ARTIST SOUP

Serves 1 for 2 evening meals

THIS STORY WAS sent to me by Ronnie Reed of Worthington, Ohio, and the story is even (or perhaps much) better than the recipe he enclosed — an inspiration to lovers everywhere. If you're trying to survive a difficult time, aren't used to cooking, wouldn't mind losing a little weight, are yearning to be with the one you love — any or all of these things — I think you'll be interested in what Ronnie has to say about soup and love.

I'm thirty-one years of age and work for an international business machine company. My wife and I have been married for twelve years. I have grown to love and appreciate soups in general lately. During my separation from my wife, I ate soup for lunch and dinner for, well, let's just say *a long time!* I went from 220 down to 190 in a matter of months. I still eat soup at least twice a week. In a nutshell, it's good for you and good for the soul. *Soup rules!*

Here's my story and recipe.

This soup was invented during a time when my wife and I were separated for a few months. I wanted to lose weight and cut back on costs but not die from starvation, so I had to learn how to cook. Man cannot live off beer and peanut-butter crackers alone. To me, if it's worth looking at, it's worth eating. So in an attempt to be as creative as I could without burning down the kitchen, I made "The Starving Artist Soup." It's easy, it's quick, and it looks good, too. What you will need are . . .

2 (10-ounce) cans Campbell's Beef Vegetable Soup
1 pound hamburger meat (ground sirloin)

Brown the hamburger meat in a pot and drain the grease (the second step is optional, depending on how hungry you are). Add the 2 cans of soup to the hamburger, then add 2 cans of water. Let it cook for 2 minutes on high heat, then bring it down to a simmer.

It makes about four bowls, so you can eat two that night and have leftovers the next night for dinner. It does taste better the second day; I'm not sure why. I lived on this stuff for four months. I lost twenty pounds, paid my expenses, and survived. My wife, after discovering that I hadn't died without her, came back. That's my story and recipe. Thanks for reading it.

10

TO STIMULATE AN APPETITE

ONCE UPON A TIME, that magnificent "Monarch of the Kitchen," Antonin Carême — chef to Talleyrand, Tsar Alexander I, George IV, and Baron de Rothschild — stipulated that soup "must be the agent provocateur of a good dinner." Nineteenth-century French gastronome and lawyer Alexandre-Balthazar-Laurent Grimod de la Reynière agreed, opining that "soup is to dinner what the portico or the peristyle is to an edifice. That is to say, not only is it the first part, but it should be conceived in such a way as to give an exact idea of the feast, very nearly as the overture to an opera should announce the quality of the whole work."

In other words, when you're in the business of *stimulating* appetites, you are not going to be tossing chunks of pure vegetable into fat-free water or broth and calling it a day. You are, rather, orchestrating exquisite creations out of precious ingredients that are designed to excite the eye, the nose, and the palate.

In today's largely overweight society, you don't hear a lot of call for this kind of appetite teasing. And yet that call is there: for those who suffer from anorexia or bulimia; those who have lost weight after medical procedures like chemotherapy; elderly people suffering appetite loss, who need to be coaxed back to strength — not to mention athletes who are trying to make weight. In all these cases, what could be better than an elegant and very thin potation that delights with delicate beauty and taste, that sharpens the appetite with a little sharpness of its own, or that teases the tongue with layers of flavor in a concentrated cream?

Each of the following recipes is set for four servings — say, for that intimate dinner party you've been thinking about hosting. But each can easily be doubled for an even bigger splash, or halved for *dîner à deux.*

THE KINDEST COURSE

Soup is cuisine's kindest course. It breathes reassurance; it steams consolation; after a weary day it promotes sociability . . . there is nothing like a bowl of hot soup, its wisp of aromatic steam making the nostrils quiver with anticipation.

—CHEF LOUIS P. DEGOUY, *THE SOUP BOOK, 1949*

CRAB TALES

- John Russell describes crab in his 1460 Boke of Nurture as "a slutt to kerve and a wrawd wight" (a perverse creature).
- Norman Douglas describes its hold over Italians when he noted "Beelzebub himself could never keep a Capri fisherman out of a sea-cave if there was half a franc's worth of crabs inside it."
- Poet T. S. Eliot plays it against type when he has his timid J. Alfred Prufrock declare, "I should have been/a pair of ragged claws/Scuttling across the floors of silent seas."

In fact, the crab is a crustacean that, as a general rule, will eat anything it runs across, and likes nothing better than to fight and procreate. So much for Eliot's image of a repressed creature.

CREAMY CRAB AND COGNAC SOUP
Serves 4

A TOTALLY DECADENT start to some heavenly meal. You might even want to double the recipe and serve it as the second course.

> *4 tablespoons (½ stick) butter*
> *3 tablespoons all-purpose flour*
> *4 cups milk*
> *2 tablespoons grated onion*
> *2 teaspoons concentrated vegetable or chicken base, or crushed bouillon cubes*
> *2 teaspoons chopped fresh parsley*
> *1 teaspoon salt*
> *½ teaspoon ground white pepper*
> *¼ teaspoon grated nutmeg*
> *½ pound backfin crab meat, with any shells removed*
> *1 tablespoon Cognac*
> *Tiny pinches of grated nutmeg, for garnish*

TO PREPARE
Prep the ingredients as directed in the recipe list.

TO COOK
1. Melt the butter in a large saucepan over medium-low heat. Whisk in the flour and cook, stirring constantly, for 3 minutes. Grad-

ually whisk in the milk. Add the onion, stock base or bouillon cubes, parsley, salt, pepper, and nutmeg. Raise the heat to high and bring to a boil, then reduce the heat to low and simmer, uncovered, until the soup begins to thicken, stirring occasionally, about 10 minutes.

2. Add the crab meat, stirring gently to keep the lumps from breaking apart, and simmer until the soup is creamy and the crab is heated through, 10 to 15 minutes.

To Serve

Adjust the seasonings, stir in the Cognac, and ladle the soup immediately into elegant cups. Lightly pinch a bit of nutmeg into each portion.

CRABBY DELIGHTS

Besides being tasty, crab meat is considered an aphrodisiac, possibly because its own history shows it to be eminently successful in the amatory arts. Having evolved during the Jurassic period, along with all those dinosaurs, the crab not only survived the period but multiplied into some 4,500 different species. Some scuttle sideways; some swim; some walk on land.

The ancients, though, set it in the skies: the Cancer constellation. Who put it there? First the Babylonians, who just noted it. Then the Greeks, who lifted it to stardom, giving it a bit role in Hercules' ninth labor, when he fights and defeats the nine-headed Hydra. Here's the story: Hera, queen of the gods and eternal hater of this illegitimate son of hubby Zeus, sent a Giant Crab out of the Lerna swamp to pinch Hercules' toes and distract him from the task at hand. Didn't faze him. Hercules smooshed that crab flat with his foot, without even a courtesy glance. Hera felt bad about the Crab's quick end and, to make up for it, gave it immortality by placing it in the heavens as the Cancer constellation. Or so Ptolemy's *Almagest* in the second century A.D. says. But modern astronomers generally think that, because it's such a dim and poorly defined constellation, ancient astrologers fudged—just made the whole story up so they could round out the heavenly map using the Hercules myth to score the twelves signs of the Zodiac.

TRUTH IN LAST RITES

An Irish nobleman, on his deathbed, summoned his heir to his bedside and told him he had a secret to communicate that might prove some compensation for the dilapidated condition of the family property. It was that crab sauce is better than lobster sauce.

—Abraham Hayward, *The Art of Dining*, 1852

STRAWBERRY BALSAMICO SOUP

Serves 4

THE EXCEPTION THAT proves the rule: practically noncaloric, but just the thing for provoking an appetite. This marvelous cold fruit soup was brought to my attention by Lisa Gitelson of New York City. She says it best: "Give it a try on a hot summer's night, don't tell your guests what's in it, and they will fall in love." Serve cold in small cups as a tantalizing first course. For larger portions, double the recipe and serve in elegant flat soup plates.

STRAWBERRIES

This member of the rose family is not a true berry at all, since it carries its tiny seeds on the outside of its flesh instead of within its tissue—and it's old, very old. So old that it's native to both the Old and New Worlds, meaning it had already evolved, like the walnut, when these continents were attached during Earth's early history. Its English name probably derives from the way it grows—originally called *strewberry* because of the way it's "strewn" over the ground; its Latin genus, *Fragaria,* is from its heady fragrance.

Strawberries didn't taste all that great in their wild state, though Romans—those omnivores—were said to relish them. Cultivation began in the fourteenth century in Europe and almost immediately captured the imagination of artistic monks, when the French king Charles V had some 12,000 strawberry plants set out in his Royal Gardens in 1386. It was a short artistic walk in the monastery for the strawberry to ramble from being a decorative element in religious paintings to becoming a rosy symbol for the Virgin Mary herself.

Strawberry lusciousness got a big upgrade in the seventeenth century, when the New World *Fragaria virginiana* was brought into the mix to create the modern strawberry. Of this New World varietal—a favorite of Native Americans that was first catalogued in Massachusetts in 1621—one colonist in Maryland wrote, "We cannot set down a foot but we tread on strawberries."

3 cups halved strawberries
³/₄ cup sugar
4 tablespoons balsamic vinegar
¹/₂ teaspoon finely grated orange zest
¹/₄ teaspoon finely grated lemon zest
1 tablespoon Grand Marnier liqueur or orange juice
3 cups plain yogurt

GARNISH
1 cup halved strawberries
¹/₄ cup sugar
1 tablespoon balsamic vinegar

TO PREPARE

1. Three hours ahead, make the garnish first by tossing the halved strawberries with the sugar and balsamic vinegar. Let the berries macerate for at least 2 hours at room temperature or in the fridge.

2. Also 3 hours ahead, puree the halved strawberries for the soup with the sugar, balsamic vinegar, zests, and Grand Marnier. Make sure the sugar has completely dissolved, and let it sit for a few minutes if it hasn't. Whip the yogurt in a separate bowl, then stir it into the puree until the soup is smooth. Chill well, at least 2 hours.

TO SERVE

Ladle the soup into small cups and top with the macerated strawberries. Drizzle a few teaspoonfuls of the strawberry juice left from the garnish over each portion in a dramatic pattern.

NOT PREJUDICE, BUT GOOD SENSE

We may say of angling as Dr. Boteler said of strawberries: "Doubtless God could have made a better berry, but doubtless God never did."

—SIR IZAAK WALTON, *THE COMPLEAT ANGLER*, 1653

TARRAGON, FROM THE STEPPES OF CENTRAL ASIA

No, really. *Fines herbes* and *haute cuisine* notwithstanding, this baby started life in Siberia and didn't make it to Europe over ancient trade routes until medieval times—a sad thing for ancient Greeks and Romans. Its name is a corruption of the French *estragon*, or "little dragon," in turn a corruption of the Arabic *tarkhun*. Perhaps its dragonish name derived from its reputation for curing the bites and stings of reptiles, venomous insects, and mad dogs, but if you saw its tortuous, coiled roots you might also see the resemblance to depictions of the deadly firebreathing "worm" that battled Saint George.

Tarragon was finally imported to England in the fifteenth century, but grown exclusively in the Royal Gardens. A hundred years later it found its way into English kitchens as a culinary herb, but it wasn't introduced to the New World until the nineteenth century.

FRANCE

TARRAGON JELLIED CONSOMMÉ
CONSOMMÉ À L'ESSENCE D'ESTRAGON EN GELÉE
Serves 4

ELEGANT AND BRACING, perhaps particularly on a hot summer day. All the steps can be done ahead so that final assembly takes only a minute. This is a favorite of the English ballerina Anya Linden, formerly of the Royal Ballet, who substitutes spoonfuls of Beluga caviar for the shrimp.

> 5 cups rich Chicken Stock, preferably homemade and clarified
> (see pages 24 and 31); if you make it with chicken feet, it
> will be naturally gelatinous and you can forgo the gelatin
> and water below
> 1 tablespoon unflavored gelatin (usually sold in 1-tablespoon
> envelopes)
> ¼ cup cold water
> 4 teaspoons minced fresh tarragon or 1 teaspoon dried,
> crumbled, and hydrated in a little warm water for 15
> minutes
> 1 teaspoon seafood seasoning (such as Old Bay)
> ¼ pound raw, unpeeled shrimp
> Lettuce leaves (Bibb or other butterhead lettuce is nice)

GARNISH
Fresh parsley
1 large lemon

TO PREPARE

NOTE: Start the soup at least 5 hours in advance to let it turn to jelly in the refrigerator.

Prep the ingredients as directed in the recipe list and, if you are not starting with gelatinous, homemade stock, dissolve the gelatin in the cold water for 10 minutes.

To Cook

1. Bring the stock to a boil in a large saucepan over medium-high heat. Reduce the heat to low and simmer for 5 minutes. Add the tarragon and the dissolved gelatin, if using, mixing well. Remove from the heat and let cool to room temperature, uncovered. Cover and refrigerate for at least 4 hours.

2. Bring about 4 cups of water and the seafood seasoning to a boil over high heat, then add the shrimp and boil them in their shells for 5 minutes. Drain and cool, remove their shells and devein their backs, then chop them into bite-size pieces. Store in the refrigerator until you are ready to assemble the soup.

3. Wash the lettuce and tear it into pieces that will fit into your serving cups. Store in the refrigerator in paper towels, to crisp.

4. Prepare the garnishes: chop the parsley, slice four thin rounds from the lemon, and cut a wedge from the remainder for squeezing.

To Serve

Line elegant cups—ideally crystal or glass so you can see the sparkling jelly—with the lettuce. Gently stir the jellied soup, then ladle it into the cups. Sprinkle each portion with the shrimp, parsley, and a squeeze of lemon juice, then slide a paper-thin lemon round down into the jelly.

SOUP WISDOM FROM THE "KING OF CHEFS AND CHEF OF KINGS"

Soup puts the heart at ease, calms down the violence of hunger, eliminates the tension of the day, and awakens and refines the appetite.

—AUGUSTE ESCOFFIER, *early twentieth-century French chef who served as Chef de Cuisine in the Franco-Prussian War, then went on to revolutionize the professional kitchen at The Savoy and other great hotels. It was Germany's Kaiser Wilhelm II who told Escoffier, "I am the Emperor of Germany, but you are the emperor of chefs."*

AVOCADOS

Known as "alligator pears" for their shape and reptilian skin, and as "poor man's butter" for their creaminess, avocados are most colorfully known as the fruit of the "testicle tree." It's no mystery why. Fully fruited, these ovulate gems hang down from the trees in twos—and have a longstanding reputation as aphrodisiacs. Their very name in Aztec, *ahuacatl,* means "testicle."

Avocados are native to Central America and can be traced back to the fifth century B.C.E. in Mexico and Guatemala, cultivated by both Aztecs and Mayans. In 1519, the Spanish cartographer Martin Fernandez de Encisco, returning from an exploration on the northern coast of South America, pronounced them "marvelous of flavor, so good and pleasing to the palate that it is a marvelous thing." U.S. President George Washington, on a visit to Barbados in his youth, reportedly ate the *avogato* with extreme pleasure.

MEXICO

AVOCADOLICIOUS SOUP
SOPA DE AGUACATE
Serves 4

PIQUANT BUT NOT too piquant, creamy but not creamy thick, and packed with calories, this Mexican soup is gorgeously elegant and brainlessly easy to make, whether you decide to serve it cold or hot. If the former, you'll make it completely in advance and be done with it; if the latter, be prepared to throw it together at the very last minute because you don't want the delicate avocado turning bitter on you if it's cooked too long. Needless to say, don't even think about trying to reheat it.

> 4 cups (1 quart) Vegetable or Chicken Stock (pages 23 and 24)
> 1 cup heavy cream
> 1 chile pepper, as hot as you dare (from banana to habanero)
> 1 garlic clove
> 2 avocados, peeled and pitted
> Salt and white pepper to taste

GARNISH
> Minced fresh cilantro
> Crisp tortilla chips or fresh tortillas fried in lard or oil

TO PREPARE

NOTE: If you are making the cold version, start at least 3 hours ahead so the soup has time to chill properly.

Prep the ingredients as directed in the recipe list.

TO COOK

1. Heat the stock and cream over medium-high heat in a large saucepan, then reduce the heat to low and keep at a simmer.

2. Either in advance for the cold soup or at the last minute for the hot soup, puree the chile pepper and garlic in a blender, then toss in the avocados. Gradually add the hot stock mixture and blend until smooth. Season with salt and pepper, remembering to overseason slightly for a cold soup.

To Serve

Either serve the hot soup immediately in elegant bowls with the cilantro topping and tortilla chips on the side, or cool slightly and refrigerate to make a cold soup that you will serve later, also with the cilantro and chips.

Cinematic Avocados

In arguably one of the most "B" movies ever made, *Cannibal Women in the Avocado Jungle of Death* (1989), Colonel Mattel (Paul Ross) warns: "Avocados are vital to this nation's security interests. With the communists already in control of Nicaragua and Guatemala and El Salvador rife with revolution, California is the last secure supply of avocados in the free world. We're on the verge of a major avocado gap!"

SPAIN

CHILLED "PUREED SALAD"
ANDALUSIAN GAZPACHO
Serves 4

I WAS PLEASED to get this recipe from José Luis Vivas, a native of Seville currently living in Brussels and working as a conference interpreter; José is a gifted polyglot, hot-air balloon crewman, and connoisseur. The following recipe, his personal version, is both authentic and wonderful. Mr. Vivas says, "Usually you make the quantities very large. This is because we usually make a large batch of this 'base cream' and thin it with water to taste, as you can either eat it from a dish like a pureed salad or, as we very often like to do in our hot summers, drink it in a glass." If you want a smoother texture you can peel the tomatoes and remove the seeds from them and from the cucumbers.

NOTE: Start the soup at least 3 hours in advance so it has time to chill properly. If you don't have time to chill it properly, just stir some ice cubes into it before serving.

> *2 slices crusty white bread*
> *2 pounds ripe or canned tomatoes*
> *1 pound cucumber, peeled and coarsely chopped*
> *1 large green bell pepper, seeded and chopped*
> *1 red bell pepper, seeded and chopped (optional for stronger color)*
> *2 large garlic cloves*
> *½ cup olive oil*
> *¼ cup sherry vinegar*
> *2 teaspoons sea salt*

Garnish

*Chopped tomato, onion, cucumber, green pepper, hard-boiled
egg, and Spanish dried ham*
Fresh spearmint leaves

To Prepare

1. Soak the bread in plenty of water. Prep the remaining ingredients as directed in the recipe list.

2. Puree all the fruits in a blender (and, yes, they are all fruits, not vegetables), saving the garlic for last. Add the soaked bread, barely drained, the oil, vinegar, and salt and blend again. Refrigerate until very cold.

3. Prepare the bowls of garnishes.

To Serve

Ladle the soup into large bowls, dropping a spearmint leaf into each. When served "formally," gazpacho is presented with an array of garnishes in separate dishes. Pass the garnish bowls for people to serve themselves.

ALICE B. TOKLAS ON
GAZPACHO

After the first ineffable *gazpacho* was served to us [Alice and her longtime lover Gertrude Stein] in Malaga and an entirely different but equally exquisite one was presented in Seville the recipes for them had unquestionably become of greater importance than Grecos and Zurbarans, than cathedrals and museums. Surely the calle de las Sierpes, the liveliest, most seductive of streets, would produce the cook-book that would answer the burning consuming question of how to prepare a *gazpacho*.... Cook-books without number, exactly eleven, were offered for inspections but not a *gazpacho* in any index. Oh, said the clerk, *gazpachos* are only eaten in Spain by peasants and Americans.

—ALICE B. TOKLAS, *in her* ALICE B. TOKLAS COOKBOOK, *written in the 1920s but not published until 1954*

GAZPACHO QUIZ

QUESTION: What does *gazpacho* mean?

ANSWER: No one knows for sure, but one theory says it's a combination of *caspa* (a pre-Roman word meaning "bits and pieces") and *-acho* (a sneering diminutive meant to identify it as a dish that only the poor and desperate would eat). The fact is, gazpacho—made of bread, garlic, olive oil, vinegar, salt, and water, all packed into unglazed earthenware pots to keep it cool—was introduced into Andalusian Spain by the Moors sometime after A.D. 800. On a good day, it might include almonds and almond milk (see page 334 for this recipe, also Mr. Vivas's, of modern *Ajoblanco*). Anyway it was white; it was thick; it filled the belly and cooled the brow of laborers during the heat of the day. It was this *gazpacho* that Sancho Panza knew and loved, saying at the end of his days as governor, "A Spade does better in my Hand than a Governor's Truncheon; and I had rather fill my Belly with Gazpacho, than lie at the Mercy of a Coxcombly Physick-monger that starves me to Death."

QUESTION: Why use vinegar, when the Moors so loved their lemons?

ANSWER: Clearly a cultural tip of the hat to Roman food traditions because those Romans, who occupied Spain by the time Augustus came to power in 27 B.C.E. and didn't leave for hundreds of years, simply adored their vinegar, especially from the wine they made from Spanish grapes.

QUESTION: Why are there no tomatoes or peppers in the original recipe?

ANSWER: They were still in the New World, patiently waiting to be discovered by early Spanish explorers. Even though Spain embraced these New World foods before the rest of Europe, it was a long time before they found their way into the gazpacho pot. Juan de la Mata's recipe for gazpacho in his 1747 cookbook *Arte de repostería* included neither tomatoes nor peppers.

QUESTION: Who gets the prize for the funniest *gazpacho* ever?

ANSWER: Filmmaker Pedro Almodóvar, hands down. In his 1988 film *Women on the Verge of a Nervous Breakdown*, poor Pepa (Carmen Maura), desolate over losing her lover Iván, stays home in hopes that he will call and makes a batch of *gazpacho*, dreamily lacing it with masses of super barbiturates. While it's chilling, people start arriving—a friend who has unwittingly abetted Shiite terrorists; young lovers; Iván and his new lover; Iván's wife; police inspectors—you name it. One by one, different characters help themselves to the soup and instantly fall into a deep and long sleep.

United States

ICED POTATO AND LEEK SOUP
Vichyssoise
Serves 4

This elegant soup needs no describing—it's a miracle of smooth tastiness, not to mention a classic chef joke, with its creator Louis Diat turning the rough and simple French "homemaker's potato soup" *(bonne femme)* into such an ooh-la-la dish.

> *2 tablespoons butter*
> *3 large leeks, white parts only, washed well and thinly sliced*
> *3 cups Chicken Stock (page 24)*
> *2 medium potatoes, peeled and thinly sliced*
> *1 teaspoon salt*
> *1 cup milk*
> *¼ teaspoon very finely ground white pepper*
> *1 cup heavy cream*
> *Finely sliced fresh chives, for garnish*

To Prepare

Note: Make the soup the day before so it has time to chill properly.
Prep the ingredients as directed in the recipe list.

To Cook

1. Melt the butter in a large saucepan over low heat, then stir in the leeks and sauté at a very low temperature, stirring occasionally, until they are golden, about 10 minutes.

2. Add the stock, potatoes, and salt. Bring to a simmer over medium-high heat, then cover, reduce the heat to low, and simmer for 40 minutes. Puree, then press the soup through a sieve to get a very fine texture.

3. Return the soup to the saucepan, add the milk and pepper, and bring to a simmer over low heat. Remove from the heat, whisk

Tales of Vichyssoise

In film director Tim Burton's *Batman Returns*, valet Alfred (Michael Gough) serves *vichyssoise* to Batman (Michael Keaton) while he's hard at work in front of his computer. Batman's reaction? He immediately complains that the soup is cold.

My personal fave memory of this soup, though, is from childhood. My family had driven from the iciness of Philadelphia to the tropics of Florida for the Christmas holiday, and we were staying at a small, elegant inn right on a corner of Miami Beach's sweeping sands. We'd smuggled fireworks into our rooms and planned to ring in the New Year by illegally blasting them off the beach, deep into the ocean. First a late dinner, when Mom ordered . . . a cold soup? Never heard of such a thing. She spooned it up with an expression of pure delight, giving us each our very first tiny taste of *vichyssoise*. Then we all ran out to the beach to fire off our rockets.

in the cream, adjust for seasoning (cold soups should be slightly overseasoned), and chill overnight.

TO SERVE

Ladle the soup into small cups — nested glass cups with shaved ice in the bottom would be nice — and sprinkle with chives.

VICHYSSOISE, REVOLUTIONARY SOUP

Pardon, mesdames et messieurs, but I must tell you the unlikely story behind this so-called American soup. Brilliant French chef Louis Diat—who created *crème vichyssoise glacée* in New York City of all places—ate hot potato soup for breakfast every day of his childhood in the tiny village of Bourbonnais Montmarault. Oh, how he loved it. In fact, the first dish he ever cooked on his own, at the age of eight, was leek and potato soup.

By 1900, Diat had apprenticed in Moulins, then was off to Paris to learn the regal craft of haute cuisine, and he practiced these arts at the Ritz Hotels in Paris and London. But then a revolution occurred! César Ritz guillotined the old regime of fantastically elaborate dishes and extravagant feasts. He sent Chef Diat to New York to raise the revolutionary standard of exquisite flavor, texture, and simple excellence at the spanking new Ritz-Carlton. Death to exotic affectation! And so, ultimately, *vichyssoise* was born. Diat says, "I remembered how *maman* used to cool our breakfast soup, on a warm morning, by adding cold milk to it. A cup of cream, an extra straining, and a sprinkle of chives, *et voilà,* I had my new soup. I named my version of *maman*'s soup after Vichy, the famous spa located not twenty miles from our home, as a tribute to the fine cooking of the region."

11

TO STRENGTHEN A
CONVALESCENT

Mrs. Goldberg refuses to believe that her husband is dead. She sits by his gurney in the mortuary and continues to force-feed him chicken soup. The doctor comes by and asks her what she thinks she's doing. "It may not help," she says, "but it couldn't hurt."

ONCE UPON A TIME, I lay in a small bed in a darkened room. Groggy. Hot and sweaty. Coughing. Then, footsteps on the stairs. The door opens a crack. Mom.

And not just Mom: Mom with a tray that's set with a napkin, a silver spoon, a plate of buttered toast points, and a small porcelain bowl of chicken-rice soup.

I whimper. She blots my forehead with a cool cloth. I sniffle. She gives me a kiss, sits me up, plumps up the pillows. Sets the tray on my lap. Suddenly I'm hungry.

How much sweeter could life be than this? I'm so happy to have the memory. It was the early 1950s on Hilspach Street in Philadelphia, city of brotherly love. My older sister was off at school; my brother not yet born. Dad was putting in long hours at the mill and longer ones at night school, still catching up from a youth stolen by B-29 missions in World War II. And I had a young, beautiful mother who brought me chicken soup on a tray when I was ailing.

I bet you have a memory like this, too, even if the details are a bit different. Think sick; think soup. Universally.

And there are good reasons for it.

BROTHS MADE FROM chickens and other creatures were prescribed as remedies for ills as far back as the second century A.D. by the Greek physician Galen, and his teachings (with those of the earlier Hippocrates) were carried forward by word of mouth for a thousand years by local docs. Also, starting in the ninth century, Arab physicians began translating and using these old texts in their communities. Al-Dakhwar in his Damascus clinic, for example, was reported by a student to specifically prescribe chicken soup to a feverish patient.

It was in 1190, though, that the brilliant Jewish philosopher Moses Maimonides, serving as physician to Saladin's court in Cairo, wrote a scientific treatise on asthma for his royal patient, forty-year-old Prince al-Afdal, in which he advised "the soup of fat hens is an effective remedy in this disease." Maimonides also collected and codified the old Galen prescriptions in some 1,500 aphorisms that included Galen's advice to use chicken soup to treat leprosy, migraine, constipation, "black humours," and chronic fevers.

Fast forward nearly a thousand more years and we've finally figured out, more or less, why and how chicken soup is good for respiratory ailments. In 1978, pulmonary specialist Marvin Sackner, of the Mt. Sinai Medical Center, published his study that demonstrated chicken broth specifically promotes the flow of air and mucous in nasal passages and clears up congestion better than control liquids of hot and cold water.

In the 1980s, Dr. Irwin Ziment, of UCLA School of Medicine, identified cysteine as an amino acid released in cooking a chicken that actively thins the mucous in the lungs, and he demonstrated increased efficacy when chiles, garlic, and spices are added to chicken soup as they loosen phlegm and act as expectorants.

Then, in October 2000, Dr. Stephen Rennard, of the Nebraska

Medical Center, published his study on the ability of Jewish chicken soup with matzo balls (a family recipe from Lithuania) to inhibit neutrophil chemotaxis — that is, could it stop the inflammation associated with colds? Emphatically yes, it turns out. Colds happen when viruses infect the mucosa of the upper respiratory tract, provoking the release of white cells (neutrophils), which in turn rush into the tissue and kick up piles of mucous in your lungs and stuffy head. Enter chicken soup, which chemically stops those neutrophils in their tracks without reducing the body's ability to fight the infection.

Tired of all the talk about mucous? Chicken soup has other benefits, too. All that liquid, for example, washing those pesky viruses down to the stomach, to be destroyed by its powerful digestive acids, not to mention all that liquid preventing dehydration — both of these noted with approval by the American Academy of Family Physicians in 2003. Then, too, there are the intangibles of warm, aromatic comfort food administered by a loving hand. And what about the goodness and power of all the other ingredients in soup?

Eileen Behan, in *Cooking for the Unwell,* notes that clear broth soups (like "beef tea" and chicken bouillon) may settle an upset stomach, but patients need protein, vitamins, and calories to actually get well. That means adding eggs, bits of meat, flu-fighting garlic, starches, and vegetables to the soup.

The following soups come from many different traditions and cultures, but all are designed to make you feel better and get better. I've made the portions very small, on the grounds that these soups are so often custom-made for one (with the obvious exception of Jewish "penicillin," of which you can never have enough). But they're awfully good soups in their own right, so if you like them, feel free to double or triple the recipes and serve them for meals or dinner parties. One last note: I regret that I haven't included Chinese soups — famously medicinal. Alas, they are too specialized: instead of being sovereign remedies, they are customized to address specific imbalances in the body. And I certainly wouldn't want you eating a yin soup if you had a yang problem.

"RECEIPT TO MAKE SOUP: FOR THE USE OF DEAN SWIFT"

Take a knuckle of Veal
(You may buy it, or steal),
In a few peices cut it,
In a Stewing pan put it,
Salt, pepper and mace
Must season this knuckle,
Then what's join'd to a place,
With other Herbs muckle;
That which killed King Will,
And what never stands still,
Some sprigs of that bed
Where Children are bred,
Which much you will mend, if
Both Spinage and Endive,
And Lettuce and Beet,

With Marygold meet;
Put no water at all;
For it maketh things small;
Which, lest it should happen,
A close cover clap on;
Put this pot of Wood's mettle
In a hot boiling kettle,
And there let it be,
(Mark the Doctrine I teach)
About — — —let me see, — — —
Thrice as long as you preach.
So skimming the fat off,
Say Grace, with your hat off
O then, with what rapture
Will it fill Dean and Chapter!

—ALEXANDER POPE, *eighteenth-century English poet,*
renowned for his "well barbered" satires

NOTE: This soup was prepared to hasten Pope's own recovery from a near fatal accident, and he versified the recipe to recommend it to his friend Jonathan Swift, recently returned to Ireland. It's full of puns and wordplay, of course: "what's join'd to a place" is celery; King William III was killed when his horse, Sorrell, stumbled; thyme, of course, "never stands still"; and the meaning of "bed where children are bred" is parsley, but I don't know why.

ARMENIA

YOGURT-RICE SOUP
PRINZOV ABOUR
Serves 1 to 2

THIS SOUP IS an excellent reflection of Armenian culture, which was forged in Asia Minor, a crossroads of trade routes between the Caspian and Black seas and consequently a battleground over the ages for Assyrians, Medes, Persians, Greeks, Romans, Turks, Russians — you name it. It was in this small spot of the world that cherries and apricots originated — and Armenians developed a cuisine heavily based on those fruits and also on dairy products, meat, grains, butter, and spices. *Prinzov abour* is rich, yet light; soft on the palate; and highly stimulating to the appetite with its sour-minty tang.

> *2 cups Beef Stock (page 26)*
> *¼ cup raw long-grain rice, washed*
> *1 small onion, finely chopped*
> *1 tablespoon butter*
> *1 tablespoon minced fresh mint leaves or ½ teaspoon dried,*
> *   crumbled between your palms*
> *1 tablespoon minced fresh parsley*
> *1 to 2 cups plain yogurt, depending on how thick you like the*
> *   soup*
> *1 small egg, beaten*
> *Salt to taste*
> *Finely minced fresh parsley and mint, for garnish*

TO PREPARE
  Prep the ingredients as directed in the recipe list.

TO COOK
  1. Bring the stock to a boil in a large saucepan over high heat,

YAB-TA-ÎL-NÊ-NÂ, OR
"THE MINT VENDOR"
(A POPULAR FOLK SONG)

*Take me home to my own
    people,
And a kiss I will allow you,
And bestow upon you riches,
And a bunch of mint, sweet
    scented.
There's the lad who sells the
    mint leaves.
How I love those leaves
    sweet scented.*

*If you take me to my mother,
On the lips a kiss I'll offer,
Treasures rare, too, I will give
    you,
And a bunch of mint, O
    sheikh Ahmad.
There's the lad who sells the
    mint leaves.
How I love those leaves
    sweet scented.*

pour in the rice, then reduce the heat to low and simmer, covered, about 20 minutes, until the rice is tender.

2. While the rice is cooking, sauté the onion in the butter in a small skillet over low heat, stirring often, until golden brown. Remove from the heat, stir in the mint and parsley, and scrape into the soup when the rice is cooked.

3. In a separate bowl, beat the yogurt until smooth, then beat the egg into it. Whisk some hot soup into the yogurt, then whisk the yogurt mixture back into the simmering soup and stir until the soup is heated through. Don't let the soup boil.

TO SERVE

Ladle the soup into bowls and sprinkle with minced parsley and mint before racing it to your patient.

England and France

BEEF TEA

Serves 1

They're a horrible pain to make, but these pure essences pack a huge strengthening punch (see page 37 for Chinese *Gee tong*, a similar essence, but of chicken). The English version is brown and opaque, tasting like the drippings of a Christmas prime rib that's been carved—and that I used to fight my brother and sister for shamelessly, dipping into those drippings with small pieces of buttered bread, elbows sharp and territorial over the carving board. The French version is rosy and clear, half the volume of the English version with twice the meat; of course it takes your breath away with its pure intensity. After drinking either, I feel like Pippi Longstocking, Paul Bunyan, and Supergirl, all balled up into one. My grandmother used to make it the English way (unfortunately administering a mustard plaster to my chest at the same time), but now I think the sophisticated French version is superior. Might have something to do with that mustard plaster, though.

ENGLISH BEEF TEA

> *½ pound boneless round steak, cut 1 inch thick and trimmed completely of fat*
> *Salt to taste*

To Prepare
Prep the meat as directed in the recipe list.

To Cook
1. Broil the steak 2 minutes per side. Then, right in the broiling pan, cut the steak into 1-inch squares and put the squares into a pint-size glass canning jar. Be sure to scrape up the bottom of the

ROBERT E. LEE'S LAST SOUP

This great American general and commander-in-chief of the Confederate Armies retained during his lifetime the habit of eating his main meal at 3 P.M.—"the old-fashioned hour," as he called it—and always began it with soup. This could be Mrs. Randolph's oyster soup, turkey soup, or his favorite tomato-vegetable bouillon with sherry. On his deathbed, however, he supped beef tea: "My dear Genl," Mrs. Lee wrote on October 10, 1870, to Francis H. Smith, superintendent of Virginia Military Institute, "the Drs. think it would be well for Genl Lee to have some beef tea at once and as I cannot get it at the market before night I send to beg a small piece [of beef]." Alas, General Smith's offering had little effect on the Genl's heart: "Robert . . . always welcomes me with a pressure of the hand," said Mary Lee as she sat behind him in her rocking chair, and two days later he died.

—From Anne Carter Zimmer's *The Robert E. Lee Family Cooking and Housekeeping Book, 1997*

pan with one of the squares and get every scrap of goodness into the jar.

2. Pour cold water over the meat to cover, screw on the top, then put the jar into a saucepan of cold water (you can put a brick on the top to keep it steady). The point here is not to cook, but to steep the meat. Turn the heat to low and let the goodness leach out of the meat slowly, over the next 3 to 4 hours.

TO SERVE

Pour off the beef tea, discarding the meat hunks, salt it slightly, and serve warm, preferably in a beautiful cup on a tray with silver spoons and linen napkins.

L'ESSENCE DE BOEUF

1 pound boneless round steak, partially frozen, then carefully trimmed of fat and chopped by hand or in a food processor
1 small onion, finely sliced
A few drops of lemon juice
A few drops of Cognac
Salt to taste

TO PREPARE

1. Prep the ingredients as directed in the recipe list.

2. Mix the chopped meat and onion and place in a quart-size glass canning jar.

To Cook

1. Screw the top on the jar tightly, place in a large soup pot filled with barely simmering water that reaches to the top of the meat inside the jar (put a brick on the top to keep the jar steady), and simmer for 3 to 4 hours, replacing water in the pot as needed to keep the level to the top of the meat.

2. Strain the "essence" carefully — ideally through several layers of moistened cheesecloth — then stir in the lemon, Cognac, and salt.

To Serve

Prepare a tray with a lace placemat, a flower in a bud vase, and *l'essence* in a delicate cup to be carefully spooned into the mouth of your invalid.

"The Sentimental Bloke"

She never magged; she never said no word.
An' when I speaks, it seems she never 'eard.
I could 'a' sung a nim, I feels so gay!
If she 'ad only roused I might 'a' smiled.
She jist seems 'urt an' crushed; not even riled.
    I turns away,
An' yanks me carkis out into the yard,
Like some whipped pup; an' kicks meself reel
    'ard.

An' then, I sneaks to bed, an' feels dead crook.
Fer golden quids I couldn't face that look —
    That trouble in the eyes uv my Doreen.
Aw, strike! Wot made me go an' do this thing?
I feel jist like a chewed up bit of string,
    An' rotten mean!
Fer 'arf an hour I lies there feelin' cheap;
An' then I s'pose, I muster fell asleep. . . .

"'Ere, Kid, drink this" . . . I wakes, an' lifts me
    'ead,
An' sees 'er standin' there beside the bed;
    A basin in 'er 'ands; an' in 'er eyes —
(Eyes that wiv unshed tears is shinin' wet) —
The sorter look I never shall ferget,
    Until I dies.
"'Ere, Kid, drink this," she sez, an' smiles at me.
I looks — an' spare me days! It was beef tea!

Beef tea! She treats me like a hinvaleed!
Me! that 'as caused 'er lovin' 'eart to bleed.
    It 'urts me worse than maggin' fer a week!
'Er! 'oo 'ad right to turn dead sour on me,
Fergives like that, an' feeds me wiv beef tea . . .
    I tries to speak;
An' then — I ain't ashamed o' wot I did —
I 'ides me face . . . an' blubbers like a kid.

—C. J. Dennis (1876–1938), Australian writer known as the "Laureate of the Larrikin"

ANCIENT FAVA BEANS

Favas originated in ancient Egypt but early spread throughout the Mediterranean and into China. In fact, it was that ancient Greek mathematician Pythagoras who forbade his followers to eat them because, according to legend, they were said to contain the souls of the dead. More likely, Pythagoras discerned the connection between eating undercooked fava beans and the anemic blood disorder now called favism. Traces of the fava's cultivation have been found in Bronze Age sites in Switzerland and in Iron Age sites in England. Epigrammatist Martial opined about them, "If pale beans bubble for you in a red earthenware pot, you can often decline the dinners of sumptuous hosts."

EGYPT

FAVA BEAN SOUP
FUL NABED
Serves 2 to 3

PLAIN AND DELICATE in flavor, this simple and nutritious version of the classic Egyptian soup is routinely prescribed for the sick. The familiar garnish of lemon and parsley used here seems to invite the patient to step back into a normal diet. Fava (or broad) beans take a long time to soak, meaning you've got to plan for when your sickie is ready to be crammed full of protein, but long soaking results in a blandly comforting soup that's made pretty quickly in the end. If you can't find the dried white skinless fava beans, look for canned whole ones, which are relatively easy to skin, or substitute chickpeas.

> 1 cup dried white skinless fava beans
> 1 garlic clove
> 3 cups water
> 1 tablespoon olive oil
> Pinch of ground cumin
> Salt and white pepper to taste

GARNISH
1 tablespoon minced fresh parsley
Lemon juice

TO PREPARE

1. Two days ahead, place the beans in a bowl with plenty of water to cover to soak. You may change the water throughout the soaking period to discharge those indigestible complex sugars that have such an impact on human digestive systems.

2. Prep the remaining ingredients as directed in the recipe list.

To Cook

1. Drain the soaked beans and put them in a large saucepan with the garlic and water. Bring to a boil over high heat, then reduce the heat to low, cover, and simmer for at least 1 hour, until the beans are very very tender and literally disintegrating to form a soup. (Depending on the beans, you might need to cook the beans another full hour, adding additional water—don't worry, you can't overcook them.) Mash with a fork to get a nice soupy consistency, adding water as necessary to thin the soup to your liking.

2. Whisk in the olive oil and cumin, then season with salt and pepper. Let simmer a few more minutes to blend the flavors.

To Serve

Ladle the soup into bowls and garnish with the minced parsley and squeezings of lemon juice. Depending on the taste and health of your sick one, you can serve the soup with more lemon slices on the side and toasted pita bread.

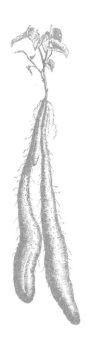

SILENCE OF THE FAVAS

It was Hannibal Lecter in the film *The Silence of the Lambs*, of course, who claimed to have eaten the liver of a census taker "with some fava beans and a nice Chianti."

MUST BE SOMETHING ABOUT OPERA

Opera composer Gioacchino Antonio Rossini doted on the Italian version of this soup, *cappelleti in brodo,* which he was said to gulp down at a tremendous rate, as if he feared someone might steal it from him— while Guiseppe Verdi made a variation he called *la squisita minestra* ("delicious soup") that he liked to serve to guests, a chicken broth with fried potato dumplings.

FRANCE

CHICKEN NOODLE SOUP
SAVOYARDE SOUPE DE FIDES
Serves 2

THIS SOUP SPECIALLY marked by farm people for the sick in the snowy Alps of France is a real beauty. It's delicate, aromatic, digestible, and filled with goodness—just the thing to pique a lagging appetite.

> 3 cups rich Chicken Stock (page 24)
> 1 garlic clove, pressed
> ½ cup broken-up fine soup noodles
> ¼ cup finely chopped fresh greens or herbs or, even better, peeled fresh asparagus, cut thinly on the diagonal and with tips whole
> Salt and white pepper to taste
> Pinch of minced fresh parsley, for garnish

TO PREPARE
Prep the ingredients as directed in the recipe list.

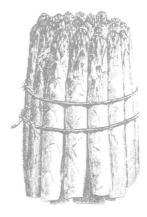

To Cook

Bring the broth to a boil in a large saucepan over medium-high heat with the pressed garlic and cook for a minute. Toss in the noodles and cook, uncovered, until they are al dente. Add the asparagus, if using; partially cover and cook for a minute or two. If you are using herbs or greens, add them just as the noodles are done and remove from the heat.

To Serve

Season with the salt and pepper. Ladle the soup into bowls and top each portion with a pinch of parsley.

Soup on a French Farm

Colette's career began with soup. Many things do, in France—the two chief meals of every day, for instance, in every family; and some things end with it also, as, in many working-class homes, there is nothing else for dinner and supper except just the soup, and a big hunk of bread to dip in it. And, on that, the boys and girls manage to grow up as strong and active and wiry as you please. For there is no more valuable article of food than well-made soup.

Mind, it must be well made. A soup square, melted down in a little hot water or a highly seasoned mess out of a tin have no food value at all, or next to none. Besides, they are very costly, and quite needlessly so: real, homemade soup should cost next to nothing, as all the odds and ends in the house can be used up for it.

—Marie Jacques, *Colette's Best Recipes: A Book of French Cookery*, 1923

ITALY

"LITTLE RAGS" EGG DROP SOUP
STRACCIATELLA
Serves 1 to 2

LITERALLY TRANSLATED, *stracciatella* means "little rags" in Italian—and so describes the classic egg rags that swirl through this comfort soup. (This also explains why *stracciatella gelato* is chocolate chip—that rag effect again.) While this soup is best known as a Roman specialty, it has many variations throughout southern Italy that have escarole or spinach added to the broth for heft, not to mention for flavor and color contrast. And it is the foundation of Italian wedding soup (see page 63), which ennobles the "little rags" by combining them with tiny meatballs of veal and sirloin seasoned with nutmeg.

> *2 cups Chicken Stock (page 24)*
> *1 egg*
> *2 tablespoons freshly grated Parmesan cheese*
> *2 tablespoons soft bread crumbs or farina*
> *Salt and white pepper to taste*

GARNISH
> *Additional grated Parmesan*
> *A sprig of fresh basil, parsley, or crossed chives*

To Prepare

Prep the ingredients as directed in the recipe list.

To Cook

1. Bring the stock to a simmer in a large saucepan over low heat.

2. In a small bowl, beat the egg with a fork and continue beating as you add the cheese and bread crumbs—and finally, ½ cup of the simmering stock.

3. Bring the remaining stock to a near boil over medium heat, then scrape in the egg mixture and whisk it feelingly, even emotionally, with a fork for 3 to 4 minutes straight. When you stop beating, let the soup come just barely to a boil. Its creaminess will then break into plump, lacy custards. Season with salt and pepper.

To Serve

Ladle the soup into bowls immediately, sprinkle with extra Parmesan cheese, and top with a single piece of fresh herb. Sit down with it. Breathe it in deeply. Get better.

THE FANTASTICAL GLORY OF PARMESAN CHEESE

Do you know about the district of Bengodi? Where "there was a mountain of grated Parmesan cheese, inhabited by people who did nothing but make macaroni and ravioli, which they cooked in chicken broth and then rolled down through the cheese so that anyone could just pick it up and eat it"?

Giovanni Boccaccio tells us all about it in the third story of the eighth day of storytelling in his *Decameron*, a collection of one hundred tales told in ten days by seven ladies and three young men who have retired to the country from Florence to escape the Black Death in fourteenth-century Italy. What's that? You didn't know this fabulous Italian cheese went back so far in history? In fact, some believe the origins of grana Parmigiano-Reggiano go back to classical times.

JEWISH

CHICKEN SOUP WITH MATZO BALLS
"PENICILLIN"
Serves 4 to 6

THIS RECIPE WAS sent to me by a gentleman in California who
said his Belgian Jewish grandmother, Omi Rosi, was renowned for
curing what ails you with this soup: "Guaranteed to make you
well." It's very similar to the Lithuanian variation tested by Dr.
Rennard in his study on chicken soup's ability to inhibit neutrophil
chemotaxis and reduce respiratory inflammations, but even more
intense by stewing the chicken in chicken stock. I've enlarged the
serving portion because, of course, you just can't have enough Jewish penicillin.

FOR THE MATZO BALLS
  1 cup matzo meal
  *⅓ cup shortening, schmaltz (rendered chicken fat), or mock
    schmaltz (simmer 1 diced onion in a cup of light olive oil
    until the onion browns, then remove the onion and stir in 1
    tablespoon chicken bouillon granules. Strain the oil into a
    jar and refrigerate. Use, when solidified, as needed.)*
  ½ cup water
  1 teaspoon salt
  Grindings of white pepper
  4 eggs

FOR THE SOUP
  *1 stewing chicken, 4 to 5 pounds, or 4 to 5 pounds chicken
    parts*
  4 celery stalks with leaves, chopped
  1 bunch parsley roots, peeled and chopped (if available)
  2 large onions, chopped
  6 carrots, peeled and chopped
  4 to 6 parsnips, peeled and chopped

1 celery root, peeled and chopped (if not available, add more celery)
1 cup finely chopped fresh parsley
½ cup finely chopped fresh dill
16 cups (4 quarts) Chicken Stock (page 24)
Salt and pepper to taste

To Prepare

1. Prepare the matzo ball dough. In a small bowl, stir together the matzo meal, shortening, water, salt, pepper, and eggs, and beat for 1 minute, then cover and refrigerate for 1 hour.

2. Prep the remaining ingredients as directed in the recipe list.

Tropical Chicken Soup

In his curious roman á clef *Ravelstein,* American author Saul Bellow fulfills his promise to real-life friend Allan Bloom (the brilliant political philosopher who died of AIDS in 1992) to write Bloom's memoir "warts and all," transforming Bloom into Abe Ravelstein and himself into Chick. It's a dark comedy that wickedly ends with Chick making himself the main character. And what does wife Rosamund do when she sees that Chick is seriously ill in St. Martin? She "walked miles through the smoke and fire of curbside grills looking for a Thanksgiving turkey. None was to be found. The skinny local hens seemed to be growing hair, not feathers. At the bottom of a freezer in the market, she found packages of stony drumsticks and wings.... On this island of yams and coconuts there were no cooking greens. Nevertheless she managed after hours of effort to produce a chicken soup. Out of gratitude I [Chick] tried to make a joke of my failure to get it down—remembering an immigrant mother of my childhood who cried out, 'My Joey can't eat an ice-cream cone. He turns his head away from it. If he won't lick an ice cream, he's got to be dying!'"

Hollywood Chicken Soup

Hollywood magnate Louis B. Mayer insisted that chicken soup with matzo balls—made from his mother's recipe—be on the MGM commissary menu every single day. And it has remained on the menu ever since, though when Sony upgraded the old deli to the Rita Hayworth Dining Room in the 1990s, the soup turned into a thin, veggie-studded shadow of itself, with one perfectly round and giant matzo taking up most of the bowl. And speaking of Hollywood, it's said that when Marilyn Monroe was married to Arthur Miller, she got tired of his mother always serving matzo ball soup. "Gee, Arthur," she said after the tenth time, "these matzo balls are pretty nice, but isn't there any other part of the matzo you can eat?"

AMAZING CHICKEN SOUP STORY #1

Hollywood mogul Louis B. Mayer forced child star Judy Garland to slim down at age fourteen on a diet of chicken soup, black coffee, and diet pills. To further kill her appetite, she smoked four packs of cigarettes a day.

TO COOK

1. Put all the ingredients for the soup, except the salt and pepper, into a large soup pot, cover, and bring to a boil over medium heat. Reduce the heat to low and simmer, lightly covered, for 2 hours, until everything is tender and soft. Skim off the foam from time to time, if needed.

2. While the soup is cooking, shape the matzo balls, in the size you prefer, from the refrigerated dough, then return them to the refrigerator until you are ready to cook them.

3. After the soup has cooked for 2 hours, take the chicken out of the pot, cool briefly, and remove all the meat from it, discarding the skin and bones. Cut the meat into bite-size pieces and reserve.

4. Fish out half or so of the cooked vegetables and whirl in a blender, then return to the soup as a thickener. Stir in the chicken pieces. Season with salt and pepper. At this point, you may cool the soup, uncovered, and refrigerate it overnight so the flavors can blend. This also makes it easy to remove the solidified fat before finishing the soup.

5. When you are ready to finalize the soup, skim the fat and bring the soup to a low boil over medium heat. Add the matzo balls, cover, and simmer for 30 minutes.

TO SERVE

Ladle the soup into bowls, evenly distributing the matzo balls, then help your sick ones to the table and watch them come back to life.

Korea

CHICKEN-RICE "WHITE" SOUP
Paeksuk
Serves 2 to 3

KOREANS MAKE MANY different kinds of curative soups, with a lot of exotic ingredients: *Kyesamt'ang*, a chicken soup with fresh ginseng roots and jujube fruits, black rooster soup, dragon and phoenix soup, black mountain goat soup, and mudfish and beef brisket soup. *Paeksuk*, though, is somewhat less dramatic—a homey and rich chicken and rice congee spiced with ginger and garlic, a little sesame oil, and a good jolt of hot pepper sauce. Traditionally, for this elixir you'd use a broth made from a tough old stewing hen that's been cooked for hours, but it's just as good, and very quick, to make it with any chicken stock you have on hand.

2 cups Chicken Stock (page 24)
1 tablespoon pressed or finely minced garlic
1 teaspoon finely grated fresh ginger
3 tablespoons sweet rice, scrubbed in water and rinsed, or any sticky rice
¼ teaspoon toasted sesame oil
½ teaspoon hot pepper sauce, or to taste
1 small green onion, minced, for garnish

To Prepare
Prep the ingredients as directed in the recipe list.

To Cook
Combine the chicken stock, garlic, and ginger in a large saucepan. Bring to a boil over medium-high heat, add the rice, then reduce the heat to low, cover, and simmer until the rice is very tender, about 30 minutes. Thin with water, as needed, to get the consistency you like.

"The Wanderings"

Among rivers and lakes I lay sick.
Lying among bamboo groves I rested.
Then the King summoned me, made me Governor;
I leave for my new post, eight hundred leagues away.
O royal favor, imperishable grace.
I enter the Yŏnch'u Gate, bow toward the South Gate,
And find a man holding a jade tally.
I change horses at P'yŏnggu Station and follow the Yŭ.
Where is Sŏm River? Mount Ch'i is here.
O waters of Soyang, whither do you flow?
When a lonely subject leaves the court,
nothing happens except that he gets old.

—CHŏNG CH'ŏL, sixteenth-century Korean poet, also a musician and politician who fell in and out of favor during the reign of King Sŏnjo, ultimately dying in exile

AMAZING CHICKEN SOUP STORY #2

American football great Joe Montana tells the story of the 1979 Cotton Bowl, when he quarterbacked for Notre Dame. The team was down. The city of Dallas was frozen in an ice storm. Montana was so cold that he was fed hot chicken soup in the locker room to stop from shaking. When he went back in the fourth quarter—Cougars 34, Irish 12—he threw a barrage of touchdown passes to finally defeat those Houston Cougars 35–34.

TO SERVE

Stir in the sesame oil and hot pepper sauce, then ladle the soup into bowls, garnish with the green onion, and serve to your patient at once.

PHILIPPINES

RICE SOUP WITH CHICKEN
Arroz caldo at manok
Serves 2

THIS SOUP IS tasty, filling, and delicately flavored. One bite is so soothing, you want another... and another... and suddenly you're feeling better in spite of those nasty germs.

> *1 tablespoon vegetable oil*
> *2 teaspoons peeled and finely grated fresh ginger*
> *1 garlic clove, pressed or minced*
> *1 small onion, chopped*
> *1 pound boneless chicken breasts, cut into bite-size pieces*
> *1 tablespoon fish sauce (*patis, nam pla, *or* nuoc mam*), or more to taste*
> *½ cup sticky (or sweet) rice, scrubbed in water and rinsed*
> *2 cups Chicken Stock (page 24)*
> *White pepper to taste*
> *Thin diagonal slices of green onion, for garnish*

TO PREPARE

Prep the ingredients as directed in the recipe list.

TO COOK

1. Heat the oil over medium heat in a large saucepan and sauté the ginger, garlic, and onion for a minute or so. Add the chicken and 1 tablespoon fish sauce, and stir to coat. Reduce the heat to low, cover, and simmer for about 3 minutes. Add the rice, stirring to coat, and pour in the stock.

2. Bring the soup to a boil over high heat, then reduce it to low, cover, and simmer for 20 to 30 minutes. The soup should be thick and the rice tender.

"SUN SERIES"

Cosmic elixir of Hermit Prince: Noon,
In the bottom of this celadon
Fish is fish and rice turns
Wine, subtler than salt or
Cane, embalmer, where none dies
The small death, sleep except
By his darkest win, Night.

—VIRGINIA R. MORENO, *twentieth-century Filipino poet*

3. Remove from the heat and season with more fish sauce and the white pepper.

TO SERVE

Ladle the soup into bowls, garnish with delicate slices of green onion, and rush in to your sick ones.

THAILAND

RICE SOUP
KAO TOM
Serves 2

THIS EXCELLENT SOUP is especially nice for invalids and babies, with its soft, digestible rice; a barely coddled, protein-rich egg; tender, ground pork bits; and appetite-stimulating spices. The soup is also traditional in Thailand for breakfast, and with lots of condiments, it serves as a "restitution soup" after a night of partying hard.

> *2 cups light Chicken Stock (page 24)*
> *¼ cup ground pork*
> *½ cup cooked rice*
> *1 tablespoon* nam pla *or other fish sauce*
> *2 eggs, the smallest you can find*

GARNISH
> *2 teaspoons finely minced fresh ginger*
> *2 teaspoons minced fresh cilantro*
> *1 green onion, minced*
> *1 teaspoon golden fried onion flakes (toss dried onion flakes in a hot oil–slicked frying pan)*
> *⅛ to ½ teaspoon red pepper flakes*

TO PREPARE

Prep the ingredients as directed in the recipe list, to include the garnishes, which can be reserved in small heaps on a flat plate.

TO COOK

Bring the stock to a boil in a large saucepan over medium heat. Add the pork, stirring to break it up. Reduce the heat to a simmer, stir in the rice, and simmer for 2 minutes. Season with the fish sauce.

FISH SAUCE

Having grown up in a small Midwestern town, I was already used to driving an hour, each way, for our family's supply of *nuoc mam*. These days, fish sauce (known as *nuoc mam* in Vietnam and *nam pla* in Thailand) appears on the short list of popular ingredients, and the heady seasoning is now much easier to find. Chefs in search of *umami*, that elusive fifth taste that follows sour, salty, bitter, and sweet, admit to stirring a spoonful of the potent sauce into the day's special, and home cooks store a bottle of fish sauce next to their black bean paste and wasabi powder. For others, though, *nuoc mam* (literally, "water of salty fish") is still an intimidating bottle of the essence of fishy-ness.

Traditionally, fishermen toss freshly caught anchovies with sea salt, pack the fish into large wooden vats, and then cover them with woven straw mats. Rocks or logs mounded on the vats weigh down the fish. Left undisturbed for six months to one year, the fish slowly ferment, giving off a clear, amber liquid that will later be drained and bottled.

—THY TRAN, the *WASHINGTON POST*, *January 29, 2003*

AMAZING CHICKEN SOUP STORY #4

International faves: Israeli prime minister Golda Meier gave her personal recipe to Dan Cooke, a spokesman for the Los Angeles Police Department, who then passed it on to some 200,000 American television viewers. Yasser Arafat practically lives on chicken soup, preferring it to most other foods. Dominican Republic president Joaquin "The Doctor" Balaguer ate it every night with his sisters and lived to the age of ninty-five.

TO SERVE

1. Bring the soup back to a boil over medium heat and carefully break the eggs into it. When the eggs are poached, transfer each to a bowl, then ladle the soup on top.

2. Garnish each portion with ginger, cilantro, green onion, onion flakes, and as much red pepper as you think your sick chicks can handle. Cover each bowl with a lid, let sit for a minute to let the flavors blend, then serve, reminding your patients to inhale the steam as they unlid the bowl.

True Confessions: The Search for Noodle Soup with Chicken in It

I spent most of my college semester in London battling the British version of the flu. The perpetual cold, damp weather didn't help much. Nor did my flatmates' legendary partying, which won my living room the nickname "Club Flat 10." The labels on over-the-counter cold medicines in the drugstore might as well have been written in Greek. So, during a particularly miserable day, I resorted to calling my mother in New Jersey to ask for advice. "Chicken soup," was her reply. "Preferably hot and clear."

It was a simple prescription, but difficult to fill in a country that likes soups creamy. (I hadn't seen a soup that escaped the blender since I arrived at Heathrow.) I consulted *England on $45 a Day*, and located a famous kosher restaurant across town. It was clear across London, but I figured there could be no better place to get some nice Jewish (hot, clear) chicken soup, so I headed out.

By the time I traveled an hour on the tube, I was feeling decidedly worse. At least the scene in the restaurant was welcoming. A long, glass deli case filled with knishes, kugels, pickled herring, chopped liver, and other delicacies stretched across the room. Salamis hung from the ceiling over the case. Seated at a small table, I thought, "This is a little piece of home that slid across the Atlantic." Ah, the Motherland. I smiled at a group of Hassidic men in a nearby booth. They ignored me.

I turned my attention to the menu. To my horror, no chicken soup was listed. I asked the waitress, "Do you have soup?" She replied, "Soup of the day is minestrone."

Minestrone? My sense of being home away from home was shattered. Miserable, I slurped my mediocre minestrone soup. I coughed and blew my nose loudly, hoping subconsciously that a little Jewish grandmother hiding in the kitchen would take pity on me and come up with some chicken soup. No such luck. The waitress gave me a dirty look and the Hassidic men continued to ignore me. So much for the Motherland.

When I got back to the flat I called my mother again and whined pathetically, "There is no hot, clear chicken soup to be had in London." "Well, try wonton soup," she said. "That will work."

Yes. Wonton soup. I can do that. Chinatown is a mere eight blocks away! I started out in the general direction of Chinatown. By this time, my fever was raging and I was probably borderline delirious. Even though I had made the trip thirty times, I got lost and found myself in a creepy-looking alley. When I turned to retrace my steps I noticed a small, dingy looking restaurant. Ducks and a variety of other critters hung in the grease-stained window. Beside the door was taped a faded menu, and on that menu I spotted "Soup." I scanned down the list:

Noodle soup
Noodle soup with pork
Noodle soup with prawns
Noodle soup with chicken

Eureka!

Inside, the restaurant was dark, the air heavy with cigarette smoke. A Chinese family sat, talking and eating at a table toward the back. Otherwise the place was empty.

A young women approached, herded me toward a table and slapped down a menu. It barely resembled the one in the window and was missing the all important entry: "Noodle soup with chicken." I asked the girl if it would be possible to get the noodle soup with chicken. She looked at me blankly. I tried again, "Could I get the noodle soup, with chicken in it?" The girl shook her head in frustration and disappeared.

A few minutes later an older women appeared, clearly the mother. She asked me what I would like. I cleared my very hoarse voice. "I would like noodle soup," I said, pointing to the appropriate menu item, "with chicken in it."

Confusion. Blank stares.

"Please, I just want the noodle soup with chicken."

The women disappeared, and I heard increasingly enthusiastic chatter coming from the back of the room. I was next approached by a small man, clearly the patriarch, who looked about 110 years old. He was flanked by a younger man wearing a messy apron. The old man smiled broadly and asked me what I would like.

I spoke very slowly, "I would like the noodle soup—with chicken in it."

"Noodle soup with chicken in it?"

"Yes, yes, that's right! Noodle soup with chicken."

He smiled again, then turned and yelled at his younger companion in Chinese. The old man tapped me on the shoulder and nodded, then disappeared. The volume of chatter coming from the back of the room continued to rise. I didn't care. All I could think of was how much I wanted that noodle soup with chicken in it.

It arrived about ten minutes later, escorted by an entourage consisting of the waitress, her mother, the patriarch, a few cousins, and pretty much everyone else in the restaurant. A huge bowl was placed in front of me containing noodle soup with a chicken in it—the whole chicken, feet and all. They had courteously hacked the bird into quadrants with a cleaver. To eat this, I was provided with chopsticks. Then the group gathered around to watch.

I was there, working on that soup, for what seemed like about six hours. I woke the next morning in my flat with no recollection of how I got home but feeling surprisingly better. Absent the delirium, and no matter how much I looked, I never found that restaurant again.

—NINA MROSE, *attorney and speechwriter,*
Washington, D.C.

12

To Woo a Lover

ONCE UPON A TIME, there was Love.

Love! You know: the thing that everyone wants . . . yearns after . . . daydreams about.

"Two minds without a single thought."

"The delightful interval between meeting a beautiful girl and discovering that she looks like a haddock."

"When a liberal wants to marry a conservative or vice versa."

"The feeling that has the power of making you believe what you would normally treat with the deepest suspicion."

"Friendship set on fire."

"Space and time measured by the heart."

"The beginning, the middle, and the end of everything."

Which reminds me of Plato's *Symposium*, or Drinking Party, when Socrates joined his friends at Agathon's house in 416 B.C.E. and undertook a discourse on the nature of Love. Before Socrates blew everyone out of the water with his thoughtful analysis on the subject, there were some pretty hilarious explanations. My favorite?

Ribald dramatist Aristophanes, who slyly explained love as a result of an earlier civilization made up of three rotund and conjoined sexes — male/male; female/female; and male/female. Although ungainly, he said, they had terrible strength and force, and they were so wild and out of control — even attacking the gods themselves — that Zeus thought he ought to just kill them off. Fortunately he had a happy inspiration that he shared with his fellow gods: "I will slice each of them down through the middle! Two improvements at once! They will be weaker, and they will be more useful to us because there will be more of them."

That Zeus always was a practical guy.

It was a little messy, Aristophanes said. And the poor split halves, as you can imagine, didn't like being separated one bit — and have ever since tried to bring themselves back together "into unity." "So you see how ancient is the mutual love implanted in mankind, bringing together the parts of the original body, and trying to make one out of two, and to heal the natural structure of man."

Okay, but what happens when you *don't* match up with your soul mate? What happens when you fall in love and yearn to "heal the natural structure," and your love is not returned?

Why you turn to aphrodisiac cookery, of course — and what a long history there is of it.

ABSINTHE MAKES THE HEART GROW FONDER

I was surprised to learn that the most ancient Western aphrodisiacs, way back in ancient Egypt, were onions, radishes, and leeks. I mean, come on: you want to dose your wannabe lover with alliums so he or she can come on like a field of garlic? And yet, when you think about it, the snap of desire is all about stimulating the senses: perfumes and unguents for the nose; jewelry, cosmetics, and suggestive clothing for the eyes; soft hands and lips for the touch; sweet nothings and music for the ears; and . . . and . . . well, what was the best bet for stimulating the palate in those ancient days? Tough barley cakes? No. Sharp, clean-tasting fresh vegetables? In fact, yes —

likely your best bet, not to mention cleansing and energizing, too. In fact, it was precisely these that the Israelites lamented leaving behind in Egypt: "We remember the fish, which we did eat in Egypt freely; the cucumbers, and the melons, and the leeks and the onions, and the garlick" (Numbers 11:5).

In classical Greece, the principle of aphrodisiacs was the same, but the foods were different. The tang of herbs. The earthy sponge of mushrooms. The smooth and salty richness of seafood. From India, the Hindu love menu offered saffron, *ghee* (clarified butter), fruits, yogurt, pulses, and those onions, garlic, and leeks again. From the *Kama Sutra:* "If *ghee,* honey, sugar, and licorice in equal quantities, the juice of the fennel plant, and milk are mixed together, this nectar-like composition is said to be holy and provocative of sexual vigor. . . ."

One last plaintive cry, from the sacred Indian text *Samayamatrika,* of an aging woman: "Aware that her youth was passing and wishing to oust all the rest of her decrepit lover's women, she took pains to enthrall him by the use of magic plants. At the same time, she re-awakened his juvenile ardor by the judicious use of fish soup. . . ."

Did you catch that? Fish soup. Not the last bowl of soup you're gonna see on the Love Menu.

Then Rome! Well, what would you expect from those decadents anyway? Ovid extols eggs, nuts, and honey. Martial advocates sharp lettuces and cabbages and opines: "If your wife is old and your member is exhausted, eat onions a plenty." Then, too, everyone swore by that sharp Roman seasoning made from fermented anchovies—a fish sauce variously called *garum, liquamen,* and *muria* and now known as Worcestershire sauce.

After Rome came the sober propriety of the Catholic Church, bent on cleaning up prodigal Europe. Forget carnality. Forget the amatory arts. Forget erotic food. Some medieval religious orders even forbade the eating of beans. Why? Precisely because of their side effects. Those airy explosions, you know: they could stimulate nether regions and cause impure thoughts. Oh, pardon me—more information than you actually wanted.

The erotic arts ultimately came back to Europe from the Mideast with returning Crusaders, along with fabulous new foodstuffs. Suffice it to say, at the dawn of the Renaissance, Europe took off her hair shirt, loosened her hair, and dabbed some perfume behind her ears, never to return to the convent. In his sixteenth-century *Dyetary of Health,* Scotsman Andrew Boorde included a chapter on aphrodisiacs that he based on his research and travels to the Holy Land. Cabbages, turnips, onions, artichokes, sugar, and other dainties were back on the boudoir table.

What about ancient China and Asian civilizations? Using food almost as a medicine to balance cold and hot natures, this culture valued—and still does—good health for good loving. But they likewise specifically favored seafood as an aphrodisiac, including the fish sauces of *nuoc mam* and *nam pla.* Also, and perhaps a little eyebrow raising for our Western sensibilities, folks in this part of the world employ oddities like animal pizzles and testicles, powdered rhino horn, cobra and fugu venom, mostly brewed in soups, as a way to light a man's fire.

And the New World? Are we going to be surprised that it was chocolate, chocolate, chocolate? Aztec ruler Montezuma was said to fortify himself with as many as fifty cups of hot chocolate before strolling into his 600-wife harem.

Soup on the Boudoir Table

Apparently there's just something about a hot, liquid delivery system for all these amorous ingredients that intensifies desire. Remember the ancient Indian woman and her prescription for fish soup to awaken her old man's juvenile ardor? Alexandre Dumas swore by almond soup as an apéritif after the theater before bedding his mistress. And it was the Marquis de Sade, in *120 Days of Sodom,* who said, "the most potent erotic dinner should start with bisque."

I most particularly want to draw your attention to that infamous scene in director Tony Richardson's film *Tom Jones,* when Tom (Albert Finney) and (all unknowingly) possibly his mother,

Mrs. Waters (Joyce Redman), meet for a sex-drenched dinner. They begin, naturally, with big steaming pewter bowls of soup, whereat Mrs. Waters leans well over the table and lustily slurps big round spoonfuls of soup, breasts tumbling out of her bodice and eyes with a more-than-come-hither look. What does Tom do in the face of all this suggestive sipping and spoon licking? Nearly overcome, he involuntarily rips a claw off the langouste he has in his hand and happily sucks on it.

The following recipes make elegant and sophisticated starts to a meal — or to whatever else you might have in mind. They are written in quantities to serve two lovers, but they could certainly be doubled for, say, a ménage à trois or couple swapping, heaven forbid, or just for a romantic dinner party with friends.

MAXIM ME THIS

It is difficult to define love: in the soul, it is a thirst for mastery; in the mind, a harmony of thought; in the body, nothing but a delicately hidden desire to possess, after many mysteries, whatsoever one loves.

—FRANÇOIS, DUC DE LA ROCHEFOUCAULD, *seventeenth-century French writer and moralist,* MAXIM #68

APHRODISIAC ALMOND SOUP
Serves 2

INSPIRED BY THE classic recipe in Norman Douglas's *Venus in the Kitchen, or Love's Cookery Book* (written under the pseudonym of Pilaff Bey), this soup stands on its own as a kind of decadent snack late on some winter's night when you and your honey are wakeful and at loose ends. Rich and thickly nutty, slightly honeyed, it is lifted to heavenly delight with the tart contrast of jewel-red raspberries. Serve it to two people with appetite, maybe with Champagne.

> *Yolks from 2 hard-cooked eggs*
> *1 cup whole almonds, blanched*
> *¼ cup fresh raspberries, crushed and lightly sugared, for garnish*
> *1 cup Chicken Stock (page 24), skimmed of all fat and heated*
> *1 cup light cream*
> *2 tablespoons honey*

TO PREPARE

1. Hard-boil the eggs, let cool, remove and reserve the egg yolks, discarding the whites or reserving them for another purpose. Soak the almonds for a minute in boiling water, then pop off their skins by pressing between your thumb and forefinger.

2. Crush and lightly sugar the raspberries and set aside.

TO COOK

1. Place the almonds and egg yolks in a blender and chop fine.

2. Slowly add the chicken stock, a spoonful at a time, until the ingredients make a fine paste. Continue blending on high speed as you slowly pour in the rest of the chicken stock and all of the cream.

3. Pour the soup into a large saucepan and heat it very carefully over low heat until it is hot and thick. It must never boil or it will curdle. Stir in the honey.

To Serve

Ladle the hot soup into two exquisite bowls. Top each portion with spoonfuls of the raspberry puree. Serve immediately.

"The Passionate Shepherd to His Love"

Come live with me and be my love,
And we will all the pleasures prove
That valleys, groves, hills, and fields,
Woods, or steepy mountain yields.

And we will sit upon the rocks,
Seeing the shepherds feed their flocks,
By shallow rivers to whose falls
Melodious birds sing madrigals.

And I will make thee beds of roses
And a thousand fragrant posies,
A cap of flowers, and a kirtle
Embroidered all with leaves of myrtle;

A gown made of the finest wool
Which from our pretty lambs we pull;
Fair lined slippers for the cold,
With buckles of the purest gold;

A belt of straw and ivy buds,
With coral clasps and amber studs:
And if these pleasures may thee move,
Come live with me, and be my love.

The shepherd's swains shall dance and sing
For thy delight each May morning:
If these delights thy mind may move,
Then live with me and be my love.

—Christopher Marlowe, *English poet, 1600*

Almond Joy

Almonds were known throughout antiquity for stimulating desire: Samson wooed Delilah with them; Sheik al-Nefzawi swore by them; Alexandre Dumas dined on a bowl of almond soup each night before enjoying the favors of Mme. Mars, a diva of the theater.

Where'd they come from? From a beautiful tree—related to the peach, apricot, and plum—that is said to have originated in the deserts of southwestern Asia—then spread into Greece and Italy, where it was cultivated from at least 200 B.C.E. on. Cato himself brought the almond from Greece into Italy. From here, cultivation spread to North Africa, Spain, Portugal, and France. In fact, in A.D. 812, Charlemagne ordered almond trees to be planted in his imperial orchards.

An early defining moment in the life of almonds: remember in Egypt when Moses and Aaron challenged Pharaoh's priests in miracle making? "Behold, the rod of Aaron for the house of Levi was budded, and brought forth buds, and bloomed blossoms, and yielded almonds" (*Numbers 17:8*).

MAXIM ME THIS

You can find women who have had no love affairs, but scarcely any who have had just one.

—FRANÇOIS, DUC DE LA ROCHEFOUCAULD, *seventeenth-century French writer and moralist,* MAXIM #73

ANDORRA/CATALONIA, SPAIN

CREAMY FENNEL SOUP WITH SHALLOTS AND ORANGE SPICE
SOPA DE FONOLL
Serves 2

SUBTLE AND FRAGRANT, this Catalan soup is as smooth as your practiced line and as brightly sharp as your desire.

> *2 tablespoons butter*
> *2 shallots, chopped*
> *1 garlic clove, minced*
> *2 cups Vegetable or Chicken Stock (pages 23 and 24)*
> *A large piece of orange rind (about the size of a tablespoon), scraped of the white pith*
> *1 large or 2 small heads of fennel, trimmed and chopped*
> *¼ cup heavy cream*
> *½ teaspoon salt*
> *Dash of white pepper*

> GARNISH
> *Fine gratings of orange zest*
> *Paper-thin slices of green onions, separated into tiny rings*

TO PREPARE
Prep the ingredients as directed in the recipe list.

TO COOK
1. Melt the butter in a large saucepan over low heat, then sweat the shallots and garlic, covered, for about 10 minutes. Pour in the stock and bring to a boil over high heat. Add the orange rind piece and the chopped fennel, then reduce the heat to low. Cover and simmer for 45 minutes.

2. Puree the soup in a blender, solids first, then strain, pressing hard. Discard the solids, then return the soup to the saucepan. Stir in the cream, salt, and pepper.

TO SERVE

Heat the soup to a boil over medium-high heat, then ladle it into elegant bowls. With a fine grater, freshly grate orange zest over each portion and decorate with a few circles of finely sliced green onion rings.

"MESTER D'AMOR"

You don't have to read Catalan to know what Joan Salvat-Papasseit is up to in this poem, strongly urging a beautiful girl to kiss and be kissed (boldface mine).

Si en saps el pler no estalviïs el **bes**
que el goig d'amar no comporta mesura.
Deixa't **besar**, i tu **besa** després
que és sempre als llavis que l'amor perdura.

If you know the pleasure of it, don't spare the kiss,
for the joy of loving cannot bear to be measured.
Let yourself be kissed, and then you kiss back,
for it's always on the lips that love endures.

No **besis**, no, com l'esclau i el creient,
mes com vianant a la font regalada;
deixa't **besar** -sacrifici fervent-
com més roent més fervent la **besada**.

No, don't kiss like the slave, like the submissive,
but like the traveler at the welcome fountain;
let yourself be kissed, a fervent sacrifice,
for the more burning the kiss, the more fervent.

¿Què hauries fet si mories abans
sense altre fruit que l'oreig en ta galta?
Deixa't **besar**, i en el pit, i a les mans,
amant o amada -la copa ben alta.

What if you had died before with no other reward
than the balmy breeze against your cheek?
Let yourself be kissed on the breast and on the hands,
lover or beloved, the chalice filled to the top.

Quan **besis**, beu, curi el veire el temor:
besa en el coll, la més bella contrada.
Deixa't **besar**
i si et quedava enyor
besa de nou, que la vida és comptada.

When you kiss, drink; take care with the glass, with
    your fear:
kiss on the neck, the most beautiful spot.
Let yourself be kissed and if longing lingers
kiss again, for the days are numbered.

—JOAN SALVAT-PAPASSEIT, early twentieth-century Catalan poet, translated by Stephen G. Gudgel

MAXIM ME THIS

It is a form of coquetry to emphasize the fact that you do not indulge in it.

—FRANÇOIS, DUC DE LA ROCHEFOUCAULD, *seventeenth-century French writer and moralist,* MAXIM #107

FROM ART TO FATALITY

Asparagus, a member of the lily family, was said, with Champagne, to have inspired the main theme of Johannes Brahms's Third Symphony. By contrast, it was considered such a delicacy in ancient Rome that Emperor Augustus ordered executions to be carried out "quicker than you can cook asparagus"—proving in a phrase his reputation for both mercy and gustatory discrimination.

CURRIED SPRING ASPARAGUS SOUP
Serves 2

DELICATE AND HIGHLY suggestive, this exquisite soup is best when you have a long campaign in front of you. Serve it as a first course, then see what develops.

> *½ pound asparagus, with tips cut off and reserved, woody*
>   *stems snapped off and discarded, and the remainder diced*
> *3 cups Vegetable or Chicken Stock (pages 23 and 24)*
> *1 tablespoon butter*
> *1 tablespoon flour*
> *1 egg yolk*
> *½ teaspoon curry powder*
> *½ cup heavy cream*
> *Salt and white pepper to taste*

TO PREPARE

Prep the ingredients as directed in the recipe list.

TO COOK

1. Place the diced asparagus spears in a large saucepan with the stock. Bring the soup to a boil over medium heat, then reduce the heat to low and cook, uncovered, for 10 minutes. Remove from the heat, cool briefly, then puree, solids first. Set aside.

2. In the same saucepan, melt the butter over low heat, whisk in the flour, and cook, stirring constantly, for 2 to 3 minutes. Whisk in the reserved puree and, keeping the heat on low, stir until the soup is hot and thickened.

3. Add the asparagus tips and let them simmer for 5 minutes.

4. Meanwhile, beat the egg yolk, curry powder, and cream in a small bowl. Stir in this enrichment and let the soup heat through on low heat for another couple minutes, stirring from time to time. Season with salt and pepper.

To Serve

Ladle the soup into flat soup plates, evenly distributing the asparagus tips, and serve immediately.

"To the Virgins, to Make Much of Time"

*Gather ye rosebuds while ye
    may,
    Old time is still a-flying,
And this same flower that
    smiles to-day,
    To-morrow will be dying.*

*The glorious lamp of heaven,
    the sun,
    The higher he's a-getting,
The sooner will his race be
    run,
    And nearer he's to setting.*

*That age is best which is the
    first,
    When youth and blood are
    warmer;
But being spent, the worse,
    and worst
    Times still succeed the for-
    mer.*

*Then be not coy, but use your
    time,
    And while ye may, go
    marry;
For having lost but once your
    prime,
    You may for ever tarry.*

—Robert Herrick,
seventeenth-century English poet

MAXIM ME THIS

True love is like seeing ghosts:
we all talk about it, but few
of us have ever seen one.

—FRANÇOIS, DUC DE LA
ROCHEFOUCAULD, *seventeenth-*
century French writer and
moralist, MAXIM #76

RIDDLE ME THIS

QUESTION: What goes into
the water black and comes
out red?

ANSWER: A lobster

THE WHAMMY

LOBSTER SWEETHEART SOUP
Serves 2

WHEN THERE'S NOTHING too good for your baby, this may be just the labor of love you're looking for. It is mightily extravagant, a pain to make, and definitely worth it. Serve this red-and-white Valentine Special bubbly hot, with crusty bread and Champagne, preferably by candlelight.

Now, how do you get this clattery crustacean ready for the soup pot? Easy. Whether you steam the lobster yourself or pick it up from the grocery steamer, start by putting your cooked lobster flat on its back on a plate (to catch the juices). Take a pair of scissors and cut from the bottom of the tail straight up its top shell, through the body, to the center of the head (but not through the eyes). Turn the lobster over and cut the same way through the other side of the shell. Now you should be able to cut the lobster in half lengthwise, from bottom to top, except still attached at the head. Break the shell apart at the head to open it up. You'll see the stomach sack—on one side or the other—right under the eyes (it's about an inch long). Twist it out with your fingers and throw it away. Also pull out the long intestinal vein that goes down the length of the lobster from the sac to the tail. Throw it away, too.

Now to work: scoop the green tomalley, or liver, located in the chest, into a small bowl. You will want to cream this with soft butter later on to serve with the bread. If you have a female lobster (she'll have hairy paddles under the legs instead of pointy sticks), you may find orangey roe—just add this to the tomalley or keep separate for its own butter.

Dismember the rest of the lobster over the plate (to catch the juices), separating claws, joints, legs, chest halves, and tail halves. Cut the meat away from the tail, the joints, and the claws and set aside. Save the shells.

1½ tablespoons butter

1 cup finely chopped combination of onion, carrot, and fennel (or celery)

1 freshly cooked lobster, ½ of the tail meat reserved for the lobster cream garnish

Salt and pepper to taste

1 cup dry vermouth

1 (15-ounce) can tomatoes, chopped with the juice, or 1 pound fresh tomatoes, peeled and chopped

1 bay leaf

1 garlic clove, mashed

Pinch of cayenne pepper

GARNISH

Lobster cream, made of ½ lobster tail, 1 tablespoon vermouth, salt and pepper, and heavy cream

TO PREPARE

1. Prep the ingredients as directed in the recipe list, including dismembering of the lobster (see headnote).

2. Make the lobster cream garnish: cut away any red markings on the reserved lobster tail half, mince it finely, then puree in a blender with the vermouth, salt and pepper, and enough cream to make a thick sauce. Set aside.

3. Make the tomalley and/or orange roe butter: soften 2 tablespoons of butter for each. Cream the tomalley and butter together and pack into a small ramekin; likewise for the roe butter. Refrigerate until you are ready to use it.

TO COOK

1. Melt the butter in a large saucepan over low heat and stir in the finely chopped vegetables. Cover and sweat slowly for 6 to 8 minutes. Be careful not to brown them.

2. Film the bottom of a Dutch oven with oil, heat to medium high, then add the lobster shells (see headnote). Toss them around

SONNET LVII

Being your slave, what
*   should I do but tend*
Upon the hours and times of
*   your desire?*
I have no precious time at all
*   to spend,*
Nor services to do, till you
*   require.*
Nor dare I chide the world-
*   without-end hour*
Whilst I, my sovereign, watch
*   the clock for you,*
Nor think the bitterness of
*   absence sour*
When you have bid your
*   servant once adieu.*
Nor dare I question with my
*   jealous thought*
Where you may be, or your
*   affairs suppose,*
But, like a sad slave, stay and
*   think of naught*
Save where you are and how
*   happy you make those.*
So true a fool is love that in
*   your will,*
Though you do anything, he
*   thinks no ill.*

—WILLIAM SHAKESPEARE

in the pot for about 4 minutes, then reduce the heat to low. Salt and pepper the shells, turn again, then pour in any saved lobster juice, the vermouth, chopped tomatoes with their juice, bay leaf, garlic, cayenne, and sautéed vegetables. Cover the pot and simmer over low heat for 30 minutes. Remove the shells and bay leaf and puree the soup.

3. Cut the reserved lobster meat into chunks.

4. Place the soup in a large saucepan and add the lobster chunks. Season with salt and pepper, then bring to a simmer over low heat.

TO SERVE

Ladle this beautifully colored soup into flat soup plates and swirl the white lobster cream in the middle of each. Slice through the cream with the flat side of a knife in a few directions to create an abstract design. Voilà. Serve with crusty bread slathered with those heavenly tomalley and roe butters.

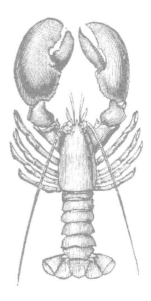

THE DOUBLE WHAMMY
OYSTER CREAM SOUP WITH LEMONY CARROTS
Serves 2

OYSTERS HAVE, APPARENTLY, always been linked with love. When Aphrodite, the Greek goddess of love, sprang forth from the sea on an oyster shell and promptly gave birth to Eros, the word *aphrodisiac* was born. The ancient Greeks served oysters with wine. Roman emperors paid for them by their weight in gold and sent thousands of slaves to the shores of the English Channel to gather them. Centuries later, Casanova himself would start the evening meal by eating twelve dozen oysters—144 of them!—fortifying himself for the evening's pleasures. Oysters themselves are coy about sex, so discreet that you can't tell a boy from a girl from the outside, and they even transform inside their shells, changing from male to female and back again during their life span. And how long may that be? As long as ten to twenty years.

This is a good recipe when you know you won't be sitting down past the first course. It's bursting with plump oysters, many layered in its brothy sophistication, and eye-catching with its tart carrots and earthy basil. It needs only a little crusty bread and wine to fill you up and get you through the night.

1 carrot, peeled
1 tablespoon lemon juice
¹/₂ tablespoon olive oil
1 tablespoon butter
1 medium onion, chopped
2 green onions, white and some green parts, chopped
1 garlic clove, chopped
2 canned tomatoes or 1 fresh, peeled, seeded, and chopped
1 teaspoon fresh basil, chopped, or pesto (page 225)
¹/₂ teaspoon dried thyme
Salt and white pepper to taste
Cayenne pepper to taste

RIDDLE ME THIS

QUESTION: What am I?
   Stouthearted men with
      naked knives
   Beset my house with all
      their crew;
   If I had ne'er so many lives,
   I must be slain and eaten,
      too.

ANSWER: An oyster

2 cups milk
½ cup heavy cream
2 cups (1 pint) oysters, with their liquor
Slivers of basil leaves or a swirl of pesto cream, for garnish

TO PREPARE

1. Bring several cups of water and the carrot to a boil in a saucepan over high heat and cook until the carrot is tender. Remove the carrot, let it cool for a minute, then slice it into very thin rounds and mix the slices with the lemon juice and oil. Refrigerate.

2. Prep the remaining ingredients as directed in the recipe list.

TO COOK

1. Melt the butter in a saucepan over medium-low heat. Stir in the onions and garlic, cover, and sweat until translucent, about 10 minutes. Add the tomatoes, increase the heat to medium, and cook until thickened, stirring occasionally, about 10 minutes.

2. Stir in the basil and thyme, salt and pepper, and cayenne. Cook until all the liquid has evaporated, then puree in a blender or food processor. At this point, you may refrigerate the soup until you're ready to serve it. Overnight just makes it better.

3. When you're ready to finalize the soup, whisk the onion mixture with the milk and cream in a large saucepan and bring to a boil over medium-high heat. Reduce the heat to low, season with salt and pepper, and add the carrots with their marinade.

4. Stir in the oysters, liquor and all, and poach until just opaque, about 2 minutes.

TO SERVE

Ladle the soup into flat soup bowls and garnish with the basil leaves, or swirl a teaspoon of pesto through each portion.

THE TRIPLE WHAMMY
SAFFRONED TOMATO-FENNEL SOUP
Serves 2

HAVE ALL YOUR other blandishments failed? Here is the soup of last resort, containing a concentration of *three* fabled aphrodisiac foods. And, once again, it's meant to be served as a one-course supper right before the victim is dragged off for a passionate kiss.

2 tablespoons olive oil
1 medium onion, diced
1 fennel bulb, trimmed and diced, reserving the fronds for garnish
1 garlic clove, minced
¼ cup dry white wine
½ to 1 teaspoon saffron threads, heated in a large metal spoon over low heat to dry, then ground to a powder and steeped in 1 tablespoon boiling water until they completely give up their color and flavor
¼ cup fresh basil leaves, finely shredded
4 cups peeled and finely chopped tomatoes, with their juice reserved (a 2-pound can of tomatoes is fine)
1 cup water
Salt and pepper to taste
¼ to ½ cup shredded basil and fennel fronds, for garnish

TO PREPARE
Prep the ingredients as directed in the recipe list.

TO COOK
1. In a large saucepan, heat the oil over medium-low heat, then add the onion, fennel dice, and garlic; cover and sweat for about 10 minutes.

2. Pour in the wine and steeped saffron, then stir in the basil. Bring to a boil over medium-high heat, then reduce the heat to low and simmer for 1 to 2 minutes.

MAXIM ME THIS

With no passion do we show so much selfishness as with love; we are always more willing to sacrifice the other person's peace of mind than to disturb our own.

—FRANÇOIS, DUC DE LA ROCHEFOUCAULD, seventeenth-century French writer and moralist, MAXIM #262

"MY DEAR MISTRESS"

*My dear mistress has a heart
    Soft as those kind looks she
    gave me,
When with love's restless art,
    And her eyes, she did en-
    slave me;
But her constancy's so weak,
    She's so wild and apt to
    wander,
That my jealous heart would
    break
    Should we live one day
    asunder.*

*Melting joys about her move,
    Killing pleasures, wounding
    blisses;
She can dress her eyes in love,
    And her lips can arm with
    kisses;
Angels listen when she
    speaks;
    She's my delight, all
    mankind's wonder;
But my jealous heart would
    break
    Should we live one day
    asunder.*

—JOHN WILMOT, EARL OF
ROCHESTER, *seventeenth-century
English poet*

3. Add the tomatoes with their juice and the water. Return to a boil over high heat, then reduce the heat to low and simmer for about 30 minutes, partially covered.

TO SERVE

Add salt and pepper, then stir in the additional basil and the reserved fennel fronds. Ladle the soup into bowls and have at it.

FABLED SAFFRON

Ah, *Crocus sativus.* Biblical Solomon crooned to Sheba, "Thy plants are an orchard of Pomegranates, with pleasant fruits; Camphire, with Spikenard, Spikenard and Saffron" (4:13). This heady yellowness—laboriously extracted from the tiny roots of purple spring crocuses—was native to Asia Minor, but it spread widely, overcoming the senses of voluptuaries world wide. Ancient Egyptians sacrificed cakes of saffron to their gods. The Greeks adored it, using it to dye their hair, their textiles, and even their fingernails. It was famously sprinkled on theatrical stages, and it was Aristophanes, in *The Clouds,* who had one of his characters drool over a woman "redolent with saffron, voluptuous kisses, the love of spending, good cheer and of wanton delights." By the time of Alexander the Great, merchants were selling it all over Europe. Rome used it for medicinal purposes, and Nero, knowing its rarity, extravagantly ordered the streets of Rome to be strewn with it for his triumphal entry. English essayist Francis Bacon said about it, "Saffron conveys medicine to the heart, cures its palpitation, removes melancholy and uneasiness, revives the brain, renders the mind cheerful, and generates boldness."

13

To Chase a Hangover

Once upon a time, man invented a reliable way to feel happy—for brief periods, anyway.

In prehistoric times, intoxication was pretty hit or miss: Stone Age women likely stumbled on plants and mushrooms with active hallucinogens and brought them back to the cave to rave reviews. Academics speculate about psychotropic-inspired "parietal" art at paleolithic sites like Lascaux, and opium seeds have been discovered at Neolithic sites. Opium use, in fact, is well documented in Ancient Egypt, Assyria, Greece, and Rome—primarily in religious ceremonies. That goes for cannabis (marijuana) in ancient Scythia too, where Herodotus, in Book IV of his *Histories,* reports that tribe members would creep into a tent, throw cannabis seed on red-hot stones, inhale the smoke, and "howl with pleasure."

Man-made intoxicants, like beer and wine, are another story. These required the miracle of chemistry: yeast fungi fermenting the sugars of natural foods into alcohol; humans tasting the result, then figuring out how to duplicate what began as an accident. Man's first cocktail was probably made from the fruit and sap of the date palm in the Mideast. Then, around the fourth millennium B.C.E., barley was fermented into beer and Mesopotamians danced in their by-ways. Beer is a big topic in early Sumerian and Akkadian texts, and no doubt it was a huge favorite with everyone in the area. It was just a matter of time before people figured out how to ferment the sugars in honey into mead, grapes into wine, apples into cider, and milk into koumish. By 400 B.C.E., physician Hippocrates of Cos was using some "boiled-down wine" remedies, a good sign that brandy and other distilled liquors were in the making.

In anthropologist Richard Rudgley's words, "the universal human need for liberation from the restrictions of mundane existence is satisfied by experiencing altered states of consciousness." Or, as Bob Dylan articulated in "Rainy Day Women #12 and 35," "E-v-e-r-y-b-o-d-y must get stoned."

What's incredibly human, though, is that people everywhere slapped rules on the use of alcohol. It has always been generally considered poor form to drink indiscriminately. Intoxicants were immediately tied into religious ceremonies and the rituals of life: asking God for help, coming of age, getting married, celebrating victories and special occasions, achieving new spiritual insight, adamantly forgetting one's misery, or celebrating the advent of a new year. But, of course, intoxication has always come with a price. No matter what the nectar or how sweet the experience, you inevitably pay with a hangover.

Believe me, this is not a new problem. Earliest man pondered the question: How can we get the "tox" out of "intoxicants"? And what was the answer? You guessed it: soup.

WHAT KIND OF SOUP? ALL KINDS

Cabbage soup has been a hangover remedy since 350 B.C.E., as referenced in the third book of the *Problemata* (ascribed to Aristotle) and demonstrated vividly in A.D. 200, when Athenaeus' *Deipnosophistai (Sophists at Dinner)* observed, "Now that the Egyptians really are fond of wine this is proof, that they are the only people among whom it is a custom at their feasts to eat boiled cabbages before all the rest of their food; and even to this very time they do so."

Then, in medieval times, the Medical School of Salerno was already recommending the hair of the dog:

Si nocturna tibi noceat potatio vini
Hoc tu mane bibas iterum, et fuerit medicina

If an evening of wine does you in,
More the next morning will be medicine.

Then there are more modern soup remedies, with the main ingredients often being stomach linings. Partly this is an association thing: *your* stomach hurts, so it will be better if you consume the tender stomach—the tripe—of a placid cow or sheep. It may not sound too appetizing, but it's tested folk wisdom. In any case, tripe soup is a nearly universal nostrum, from El Salvadoran *sopa de patas,* Mexican *menudo,* and Puerto Rican *mondongo* to Italian *busecca;* from Polish *zupaz flaczow* and Georgian *khashi* to Greek *pastas* and Turkish *iskembe çorbasi,* all the way to Balinese *soto babat* and Chinese *moh thong leung.* Korean *Haejangguk,* sold on street corners, combines all of the old standbys: cow-bone soup with tripe, cabbage, black pepper, bean sprouts, herbs, and spices that make you sweat like a pig. The aspartic acid in the bean sprouts reputedly removes poisons from your bloodstream.

But Why Is Soup the Universal Nostrum?

In fact, soup goes to the heart of alcohol impacts. Because it's liquid, it helps rehydrate poor dehydrated you, flushing out poisons and plumping the brain back up. Because it's nutritious, it raises your blood-sugar levels, calms your stomach, and helps you stay energized while the alcohol metabolizes in its own sweet time. As for specific ingredients, well, who knows? There are lots of claims, but not much science. The bottom line is, if you want to chase that headache, no matter where you are in the world, think soup, eat soup. Thus I've stipulated big potfuls of the stuff in the recipes that follow. The more the better.

DENMARK

BEER SOUP
OLLEBROD
Serves 6 to 8

THIS SOUP IS effective because it's belly calming—and also because it's a bit of the hair of the dog. One thing only: you've got to be planning your debauch the night before to take advantage of this recipe, as the bread needs an overnight soaking. But once the soaking is done, this takes only a minute to cook and eat. And did I mention it is sweet-tart, soft on the palate, and, yes, belly-calming comfort food?

> *12 slices pumpernickel bread, broken by hand into small pieces*
> *6 cups dark ale (preferably Danish* hvidtol)
> *1 cup water*
> *2 lemons, juiced and rind grated*
> *Sugar to taste*

> GARNISH
> *Heavy cream, plain or whipped*
> *Small pinches of cinnamon*

TO PREPARE

1. The night before (or a minimum of 3 hours ahead), place the bread pieces in a deep saucepan and pour in the ale mixed with the water.

2. Prep the lemon.

TO COOK

Put the saucepan with the bread mixture over low heat and simmer until it thickens. Puree in a blender, adding the grated lemon zest and juice and sweetening to taste.

TO SERVE

Return the soup to the saucepan and bring it to a boil over medium-high heat. Ladle the soup into bowls and serve immediately, topped with plain or whipped cream and a pinch of cinnamon.

BEER SOUP FOR BREAKFAST

Frederick the Great of Prussia (1712–1786) loved this traditional northern European beer soup for breakfast, calling it *Heisse Biersuppe*. In fact, in 1777 he enacted a formal proclamation against coffee for breakfast, reasoning that if beer soup was good enough for him, the monarch, it should be good enough for the common folk.

LES HALLES AND THE HANGOVER SYNDROME

I'd always heard about onion soup at Les Halles, the central market of Paris, sold as a hangover remedy in its all-night cafés, but now I've seen it, pictured in James Whistler's *Soupe à Trois Sous* (1859), showing four bums dozing at two tables over wine and cups while a soulful-eyed, sharp-bearded *bohème* on the left stares straight over his empty onion soup plate at the artist.

FRANCE

LES HALLES ONION SOUP
SOUPE À L'OIGNON GRATINÉE
Serves 6 to 8

HERE IS PARIS'S answer to *la guele de bois*—that "wooden mouth" you get when you pour too much alcohol through it. It's a marvelous soup, rich and fragrant, packed with restoratives, and very simple to make, in the spirit of rushing a bowl to one in pain. Speaking of which, some bars are savvy enough to have onion soup on the menu. A former U.S. diplomat told me about one bar in Abidjan, the capital of Côte d'Ivoire, that had a barman-in-training who would traverse the length of the bar with scissors, snipping the molten cheese strings from the customers' lips so the cheese would fall back into the bowl.

> *½ cup (1 stick) butter*
> *8 cups thinly sliced onions*
> *3 tablespoons flour*
> *12 cups (3 quarts) Beef Stock (page 26)*
> *1 cup brandy*
> *1 tablespoon salt, or to taste*
> *1 teaspoon pepper, or to taste*

> GARNISH
> *Grated Gruyère cheese*
> *Dry toasts of French bread drizzled with olive oil*
> *Freshly grated Parmesan cheese*

TO PREPARE

1. Prep the ingredients as directed in the recipe list.

2. Prepare the garnish: cut 6 to 8 slices of French bread ½ inch thick and toast them in a 350°F. oven for about 15 minutes, until they are dry toast. Drizzle each with a little olive oil and set aside. Grate the cheeses and set aside.

To Cook

1. Melt the butter in a large soup pot over very low heat and add the onions, stirring constantly. Sweat for 5 to 10 minutes, covered, until they are soft and golden, then sprinkle them with flour, stirring, and add 2 cups of the stock. Turn up the heat to medium high and stir until the mixture is thickened.

2. Add the remaining stock and the brandy. Return to a boil, then reduce the heat to low and simmer, covered, for 30 minutes to 1 hour. Season with salt and pepper.

To Serve

Ladle the soup into individual, oven-resistant bowls and top each portion with a handful of Gruyère cheese. Place a piece of toast on each portion, sprinkle with the Parmesan, then run the bowls under a broiler for a few minutes until the cheese is melted. Carry to the table immediately on a tray — those bowls are hot.

Playwrights Pixilated in Paris

British playwright Harold Pinter recalls the night he spent carousing Paris with his friend Samuel Beckett, the Irish playwright, in the 1960s. "He was showing me his Paris and after a night of drinking he took me to Les Halles for a bowl of onion soup at 4 A.M. I collapsed with fatigue and awful stomach cramps and fell asleep on the table. When I woke, as if from a dream, Sam had gone, so I slept some more. Over an hour later he returned with bicarbonate of soda and said simply: 'For your stomach.' It was then I knew that this was a man who understood everything about the human condition."

RIDDLE ME THIS

QUESTION: What am I?
  In marble walls as white
    as milk
  Lined with a skin as soft
    as silk;
  Within a fountain crystal
    clear,
  A golden apple doth
    appear.
  No doors there are to this
    stronghold,
  Yet thieves break in and
    steal the gold.

ANSWER: An egg

GUATEMALA

SPICED TOMATO-EGG SOUP
CALDO DE HUEVO PARA LA GOMA
Serves 6 to 8

WOW! PIQUANT AND astringent until you bite into that rich and creamy egg. This is a beautiful and unusual soup, quite nice with corn bread as breakfast on a cold day (make the broth the night before) or as a warming lunch, using two eggs per person instead of one.

4 large ripe tomatoes or 8 canned, peeled, seeded, and finely chopped, reserving the juice for another purpose
2 garlic cloves, minced
2 hot chile peppers, seeded and minced (serrano or jalapeño is nice)
8 green onions, white and some green part, finely chopped
2 cups fresh epazote leaves, finely chopped (or hydrate 2 tablespoons sifted dried epazote leaves in 1/2 cup hot water for 30 minutes and mix with 1 cup finely chopped fresh flat-leaf parsley; if you can't find the dried epazote, substitute 2 cups of the finely chopped parsley with 1 tablespoon dried oregano)
8 cups (2 quarts) water
2 teaspoons salt
6 to 8 eggs (1 per person)

TO PREPARE
Prep the ingredients as directed in the recipe list.

TO COOK
1. In a large soup pot, stir the tomatoes, garlic, chile peppers, green onions, and epazote leaves (or substitutes) together and place over medium heat. Cook, partially covered, until the mix is concentrated and thick, 10 to 15 minutes.

2. Pour in the water and bring to a boil over high heat, stirring. Add the salt, then reduce the heat to low and simmer, uncovered, for 15 minutes.

3. Carefully break the eggs into the simmering broth at places where you can see the bubbles rising to the surface. Cover the pot and poach the eggs until they are just firm, about 4 minutes.

To Serve

Carefully ladle one egg into each of the bowls, then ladle the broth on top and serve immediately.

GAY GUATEMALAN GALA

In Mike Nichols's film *The Birdcage,* gay couple Armand (Robin Williams) and Albert/Starina (Nathan Lane) are putting on their best straight act to host the parents of Barbie, just engaged to Armand's son, Val. Uh-oh, Barbie's parents are the archconservative senator Kevin Keeley (Gene Hackman) and his wife, Louise (Dianne Wiest). What better way to meet and bond than over a nice dinner? So housekeeper Agador (Hank Azaria) whips up a little native Guatemalan soup with whole hard-boiled eggs in it—serving it up in pornographic Greek boy soup bowls—and no entrée. "No entrée? *No entrée?*" "Thees peasant soup *is* an entrée . . . it just *like* a soup. What you think? I should put in shrimp?"

HONDURAS

"MAN" SOUP
SOPA DE HOMBRE
Serves 6 to 8

YOU DON'T HAVE to be an hombre, much less an inebriated one, to fall in love with this extraordinary seafood soup. It's a tropical version of the American cioppini — beautiful to see, filled with chunky bits of seafood, tomato, peppers, and plantain, all in a piquant and sweet-tart coconutty broth. Heaven.

RIDDLE ME THIS

QUESTION: What am I?
  Alive without breath,
  As cold as death;
  Never thirsty, ever drinking,
  All in mail never clinking.

ANSWER: A fish

Assortment of hard-shell seafood: clams, crab, and/or mussels
2 cups Fish Stock (page 22)
1 small onion, finely chopped
½ red bell pepper, seeded and finely chopped
1 hot chile pepper, seeded and finely chopped (serrano or jalapeño is nice)
2 cups peeled and chopped tomatoes, with juice
1 small green plantain, peeled and diced
Salt and pepper to taste
¼ cup tomato paste
1 pound assorted fish fillets, cut into bite-size pieces
½ pound raw shrimp, peeled and deveined
2 cups coconut milk (one 13.5-ounce can)

GARNISH
  6 to 8 toasted croutons
  Finely chopped fresh parsley
  Thick wedges of lime

TO PREPARE
  1. Scrub the hard-shell seafood clean, then let soak in cold water until you are ready to use it.
  2. Prep the remaining ingredients as directed in the recipe list.

3. For the croutons, cut crusty bread into ½-inch slices and toast in a 350° F. oven for about 15 minutes.

To Cook

1. Bring the fish stock to a boil in a large soup pot over medium heat. Stir in the onion, peppers, tomatoes with their juice, plantain, and salt and pepper. Bring to a boil, then reduce the heat to low and simmer for 10 minutes.

2. Stir in the tomato paste, then add all the fish and seafood. Cover tightly and stew over low heat for about 30 minutes.

3. Stir in the coconut milk, being careful not to break up the seafood. Cover the pot and cook gently just until the soup comes to a bubble (otherwise the coconut taste will degrade).

To Serve

Ladle the soup into bowls. Top each portion with a crouton, sprinkle with parsley, and put a lime wedge on the side of each bowl.

"NUMBERS, IX"

*What a thin life the girl
fish-vendor leads . . .*

*She goes about dirty and
    smelly,
half-clothed in rags,
tumbling around noisily
in a near faint.
What a sickly girl!
Ah, what a pale face!*

*She has such sad eyes,
and her eyes are as blue
as the dark herons.
Ah, the girl, girl, girl
fish-vendor!*

—Constantino Suasnavar,
twentieth-century Honduran poet

HUNGARY

"NIGHT OWL" SOUP
KORHELYLEVES
Serves 6 to 8

TRADITIONALLY SERVED IN Budapest and throughout Hungary after all-night parties to fend off next-day hangovers, this hearty soup is awfully good for a cozy winter dinner as well. The potatoes are my idea — you may omit them if you want to be a purist.

10-ounce piece of ham shank (you will reserve some of its cooking liquid from step 2, below)
4 cups plus 2 tablespoons water
2 tablespoons butter
1 large onion, chopped
2 teaspoons paprika
2 cups sauerkraut, soaked in 2 cups water and drained (reserving the liquid), rinsed, and chopped
4 to 6 cups Beef Stock (page 26)
6 potatoes, peeled and diced
1 bay leaf
Freshly grated black pepper to taste
1 cup sour cream
5 ounces spicy dried sausage, diced (the traditional Hungarian Debrecen sausage is best, but Polish sausage is a good substitute)
Chopped fresh parsley, for garnish

TO PREPARE

1. Three hours ahead, soak the ham shank in cold water, changing the water several times. Drain and scrub the shank to remove any impurities.

2. Bring the 4 cups of water to a boil in a large soup pot over medium heat with the ham shank and let boil for at least 30 minutes. Let the meat cool in the broth, then cut it into small pieces, discard-

ing the bone. Set the meat aside and reserve 1 cup of the broth, discarding the rest.

3. Prep the remaining ingredients as directed in the recipe list.

To Cook

1. Melt the butter in a large soup pot over medium-low heat, then add the onion and cook, stirring, until golden. Take the pan off the heat, add the paprika, and stir. Add the remaining 2 tablespoons of water and the drained sauerkraut, and put back on the heat, stirring.

2. Pour in the reserved sauerkraut juice (add water to bring it up to 4 cups of liquid) and combined stocks, bring to a boil over high heat, and add the potatoes, bay leaf, pepper, and reserved meat pieces. Reduce the heat to low and simmer, partially covered, for 15 to 20 minutes, until the potatoes are tender. Remove the bay leaf.

3. Stir in the sour cream and diced sausage, and simmer for 5 minutes to heat through.

To Serve

Ladle the soup into generous bowls and garnish with parsley.

Petur Ban's Bitter Drinking Song

If ever two dark eyes
your heart's affection gain,
and all your loving sighs
meet nothing but disdain,
until she yields and says
her love for you will never fail—
but when your back is turned
you find it's quite another tale.
Just ponder as you drink.
Can the world really last, do you
   think?
Tomorrow it may fade away,
like moonbeams at the break of
   day.
So drink, so drink, so drink!

When sorrow comes your way
and puts you out of sorts,
and visions of dismay
are preying on your thoughts.
Think up a bold adventure
and set to with all your might.
Have faith that you can see it
through and all will come out
   right.
Just ponder as you drink.
Can the world really last, do you
   think?
But while it lasts and while it
   lives,
it does good or wrong but never
   peace.
So drink, so drink, so drink!

—Ferenc Erkel, nineteenth-century composer, from Act I of his opera Bánk Bán, *a grim song that sets the scene for the disasters in thirteenth-century Hungary that are to come; it is based on a poem by the Hungarian romantic poet Mihály Vörösmarty.*

PUERTO RICO

TROPICAL TRIPE SOUP
MONDONGO
Serves 6 to 8

DON'T BE PUT off by the tripe! This is a beautiful soup, a feast for the eyes and stomach. It's bright and chunky, multitextured, and all cut into a fine bite-size dice. If you can't find the taro and cassava, you may substitute white and sweet potatoes. This soup goes down easy and has you feeling better in no time—even if, like the poet Matos, you're only drunk on the ecstasy of night visions.

FOR THE TRIPE
6 cups cold water
1 tablespoon salt
1 pound honeycomb tripe, washed and cut into a small dice (these pieces can be soaked in lemon or orange water for 30 minutes to flavor and bleach, if you like)

FOR THE SOUP
1 tablespoon annatto oil (see sidebar)
1/4 cup diced smoked ham
1/4 cup recaíto (see sidebar)
1/4 cup tomato paste
1/2 cup alcaparrado (see sidebar)
2 cups peeled and diced taro root
2 cups peeled and diced cassava
2 cups peeled and diced pumpkin or butternut squash
1/2 green plantain, peeled and diced
3 bay leaves
Salt and pepper to taste

SPECIAL PUERTO RICAN SEASONINGS

- *Annatto oil,* for 1 tablespoon: sauté 1 teaspoon annatto seeds in 4 teaspoons corn oil over low heat for 3 minutes, then strain.
- *Alcaparrado,* for 1/2 cup: mix 1/4 cup small green olives *(manzanillos),* 2 tablespoons whole capers with juice, and 2 tablespoons chopped pimiento.
- *Recaíto,* for 1/2 cup: in a blender, puree 1/4 diced onion, 1 garlic clove, 1/2 small green bell pepper, 2 recao leaves (or substitute 1 tablespoon fresh parsley), and 1 tablespoon fresh cilantro.

To Prepare

1. Three hours ahead, bring the water to a boil in a large soup pot, salt it, then add tripe pieces, lower the heat, cover, and cook for 2 to 3 hours, until tender. Drain and rinse, discarding the water.

2. Prep the remaining ingredients as directed in the recipe list.

To Cook

1. Heat the annatto oil in a large soup pot over medium heat, then stir in the ham pieces, *recaíto*, tomato paste, and *alcaparrado*. Cook for 5 minutes, stirring.

2. Add the tripe, taro, cassava, squash, plantain, bay leaves, and water to cover. Bring to a boil over high heat, then reduce the heat to low, cover, and simmer for 45 minutes. Remove the bay leaves. Add salt and pepper.

To Serve

Ladle the soup into large bowls. This colorful soup needs no garnish.

"Clair de Lune"

In the moonlight, in this night
Of clear and glossy moon-light,
My heart like a dark frog
Leaps upon the grass.

How gay is my heart now!
With what delight this fearful
Tragic frog uplifts its head
Beneath the pensive bright-ness of the moon!

High up, among the trees,
The soft birds dream,
And higher still, above the clouds,
The stars gleam newly washed.

Ah let morning never come!
Lengthen out this slow
And blessed hour when things
Take on a supreme unreality,

And when my heart like a frog
Emerges from its swamps
And sets out in the brightness of the moon
Upon its sidereal flight among the stars!

—Luis Pales Matos, *twentieth-century Puerto Rican Afro-Antillean poet*

POKHLEBKIN SPEAKS

Viliam Vasilievich Pokhlebkin, eccentric encyclopedic food historian and nationalistic Marxist, describes *rassol'nik* in his authoritative dictionary of cuisine as stuffed with pickles, pickle juice, meats, dill, and sour cream, and he extols its curative properties. He also notes that *zurek*, or white *borshch*, is a rye-based soup that's traditionally served at the end of the wedding to sober up the guests. Alas, this great scholar was slain as a very old man in the year 2000 by thieves who broke into his home outside Moscow to steal his valuable book collection.

RUSSIA

KIDNEY-PICKLE SOUP
RASSOL'NIK
Serves 6 to 8

ANDREI RADCHENKO FROM Miami, Florida—mechanical engineer, computer professional, and native of Kiev—has been kind enough to share this extraordinary recipe for *rassol'nik* with me. It's complicated to make and must be prepared in stages, but is well worth the trouble. Please feel free to use prepared beef stock to eliminate the first step altogether.

FOR THE BEEF BROTH
10 cups (2½ quarts) cold water
2 pounds meaty beef bones
2 celery stalks with leaves
1 carrot, scrubbed and trimmed
1 medium onion, quartered

FOR THE KIDNEYS AND KIDNEY BROTH
1 beef or 2 veal kidneys (some recipes use 2 pounds of chicken gizzards)

FOR THE SOUP
1 cup barley
1 tablespoon butter or oil
1 small onion, diced
1 carrot, peeled and diced
1 parsley root, peeled and diced (or substitute parsnip)
1 medium potato, peeled and diced
1 bay leaf
Freshly ground black pepper to taste
2 large dill pickles, peeled and diced
Fresh herbs and spices to taste (thyme, parsley, coriander, etc.)
Salt and pepper to taste
Sour cream and chopped fresh dill, for garnish

To Prepare

1. Two hours ahead, place the cold water and bones for the broth in a large soup pot. Bring to a slow boil over medium heat, skimming as long as necessary, then add the celery, carrot, and onion. Reduce the heat to low, partially cover, and let simmer for at least 1 hour. Strain, discarding the vegetables and bones.

2. Also 2 hours ahead, cut all the fat from the kidneys and place in a large saucepan. Cover with cold water, bring to a boil over medium heat, partially covered, and let boil for 10 to 15 minutes. Strain, discarding the broth with its impurities, and wash the kidneys well. Return to the saucepan with fresh water to cover, bring to a boil over medium-high heat, then reduce the heat to low, cover, and simmer for 1 hour. Reserve both the kidneys and the broth. Remove the kidneys from the broth, let cool, then cut away any last scraps of fat, and cut into bite-size pieces.

3. Prep the remaining ingredients as directed in the recipe list.

To Cook

1. Put the beef stock, kidney broth, kidney pieces, and the barley in a large soup pot and bring to a boil over medium-high heat. Reduce the heat to low and simmer, covered, for at least 1 hour.

2. Heat the butter or oil in a skillet over low heat. Toss in the onion, carrot, and parsley root and sweat, covered, until the onion is soft and yellow. Scrape into the simmering soup.

3. Add the potato, bay leaf, and pepper to the soup and simmer until the potato is soft, 15 to 20 minutes.

4. Meanwhile, sweat the pickles, covered, over low heat in the skillet you used for the vegetables and add them to the soup when the potatoes are soft. Add the herbs and spices; simmer for another 10 minutes. Remove the bay leaf and taste for seasoning — the broth should have a strong sour note but not be flagrantly sour. If you like, add some pickle juice to get the right flavor.

To Serve

Ladle the soup into bowls and top each portion with a dollop of sour cream and a sprinkling of chopped dill. Wonderful!

"Gay Feast"

I love the festive board
Where joy's the one presiding,
And freedom, my adored,
The banquet's course is
    guiding.
When "Drink!" half-drowns
    the song
That only morning throttles,
When wide-flung is the
    throng,
And close the jostling bottles.

—Alexander Pushkin, *nineteenth-century Russian poet*

SENEGAL

CHICKEN STEW
YASSA
Serves 8

OKAY, STRICTLY SPEAKING, this is not a soup, but it's close and so extraordinary, not to mention fiery, that I have to include it for your own good. Imagine buttery chicken and thick sweet brown onions in a lemon-chile pepper broth, all poured over rice so your mouth doesn't go up in flames. Traditionally it is eaten communally, with your fingers, straight from the dish.

WOLOF PROVERB

"Much soup is better than much broth."

2 chickens, 3 pounds each, cut into 16 to 20 serving pieces
8 large onions, cut into thick slices
4 habanero or other hot chile peppers, seeded and quartered
1 cup fresh lemon juice
¼ cup peanut oil
2 cups hot water
Salt and pepper to taste

4 cups raw white rice

TO PREPARE

1. The night before, prep the ingredients as directed in the recipe list, then mix the chicken pieces, onion slices, and chile peppers in a flat-bottomed dish and pour the lemon juice, then the peanut oil over the chicken. Mix well. Seal the dish with plastic or aluminum foil, refrigerate, and let marinate overnight.

2. Fire up the grill (to be most authentic) or turn on the broiler.

TO COOK

1. Brown the chicken pieces as quickly as possible with a very hot flame, either on the grill or under the broiler.

2. Put the browned chicken pieces in a Dutch oven and add the marinade and onion mixture. Pour in the hot water, season with salt and pepper, seal with aluminum foil, top with the cover, and cook at 275 to 300°F. for 2 to 2½ hours.

3. Thirty minutes before serving, bring 8 cups of water to a boil. Add the rice, reduce the heat to low, and cover. Simmer for 20 minutes, then remove from the heat.

TO SERVE

Mound the rice in a large serving dish. Unseal the chicken—it should be tender and the onions should be lightly browned and very sweet—and pour it over the rice. Invite your guests to sit down and dig into the pot, with their choice of fingers, spoons, or forks.

"MAN AND THE BEAST"

. . . *The struggle is too long!*
In the shadow long as the
three ages of millennial
night.
Strength of the heavy Man
his feet in the fruitful mud
Strength of the Man, the
rushes entangling his
strength.
His heart the heat of the pri-
mal bowels, the strength of
the Man in his drunken-
ness
The hot wine of the Beast's
blood, the foam that
sparkles in his heart
Here's to the millet beer
brewed for the Initiate!

—LÉOPOLD SÉDAR SENGHOR, twentieth-century Senegalese poet, called the "Walt Whitman of Africa"; also a political thinker and the president of Senegal from 1960 to 1980, passionately connecting himself to Africa and his black heritage

PART IV

SOUPS

OF

PIETY

AND

RITUAL

Like the bee gathering honey from different flowers,
the wise person accepts the essence of different scriptures
and sees only the good in all religions.

—*Sacred Hindu text of* SRIMAD BHAGVATAM 11.3,
quoted by Mahatma Gandhi

14

NEW YEAR'S DAY

ONCE UPON A TIME, New Year celebrations had nothing to do with January 1. For that matter, they still don't in many parts of the world.

Why? It's a calendar thing.

In the Beginning, there was no concept of measuring and recording the passage of time. It got cold; it got hot; people adapted. Not until Neolithic man — or, more likely, woman — started growing things did it become important to keep track of time. People kept their eyes on the growing season and marked the end of one natural cycle (winter) and the beginning of the next (spring) according to when the first new moon appeared in the sky after the vernal equinox. New *year* celebrations and rituals logically began with new *life*, the renewal of the earth, sprouting plants and animals popping babies, all based on the lunar calendar — you know, sometime around May, give or take a month, depending on where you lived.

There was, however, one problem: "lunar" accounting doesn't add up right in the larger planetary rhythms of timekeeping. The moon waxes and wanes and waxes and wanes and still adds up to only 354 days in its annual cycles, so its calendar didn't and doesn't add up to a true 365-day year of earth orbiting the sun. And so began the battle of cultural calendars — lunar versus Zodiac versus solar.

ON THE LUNAR SIDE:

- Babylonians, who were the first, apparently, to come up with a lunar calendar around 2000 B.C.E., and they intercalated an extra month from time to time to true the seasons.
- Chinese, who—since 2637 B.C.E. and the legendary Emperor Huangdi—observe twelve 29- or 30-day months that repeat seven times in the course of a nineteen-year period and generally stay in line with the seasons. New Year? It starts at the second new moon after the beginning of winter, falling somewhere between January 20 and February 20.
- Koreans, Vietnamese, and Tibetans, who celebrate Sol-nal, Tet, and Losar based on the same Chinese calculations.
- Hebrews, who add an extra 29-day month *Veadar* every nineteen years and celebrate the New Year in the fall as Rosh Hashanah (page 261).
- Muslims, who begin their calendar from Mohammed's flight from Mecca to Medina, count 354 days for nineteen years and 355 days for eleven, so their New Year's Day moves backward through all four seasons.

ON THE ZODIAC SIDE:

- Persians (Iranians), who celebrate the New Year on March 21. Their pre-Zoroastrian calendar, which was formalized by Zoroaster and perfected by the astronomer/poet Omar Khayyam, featured twelve months—named after the guardian angels of the holy book of Zoroastrianism—of 30 days each, thereby giving 5 extra days for ancestors to visit their children on earth. New Year, or *No Ruz,* was the most important festival of all for this sacred time.

ON THE SOLAR SIDE:

- Ancient Egyptians, who fixed a 365-day calendar based on the confluence of the Dog Star Sirius reappearing in the eastern sky about the time of the Nile's annual flood.
- Romans, who progressed from a 304-day calendar that just flat ignored the 60 days of wintertime, to Numa Pompilius' faulty solar calendar that first made Januarius 1 the official start of the New

Year, to Julius Caesar (in consultation with the astronomer Sosigenes) banning the use of lunar calculations and declaring a year of 445 days in 46 B.C.E. to correct Rome's calendar, a time known as "the year of confusion."

• Roman Catholic Europeans, who corrected the Julian calendar in 1582 under Pope Gregory XIII, then exported this new Gregorian calendar all over the world with their explorers, conquerors, missionaries, and colonialists. Germans stuck with the Julian calendar until 1700; England and the American colonies until 1752; Russia, 1918; and Turkey, 1927.

Okay, you're likely saying, but now it's the twenty-first century and most everyone marches to a 365-day solar calendar. So why does the Christian Church still have moveable feasts for Ash Wednesday, Palm Sunday, and Easter? Good question. Because, as a historical footnote, the church calendar is partly regulated by throwback lunar cycles. Why? Because, despite its best efforts, the church was not able to completely ban pagan fertility rites at the vernal equinox's new moon, so it turned them into church holidays that fluxed along with the lunar cycles.

Now we're through the hard part and can get on with the whys and wherefores of New Year celebrations, not to mention which soups traditionally fuel them in kitchens across the world.

It's a pretty simple and totally universal proposition, when you think about it. People want and need fresh starts, so they create appropriate times for them, bundle them up with a lot of traditions and rituals, and declare themselves reborn at the end.

In the old days of agricultural societies, what better time to ritually honor that rebirth than when the earth was renewing itself? For peoples bound to church calendars, like Muslims and Christians, the ritual date is important, not the season in which it falls. For the modern world, driven as it is by the need for global coordination of commerce and contracts, January 1 is a convenient consensus. And if January 1 isn't your new year of choice, it's still perfectly fine to celebrate — just don't ignore the "other" New Year's Day that's traditional for you, too.

HAITI

PUMPKIN SOUP
SOUPE JOUMOU
Serves 6 to 8

THIS IS A fabulous stuffed soup — bright yellow-orange and sensu-
ously African with an opulence of meat, vegetables, and the
Caribbean bite of lime and chiles. In Kreyol, you'd say it was
stuffed with *dub, joumou, kawot, seleri, zanyon, nave, pomdete,
malanga,* and *shou* — and spiced with *piman bouk, ten, lay,* and *sit-
won.*

*Meat spice rub (grind 4 garlic cloves, 1 teaspoon thyme,
    ¹⁄₄ teaspoon pepper, and 2 sliced green onions into
    2 teaspoons salt)*
1-pound piece of boneless beef stew meat
16 cups (4 quarts) cold water
1 Scotch bonnet or habanero chile pepper, with stem attached
*2 pounds pumpkin (or other winter squash like butternut),
    peeled and chopped*
2 carrots, peeled and sliced
2 celery stalks with leaves, sliced lengthwise and cut into pieces
1 large onion, cubed
2 medium turnips, peeled and cubed
2 medium potatoes, peeled and cubed
*1 pound malanga, peeled and cubed (or substitute another
        pound of potatoes)*
1 pound cabbage, chopped
*¹⁄₄ pound vermicelli or other thin pasta, broken into
        short lengths*
Salt and pepper to taste
2 limes, juiced, plus thick wedges of lime, for garnish

TO PREPARE

1. Rub the meat with the spice paste and let marinate at room temperature for 1 hour.

2. Prep the remaining ingredients as directed in the recipe list.

TO COOK

1. Bring the meat, water, and chile pepper to a boil in a large soup pot over medium heat, then reduce the heat to low and simmer, covered, for 2 hours.

2. Add the pumpkin and carrots, cover the pot, and cook until very tender, about 20 minutes.

3. Remove the meat and chile pepper from the pot, discarding the pepper. In a blender, puree the pumpkin and carrots in the broth, then pour back into the pot. When the meat is cool enough to handle, cut it into cubes and stir them into the soup.

4. Add the celery, onion, turnips, potatoes, and malanga to the soup; bring it to a boil over high heat, then reduce the heat to low and simmer, covered, for 15 minutes. Thin the broth with as much water as needed — it should not be too thick.

5. Add the cabbage and cook 15 more minutes. Thin the soup again with water, as needed.

6. Add the vermicelli and cook until tender. Thin the soup again with water, as needed. This is a soup full of thirsty ingredients.

7. Taste and correct for seasoning with salt and pepper. Stir in the lime juice. Turn off the heat, cover the pot, and let it sit until you are ready to serve it.

TO SERVE

Carefully bring the soup back to a simmer, stirring so the pumpkin doesn't burn, and ladle the soup into bowls. Serve some lime wedges on the side for people to help themselves.

THE BIRTH OF *SOUPE JOUMOU*, JANUARY 1, 1804

People started gathering at dawn at Gonaïves' Place d'Armes. General Dessalines mounted the Autel de la Patrie to speak. He recited the cruelties of the people's enslavement in Kreyol, so everyone could understand him, and he declared that Haitians would forever after live free and die free. "Long live independence!" he shouted at the end of the ceremony, having no idea what a difficult life it would be. Cannons were fired; church bells rung; people cheered; and, they say, kettles of fragrant *soupe joumou* perfumed the air, ready to be ladled up in a mass communion. This soup symbolizes Haiti's fervent wish for peace and freedom—its symbol of communion and brotherhood. And one thing is sure: on January 1, Haitians around the world make it and eat it for lots of reasons.

Some say, pure and simple, it's a good luck charm for the New Year—and you *better* eat it because it's bad luck if you don't. Others say, no, it's really to cleanse and purify the body for the New Year. Others yet say it honors the Vodou god Papa Loko, keeper of African spiritual traditions, and that it reliably "lifts up a man's soul and makes him prophesy."

Haitian History in a Soup Bowl

What a tangled web this soup symbolizes. From the time King Ferdinand of Spain congratulated Columbus on his Christmas Day landfall near Cap Haïtien in 1492, then declared open season on West Africans to work his New World sugar plantations there, Haiti has been a land of warm and gracious people racked by violence and suffering.

Here's some history behind this heavily symbolic kettle of New Year's soup: After the 1492 landfall, Spain stayed long enough to kill off the natives, import sugarcane cuttings from the Canary Islands, and establish plantations with African slaves, but then left Haiti to the French in 1697.

France wasted no time. Under Kings Louis XIV, XV, and XVI, it transformed those depopulated mountains and valleys into cash-crop factories of sugar, indigo, and cotton. How? With African slaves culled largely from tribes in Congo, Angola, Dahomey, Guinea, and Senegal. When the slaves died, often from nearly unbelievable cruelty, they were replaced by new shipments from Africa.

So what happened in 1789 when the French rose up and proclaimed *Liberté! Egalité! Fraternité!*? After all, the French National Assembly's Declaration of the Rights of Man clearly stated, "Men are born and remain free and equal in rights." National Assemblymen in Paris said, Oh yes, we guess that means Haiti, too—or at least the freed mulattoes there, those fine sons of Frenchmen and their African slaves. No way, said the racist colonialists in Haiti, and they conducted such a tough lobby that the National Assembly reversed itself in 1791.

Haiti's mulattoes could not believe their ears. It was the last straw. They immediately joined their education, knowledge, and considerable military experience to those 500,000 enslaved Africans—and Haiti exploded in revolt. In August 1791, Vodou priest Boukman Duffy convened slave rebel leaders in the forest overlooking Le Cap. Illuminated by flashes of lightning, they made incantations; they slit the throat of a pig and drank its blood; and they formally swore death to all *blancs,* which they carried out to the letter with pruning hooks, machetes, and fire. In November, Louis-Jacques Bauvais's mulatto troops attacked and burned Port-au-Prince, slaughtering whites wherever they found them. They sported white ears as cockades in their caps and committed nearly unbelievable atrocities against women and children. And that was just the start.

Thirteen long years, all told, of tit-for-tat torched cities, slit throats, scorched earth, attacks, betrayals, mass executions, sieges, torture, encirclements, and despair, not to mention 10,000 deaths from malaria and yellow fever. Uprising leader Dessalines's ultimate winning strategy: *koupe tèt, boule kay,* "cut off heads, burn down." In the end, some 300,000 Haitians died and 50,000 French—and in the end, the French were defeated. French General Rochambeau was given ten days to pack up his army and ship home.

When the last French ship had cleared Le Cap, Dessalines sent word: "There is no more doubt, *mon cher général,* the country is ours, and the famous *who-shall-have-it* is settled." He divided up the war chest—8 *gourdes* per man; he dispersed his army to the principal towns; and he sat down with his generals "to ratify in ink what they had written in blood" and to celebrate with *Soupe joumou.*

IRAN (PERSIA)

NOODLE SOUP
ÂSH-E RESHTEH
Serves 6 to 8

THIS ANCIENT SOUP to celebrate *No Ruz* (New Year) on March 21 began life in Zoroastrian Persia, made then of spinach and clover that was freshly sprouting in mid-March and thickened with a paste of flour and water. Over time, the flour-and-water paste thickened into dumplings, and by A.D. 500, at the court of Sassanian King Kobad, tales from Old Persian literature indicate those dumplings had forever turned to noodles, 700 years before pasta turned up for the first time in Italy. This recipe is rich in native Iranian ingredients, but also reflective of its central position on the hump of the Silk Road, with traders and their fabled foodstuffs endlessly peregrinating through it, east to west and west to east and back again.

Âsh-e reshteh is a glorious soup, stuffed with grains and greens, multicolored, multitextured, and oh-so-exquisitely aromatic for all the stumpingly hearty foods in it. You can ladle it into separate bowls and garnish individually, but it's really lovely in one big tureen ladled out to hungry guests who are anxious for a lucky New Year. Be sure to have warm bread and lemon juice on the side.

Now the New Year reviving old Desires,
The thoughtful Soul to Solitude retires,
Where the white hand of Moses on the bough
Puts out, and Jesus from the ground suspires.

—OMAR KHAYYAM, eleventh-century Persian poet, from THE RUBIYAT, verse 4

¼ *cup dried red kidney beans*
½ *cup dried chickpeas*
¼ *cup dried white navy beans*
1 *tablespoon olive oil*
1 *medium onion, sliced in half from stem to top, then thinly into half-moons*
Pinch of saffron threads, crushed to a powder with a few grains of sugar and dissolved in 2 teaspoons of hot water
½ *teaspoon finely ground black pepper*
8 *cups (2 quarts) Vegetable Stock (see page 23)*
¾ *cup brown lentils*
1 *lemon, juiced*

DUALIST SOUP MEETS
DUALISTIC ZOROASTRIANISM

Once upon a time, the
Zoroastrian god Ahoura-
mazda set out to create the
world. Instantly, his act of
creation provoked an opposite reaction in the cosmos.
His evil twin Angromainyous
sprang into being, dedicated
to destroying the harmony of
the universe. Eternally these
two gods face each other off,
and humans must balance
their lives in careful equilib-
rium between their extreme
forces of good and evil. Likewise, Zoroastrians ate as
they lived: their foodways
developed to carefully balance opposing flavors, as in
this sweet-and-sour New
Year's soup.

½ teaspoon dried dill, crumbled between your palms

1 cup chopped fresh parsley

1 cup chopped green onions, white and some green parts

2 cups fresh spinach, washed, stemmed, stacked, and thinly
  sliced

Salt to taste

1 cup Persian noodles or linguine, broken into short lengths

2 tablespoons sour cream (a substitute for Persian kashk, or
  dried buttermilk)

GARNISH

¼ cup na'nâ dâgh (1 small minced onion and 1 teaspoon dried
  mint fried in 1 tablespoon oil)

Dollop of sour cream (or kashk)

Sprinkling of turmeric

RESHTEH AND NO RUZ

Reshteh, the name of this flat noodle, actually means "string"
or "reins of life" in Persian, and it is traditionally cooked into
dishes when momentous ventures are to be undertaken. Not
just at *No Ruz*, when families wish to "cut the knots of trouble"
in their lives and at the same time "tie themselves together,"
but also before journeys or when important decisions are to
be made—in fact, at any time when a fresh start in life is
needed.

As for *No Ruz* itself, it has always been a time of renewal and
family celebration. From earliest times, homes were scrubbed,
ceramic pots broken and replaced (hygiene reasons!), and
fires lit on roofs to guide one's ancestors safely home from
heaven on the cusp of the New Year to feast with the family
for the next ten days. Today, Islamic faith and New Year
notwithstanding, the festival carries on for twelve days, ending
in *Seezdah Beedar*, the thirteenth day of the New Year—and
since it's considered a very unlucky time to stay home, people
troop off to the countryside for a last blast picnic feast.

To Prepare

1. The night before, soak the beans and chickpeas overnight in plenty of water. Drain, rinse, and reserve the beans.

2. Prep the remaining ingredients as directed in the recipe list.

To Cook

1. Heat the oil in a large soup pot over medium heat and sauté the sliced onion until golden brown; this shouldn't be rushed. Stir in the liquid saffron and pepper, the drained beans and chickpeas, and the stock. Bring to a boil over high heat, then reduce the heat to low, cover, and simmer for 1 hour.

2. Add the lentils along with the lemon juice and dill, return to a boil over high heat, and again reduce the heat to low and simmer for another hour.

3. Stir in the parsley, green onions, and spinach, and simmer for 10 minutes.

4. Bring the soup to a boil over high heat, adding more stock or water (as much as 3 cups) to your taste of soupiness. Season with salt, then add the pasta. Reduce the heat to medium and cook, un-covered, stirring from time to time, until the noodles are tender, about 12 minutes.

5. Meanwhile, make the *na'nâ dâgh* by frying minced onion in 1 tablespoon of oil until golden brown, then stirring in the dried mint, crumbled between your palms. Remove from the heat and set aside.

To Serve

Ladle the soup into a large bowl. Sprinkle the *na'nâ dâgh* all around the edges of the bowl, then swirl a dollop of sour cream or *kashk* in the center and sprinkle lightly with turmeric.

JAPANESE SOUP ETIQUETTE

Planning to serve this soup with those lovely Asian ceramic spoons? Be my guest, but you'll be breaching Japanese etiquette. The ultimate standard of whether a food is Japanese or not is this: can it be eaten with *hashi* (chopsticks) or drunk from a bowl? If not, not Japanese. Besides, it really is easier to consume this sometimes dangerously sticky soup by delicately picking up that gooey *mochi* and other tasty bits to eat and nibble with chopsticks, then drinking the broth straight from the bowl. Not to scare you, but every New Year, a number of elderly Japanese over-estimate how much *mochi* they can eat at a bite and suffer the consequences of choking on it.

JAPAN

NEW YEAR MISO SOUP WITH RICE CAKE

O-ZONI

Serves 8

> *Shinnen akemashite, o-medeto gozaimase!*
> "The new year has dawned, indeed a matter for congratulation."

I'VE GOT TO give this soup a big wow. It may not be easy to find the pounded *mochi* rice cakes, which look like opaque white blocks in clear plastic packaging, but they're worth searching out. You take off the plastic wrap, stick the block under a broiler, turning on all sides with tongs as it blackens like a marshmallow at a cookout, and you've got yourself a sticky, runny, yummy hunk of molten, crispy rice goo. It's wonderful at the bottom of a bowl of *dashi* with some chicken and leeks thrown in — the perfect way to bring in the New Year, whether that means January 1 or the more proper lunar calendar end-of-winter-and-time-for-spring-planting *Osho gatsu* festival, when you leave ill luck behind and craft a new beginning for yourself. The *mochi* rice cakes date back to the early ninth century, Heian-cho times, when they signified health, rebirth, vitality, and resurrection.

> 8 mochi *rice cakes*
> 4 *raw chicken breast halves, boned, trimmed, and sliced into thin strips*
> 8 *cups Japanese Soup Stock* (dashi; *page 28*)
> 6 *tablespoons white miso*
> 4 *slender leeks or* negi, *white part only, sliced very finely on the diagonal*

MOCHITSUKI, OR MAKING MOCHI

It's a pretty hilarious family or community outdoor sport that has you wielding huge hammers to pound steamed rice into a sticky ball, but this practice is based, of course, on millennia of serious Shinto and Buddhist tradition. In earliest days, rice was precious and a worthy offering to the gods at the New Year. In Shinto, each grain of rice symbolized a human soul, so pounded rice cakes offered millions of conjoined souls to the gods. Carried forward by Buddhists, the very act of making the cakes provided an opportunity for self reflection and purification. Try it and you'll see why.

First, you steam lots of glutinous rice for several hours in a wooden steamer over an open fire, then you turn the rice into a stone or hardwood mortar (*usu*), and give everyone a shot at beating it with a big wooden mallet (*kine*) until it becomes a sticky ball, while some brave soul turns it between whacks. The ball is briefly kneaded until it's a thick white springy mass, then it's shaped into smaller balls or pressed into flat molds, an inch thick, to dry.

Here's what the great seventeenth-century poet and maker of haikus Bashō Matsuo had to say about *mochi* and the New Year in *Narrow Road to the Interior:*

> *It is New Year's Day*
> *for each rice field's own sun—just*
> *as each yearned for it*

> *Ganjitsu wa*
> *tagoto no hi koso*
> *koishikere*

> *and*

> *O bush warblers!*
> *Now you've shit all over*
> *my rice cake on the porch*

> *Uguisu ya*
> *mochi ni fun suru*
> *en no saki.*

To Prepare

1. Broil the *mochi* cakes in a metal pan under a hot broiler on all sides, turning with tongs, until the cakes are crisp and brown, but not burnt. Remove from the heat, pierce with a fork, and set aside.

2. Prep the remaining ingredients as directed in the recipe list.

To Cook

1. Dip the chicken strips into salted boiling water for 2 minutes, then drain, discarding the broth or using it for another purpose.

2. Bring the *dashi* to a boil in a large saucepan over medium heat, then add the chicken pieces and simmer until tender, about 4 minutes.

3. Put the miso into a small bowl and whisk 1 cup of hot *dashi* into it until well blended. Pour back into the soup, bring just to a boil over medium heat, then remove from the heat.

To Serve

Place a broiled rice cake in the bottom of each of eight bowls, then ladle the soup over them, evenly distributing the chicken pieces. Top with slivered leek, cover the bowls with lids, and serve immediately.

KOREA

BEEF AND RICE COIN SOUP
TTOK-KUK
Serves 6 to 8

TTOK-KUK IS A beautiful and festive soup: delicate strips of yellow egg and bright green scallion slices setting off a rich beef broth that is crammed with color and texture—chewy white rice-cake medallions, tender meatballs, and juicy beef strips. At serving time, it gets an aromatic boost with a last-minute crumble of dried seaweed, cayenne, and green onion. If it weren't for the penalty of aging a year with each serving, I'd recommend a bowl at least once a month.

FOR THE RICE COINS
  6 to 8 rice cake sticks

FOR THE TOPPINGS
  2 teaspoons peanut oil
  ¼ pound boneless beef, partially frozen, then cut into fine strips
  Salt and pepper to taste
  2 ounces ground beef, formed into marble-size meatballs
  1 teaspoon flour
  1 egg, beaten

FOR THE SOUP
  8 cups (2 quarts) Beef Stock (page 26)
  1 tablespoon soy sauce
  1 teaspoon salt
  1 green onion, thinly sliced on the diagonal
  1 teaspoon chopped garlic
  1 teaspoon hot chile sauce

HOW MANY BOWLS OF *TTOK-KUK* HAVE YOU EATEN?

This soup is associated with adding age—if you eat a bowl, you automatically turn a year older. Needless to say, you don't want to eat a bowl any more than one time a year, lest you age prematurely. Indeed, it's tradition in Korea to ask a child's age by asking how many bowls of *ttok-kuk* he or she has eaten. So when do you eat that bowl? Not on your birthday, but on *Sŏl-Nal*, the New Year.

Before the holiday, Koreans scrub their homes to wash away the year's misfortunes; they burn sticks of bamboo to cast off demons; they fill the house with brightly lit lamps; and they stay awake all night for good luck. At dawn, they offer freshly harvested foods on their home altars to honor their ancestors—and they place a bowl of *ttok-kuk* in front of each ancestor's tablet before sitting down to enjoy a bowl themselves.

GARNISH

*1 tablespoon chopped green onion
1 tablespoon crushed dried seaweed
Pinch of cayenne*

TO PREPARE

1. The night before (as needed), depending on whether your rice sticks are soft or hard as a rock, you may leave them out overnight to harden or soak them in water overnight to soften. They should be soft enough to cut with a knife yet hard enough to hold their cut shape.

2. An hour ahead, carve away the edges of the rice sticks, then slice them into thin rounds (like thick wooden coins, symbolizing wealth and prosperity in the New Year) and soak them in cold water for 30 minutes.

3. Prep the topping ingredients, separately, but all in the same skillet:

- Heat the peanut oil in a small skillet over medium-high heat and fry the beef strips until just cooked through. Remove them with a slotted spoon, season with salt and pepper, and reserve.
- Season the ground beef and shape into small meatballs. Sprinkle with flour, then dip them in the beaten egg (reserving the remaining egg) and fry in the skillet in the same oil. Remove with a slotted spoon and reserve with the beef strips.
- Pour the unused egg into the skillet (adding oil if needed) and let it cook into a thin sheet. Flip once to cook on the other side. Slice into four quarters, stack, then cut into thin strips and reserve with the fried meats.

TO COOK

Bring the beef stock to a boil in a large soup pot over medium-high heat. Add the rice cake slices, reduce the heat to medium-low, and cook, covered, until they are tender and chewy, about 10 minutes. Season the soup with the soy sauce, salt, sliced green onion, chopped garlic, and chile sauce.

To Serve

Ladle the soup into individual serving bowls, evenly distributing the rice cake, meat strips, meat balls, and egg strips. Top each portion with some slices of green onion and the seaweed that has been crushed into a powder, and sprinkle a pinch of cayenne over all.

MEXICO

GOOD LUCK SOUP
POZOLE
Serves 6 to 8

Hacer caldo, *or "to make soup," means to kiss and cuddle*

TRADITIONALLY SERVED IN Jalisco, Mexico, and in the American Southwest as good luck for the New Year, *pozole* is also commonly served as a special Christmas Eve dish. It's one of those "poor people foods"—like Indian curry—that ends up knocking your socks off with how the variety of condiments that can accompany it surprise and transform the rich *pozole* base.

Pozole itself is an old Pueblo treatment of ancient corn, but it was born to make music with Old World pigs in this great and festive stew. There are lots of variations, and all of them wonderful: white *pozole* of pork and corn served with accompaniments. Red *pozole* that includes red chile sauce. Green *pozole* that is made with tomatillos, green chiles, and green herbs. I include here very easy recipes for all three so you can make your choice; each is served with different accompaniments, but all with warm tortillas. And don't forget to check out the process of making your own hominy from scratch (see page 192).

POZOLE JALISCO (WHITE)

EARTHY AND SWEET, this rich white version serves as a homey base to support and set off the beauty and flavor of the garnishes.

5 pounds boneless pork, including tenderloin, shoulder, butt,
and neck bones (and use at least one split pig's foot to give
the broth a silky, gelatinous texture)
15 cups (3¾ quarts) cold water
1 pound whole white dried corn kernels, made into hominy
(page 192), or 4 (15-ounce) cans hominy, drained
Salt to taste

GARNISH
Spicy tomato salsa (chopped tomato, chiles, garlic, cilantro,
onion, and lime juice, to your taste)
Thinly sliced radishes
Finely shredded red cabbage
Dried and crumbled oregano
Lime wedges

TO PREPARE

1. Two days ahead (optional), if you are making the hominy from scratch; see the instructions on page 192.

2. Prep the remaining ingredients as directed in the recipe, including the garnish.

TO COOK

1. Bring the meats and cold water to a boil in a large soup pot over medium heat and let boil, partially covered, for 1 hour.

2. Add the drained hominy and salt (as much as several tablespoons), reduce the heat, and simmer, uncovered, for another hour.

3. Remove the pork, cut the meat off the bone, and return the meat to the pot, discarding the bones. Cover the pot and let simmer over very low heat for 4 hours.

TO SERVE

1. Place the garnishes in individual dishes.

2. Ladle the soup into deep bowls and serve immediately, passing the condiments for your guests to serve themselves.

CORN IN HISTORY

Corn was born in the western Sierra Madre of Mexico, a wild plant, *Zea mays ssp. Parviglumis*, that goes back at least 70,000 years. That mama plant went extinct in prehistoric times, but its fortuitous crossing with the related plant *teosinte* survived, and its offspring has been nicely domesticated, for some 3,000 years, into today's lovely varieties of sweet and popcorn. Even so, domesticated corn is high maintenance, has to be endlessly babied—sown by hand and protected from sprout to reap. Ancient Mesoamerican Indians wore popcorn decoratively in their hair and around their necks, and they brewed a pretty potent popcorn beer.

Make Your Own Hominy*

1 pound whole white dried corn kernels
*1 heaping teaspoon unslaked lime (calcium oxide), which you
must slake in cold water (see below) or "burn" as Mexicans
say, since it sizzles, vaporizes, and heats up. When the action is over, it's slaked, and it will have a slightly acrid taste
or, as the expression goes, "grab your tongue."*

1. Put the dried corn kernels in a large pot, cover with water, and let soak overnight.
2. Drain the corn, discarding the water, then add more water to cover and bring to a boil. Dissolve 1 heaping teaspoon of unslaked lime in 1 cup of cold water until the action subsides, then add it to the boiling corn through a strainer. Let the corn boil for 15 minutes, uncovered, then remove from the heat, cover, and let stand for 30 minutes.
3. Drain the corn and wash it in several changes of warm water, rubbing the kernels against each other to remove and discard their husks. Rinse one last time, then drain, place in a bowl, and refrigerate, covered, until you are ready to start the soup.
4. To cook, put the kernels in a soup pot with 15 cups of cold water. Bring to a boil and let cook uncovered until the kernels puff out into "flowers," about an hour.

Start 2 days before you want to cook and eat it.

Pozole Rojo

THIS VERSION GIVES the earthiness of *pozole* a profoundly rich bite with the addition of red chile sauce. It pleasantly warms up the back of your throat and there you are, suddenly all busted out in a bit of a sweat. The purple cabbage, red salsa, and white radish garnishes look smashing on the dark brick background of the broth—and here they compete for attention with the flavor and heat of the broth, creating an entirely different culinary experience from eating white *pozole* with the same garnishes.

INGREDIENTS FOR POZOLE JALISCO (SEE PAGE 191), plus
> *6 dried ancho or guajillo chile peppers*
> *Boiling water, to cover*
> *6 garlic cloves*

TO PREPARE

Make Pozole Jalisco, and while the soup is simmering, make the red chile sauce, below.

TO COOK

1. Toss the chiles in a hot skillet until they have begun changing color (don't let them burn!), then remove from the heat and let cool. Cut away the stems and most of the seeds, place in a bowl, and pour in boiling water to cover. Let sit for 15 to 20 minutes.

2. Puree the chile mixture in a blender with the garlic cloves, then press through a sieve to remove large pieces of skin and seeds.

3. Pour the sauce into the soup and let it simmer until the soup is done.

TO SERVE

Proceed as in the last step for Pozole Jalisco, with the same accompaniments.

POZOLE VERDE

GLORIOUSLY SOUR AND piquant, Pozole Verde needs creamy avocado, cool cilantro, and crisp pork rinds as a foil for the broth. Somehow this combination of soup and garnish makes the sweetness of the corn positively burst on your tongue with each mouthful.

INGREDIENTS FOR POZOLE JALISCO (SEE PAGE 191), plus
> *1 pound tomatillos, husked, washed, and quartered*
> *2 tablespoons water*
> *1 tablespoon lard or vegetable oil*
> *1 small onion, chopped*

*4 hot green chile peppers (serrano or jalapeno), seeded and
    chopped*
1 tablespoon fresh epazote,* chopped (omit if not available)
Pinch of dried tarragon, crumbled between your fingers

Garnish
Diced avocado
Chopped fresh cilantro
Fried pork rinds (chicharrons)

To Prepare
1. Make the Pozole Jalisco.
2. Prepare the garnishes and reserve. (You should dice the avocado at the last minute, though, so it doesn't turn brown.)
3. When the *pozole* has been simmering for 2 hours, puree the tomatillos in a blender with the water.

To Cook
Heat the lard or oil over medium-high heat in a saucepan, then pour in the tomatillo puree and fry for a few minutes, until it is a thick paste. Add the onion, chiles, epazote,* and tarragon; stir for a few more minutes, then scrape into the soup, washing the pan out with broth to get every scrap of flavor.

To Serve
Finalize the garnishes, peeling and chopping the avocado and putting it, the chopped cilantro, and the pork rinds into individual dishes. When the *pozole* is finished, ladle it into deep bowls and pass the garnishes for people to help themselves.

*This pungent Mexican herb is also known as pigweed.

HOW CORN WAS MADE MAN

An ancient Mayan document, *Popol Vuh*, tells how Heart-of-Sky and his helpers created the universe. He cried "Water"—and water appeared. He cried "Earth"—and the land was formed. He brought forth a glorious plenty of plants and animals, and it was good . . . but not so good that Heart-of-Sky was happy. "There is no one to speak my names. There is no one to praise my glory. There is no one to nurture my greatness. . . ." And Heart-of-Sky tries again. Tries to make a giver of respect. Tries to make a giver of praise.

Heart-of-Sky tries to make men of mud, but they speak nonsense, so he lets them melt away in the rain. He tries to make men of wood, but they're brainless and soulless. Finally he turns to the most precious material on Earth: he makes four men from the finest white and yellow cornmeal. At last, he has made creatures that are wise and noble. He is happy, but not for long. When he realizes they are too wise, he covers their eyes with a veil so they cannot see too far. He puts them to sleep and creates four women to keep them busy. When they wake, these new corn people watch the first sunrise on Earth.

POLAND

HUNTER STEW
BIGOS
Serves 6 to 8

NOT FOR VEGETARIANS! This soup is just crammed with meats and sausages, with the sweetness of apples more than balanced by the sharpness of sauerkraut, but it's hearty and delicious and really quite unforgettable. Traditionally served in Poland as a good luck dish on New Year's Day, it was originally eaten only by the Polish aristocracy (they being the only ones allowed to hunt game on their estates and the only ones who could afford so much meat). It's tough trying to find game these days unless you're a hunter, of course. Venison, rabbit, and pheasant will hugely add to the authenticity of this dish, but in the last analysis, it's the sauerkraut, sausage, paprika, and mushrooms that define the taste. Serve it hot as a filling meal, with boiled potatoes, a dish of sour cream, lots of rye bread on the side, and good beer or dry mead. *Wesolych Swiat!*

> 1 cup chopped raw bacon
> 1 pound boneless pork, cut into small cubes, or a mixture of
>   boneless pork, venison, rabbit, pheasant, and/or other game
> 3 garlic cloves, minced
> 3 medium onions, diced
> ½ pound fresh mushrooms, wiped clean and quartered
>   (preferably boletes—and it's fine to use ½ to 1 cup dried
>   mushrooms that have been rehydrated with warm water;
>   of course you'd want to stir the mushroom liquid right into
>   the soup broth)
> 2 cups Beef Stock (page 26)
> 2 cups diced canned tomatoes, with juice
> 2 tablespoons sugar
> 2 bay leaves
> 2 cups sauerkraut, rinsed under cold water and drained

3 apples, peeled, cored, and diced
1 cup diced cooked ham
1½ cups diced Polish sausage (kielbasa)
Salt and pepper to taste
Sour cream, for garnish

To Prepare

Prep the ingredients as directed in the recipe list.

To Cook

1. Fry the bacon in a large soup pot to render the fat, then toss in the pork chunks, garlic, onions, and mushrooms. Sauté over medium-high heat until the meat is browned, about 5 minutes.

2. Pour in the stock (including any reserved mushroom liquid), tomatoes with their juice, sugar, bay leaves, sauerkraut, and apples, and bring to a boil over medium-high heat. Reduce the heat to low and simmer, covered, for about 2 hours. Stir in the ham and sausage, then cover and cook over medium-low heat for about 30 minutes more.

To Serve

Remove the bay leaves and taste the soup for seasoning. Ladle the soup into bowls and serve with boiled potatoes, a bowl of sour cream, and thick, crusty bread on the side.

Bringing In the New Year with the Sylvesters

New Year celebrations in Poland are linked with the December 31 feast day of St. Sylvester, who served as Pope from A.D. 314 to 335 and was one of the first non-martyrs honored as a saint. Interestingly, it is another Pope Sylvester who is the real hero—credited with saving mankind on December 31, 999, when the dragon Leviathan was supposed to be released onto earth to devour all life and set fire to the heavens. At midnight, on the cusp of the year A.D. 1000, all the bells of Rome began to toll. People crowded into the streets. Then Pope Sylvester II stepped out in torchlight onto the balcony of the Lateran Palace and blessed the Eternal City and the world, ushering in the new millennium. What a relief! St. Sylvester vespers and parties on New Year's Eve have been traditional ever since.

"PAN TADEUSZ"

Bigos is being cooked in every kettle.
In human language it is hard to settle
The marvels of its odour, hue and taste;
In poetry's description one has traced
Only the clinking words and clanking rhymes;
No city stomach to its rapture climbs.
To savour Lithuanian songs and cooks,
One must have health, reside in country nooks
And be returning from a hunting party.

Even without such sauce to make one hearty,
This bigos is no ordinary dish,
For it is aptly framed to meet your wish.
Founded upon good cabbage, sliced and sour,
Which, as men say, by its own zest and power
Melts in one's mouth, it settles in a pot
And in its dewy bosom folds a lot
Of the best portions of selected meat;
Scullions parboil it then, until the heat
Draws from its substance all the living juices,
And, from the pot's edge, boiling fluid sluices
And all the Air is fragrant with its scent.

The bigos was soon done. With armament
Of spoons, with triple shout, the hunting gang
Assailed the kettle; then the copper rang;
The steams burst forth; by hungry valour banished,
The bigos flew away, like camphor vanished;
Only the steams remained, the pots' curators,
As in extinct volcanoes' smoking craters.

—ADAM MICKIEWICZ, *nineteenth-century Polish poet*

TIBET

FORTUNE NOODLE SOUP
GUTUK
Serves 9

NEVER THINK THAT *gutuk* is too exotic to make. It's a rich, thick, and deeply beefy soup, enlivened by the green of peas and the greens and also by the white of barley and radish — only exotic in its fragrant use of fenugreek. Not only is it a wonderful — and humorous — way to bring in the New Year, it is also, without the fortune dumplings, a great stick-to-the-ribs wintertime soup.

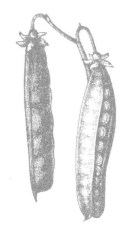

FOR THE DUMPLINGS
1½ cups whole wheat flour
1½ cups all-purpose flour
1 cup water, or more as needed
1 egg, beaten with a few teaspoons water
9 "fortunes" to put in 9 stuffed dumplings, either traditional or tasty fillings, but never meat, as this would signify sealing off good luck (see page 201)

FOR THE SOUP
12 cups (3 quarts) Beef Stock (page 26)
2 hot chile peppers
2-inch piece of fresh ginger, peeled and crushed
1 cup barley
1 tablespoon butter
1 teaspoon fenugreek seeds
1 large onion, chopped
½ cup chopped green onion, white and some green parts
4 garlic cloves, chopped
1 pound boneless beef, partially frozen (for ease in cutting), trimmed, and cut into strips
Salt to taste

*1 daikon radish, peeled and cut into a dice (2 to 3 cups) — if it
    comes with leaves, you should wash and slice them and use
    them in place of the greens below*
1 cup fresh peas
*½ cup greens (spinach, watercress, etc.), washed, stems
    removed, stacked, and sliced*

To Prepare

1. In a large bowl, mix the flours for the dumplings and work
in the water to a stiff dough. Depending on the dryness of the flour,
you may have to use more water. Knead well, for at least 15 minutes,
until the dough is elastic. Let the dough rest under a damp towel.

2. Prep the remaining ingredients as directed in the recipe list.

To Cook

1. In a large soup pot, bring the stock to a boil over medium-
high heat with the whole chile peppers and crushed ginger. Pour in
the barley, reduce the heat to low, and let simmer while you prepare
the vegetables and seasonings.

2. In a skillet or wok, heat the butter over medium heat and
sauté the fenugreek seeds, stirring, until they are deep brown; be
careful not to burn them. Remove from the pan and discard. Stir in
the onion and garlic and sauté until lightly browned. Toss in the
meat strips and sauté until they have lost their red color.

3. Remove the peppers and ginger from the soup pot, discarding them, and scrape the contents of the skillet into the soup. Wash
the skillet out with some of the broth and pour back into the soup.
You don't want to miss a drop of flavor. Continue to simmer for another hour.

4. Break the rested dumpling dough into four equal pieces and
roll three of them between your palms or on a flat surface to make
long snakes about ½ inch thick. Cut these into thin good-luck
"coins," sprinkle them with flour if they're sticky, and set aside
under the damp cloth.

5. Take the last piece of dough and roll it between your palms
into a "snake" about 1 inch thick; pinch off nine balls of dough —

you'll probably have dough left over that you can discard it or use it for another purpose. Roll each piece of dough out on a floured board into a thin 4-inch round, brush all around the edges of each one with the beaten egg, place one of the "fortunes" (see below) in the middle, then fold in half to make a half-moon and press with fork tines all around to seal. Turn each one over and press the fork tines all around the edges of the opposite side, too. Sprinkle with flour if they're sticky and let rest briefly under the damp cloth.

TELLING GUTUK FORTUNES AT LOSAR

Traditionally, *gutuk* is a thick soup made of things like dry cheese, radish, peas, highland barley, pasta bits, and beans, and brimming with little noodle coins and nine big doughy dumplings, or *momos*, stuffed with special "fortunes." Interpretations vary, but **salt** in your dumpling generally means good luck for the coming year; **wool**, you'll be lazy; **coal**, malicious; a **pebble**, long-lived; if it's a **hot pepper**, you'll be sharp-tongued; **butter**, very sweet; and **sheep pellets?** You might not want to eat them, but they signify you'll be wise. Dumpling shapes are also important: round ones suggest the sun and a bright future; a rectangular "book" made of flour will bring good luck on exams and studies.

Gutuk is eaten only once a year, at *Losar* on the night of the dark moon, and its very name means "nine," deriving from the calendar, so that the soup must contain nine ingredients, including those nine "fortune" dumplings, and everyone present must eat nine bowls, saving the big dumpling for last. At meal's end, after the dumplings have been opened amid general hilarity, all family members scrape the last spoonful of their last bowl of soup into a kettle with a piece of their clothing, a fingernail cutting, and some hair. Soot from the hearth is dumped on top and then all is crowned with a little dough human effigy. The kettle, with its "ransom" of last year's evil, is then carried to a crossroads and set on fire, burning all negativity away before the advent of the New Year.

5. In a separate large saucepan, bring a few inches of water to a boil over high heat, fit in a steamer basket, then place the dumplings in the basket, not touching, and steam for 10 to 12 minutes. Remove from the heat, use tongs to place them in a serving dish, cover, and set aside until serving time.

6. After the meat has cooked in the soup for 1 hour, return the soup to a boil over medium-high heat, adding water if necessary, and add the salt, daikon, peas, greens, and reserved dumpling coins. Boil for 8 minutes, until the dumpling coins are tender.

To Serve

Ladle soup into each bowl (they should be very small, if you expect your guest to eat nine bowlfuls), then ask your guests to pick out their "fortune *momo*" from the serving dish for you to place in their bowl.

"UNCLE TOMPA MAKES THE KING BARK LIKE A DOG"

It was the first day of the Tibetan New Year. Everybody was busy celebrating. According to tradition, one member of each family must go to see their king with offerings, such as Tibetan breads, fruits, fabrics, and white scarves for good luck.

Uncle Tompa told everyone there that he could make the king bark like a dog on this occasion, but nobody believed him. "He won't do that. It's too inauspicious." But Uncle promised that he would.

That whole day the king was busy receiving his people for the New Year's greetings. The king was sitting on his throne wearing his most expensive clothes and crown. Many people were sitting down having a meal with him. All of a sudden the king saw Uncle Tompa rush in.

The king asked Uncle, "Where have you been all this time? You're normally the first one here."

Uncle said, "My lord! There was an outstandingly beautiful dog for sale. I was trying to buy it as a present for you."

In Tibet dogs are judged by the strength of their barking, as well as by their appearance. So the king asked, "What does the dog sound like?"

Uncle made a sound just like a cat. "Meow, Meow!"

The king shook his head and exclaimed, "That's not the sound of an outstanding dog. That sounds just like a cat!"

"My lord, what does a good dog sound like then?" Uncle Tompa asked curiously.

The king put his hands on the table in front of the throne. He stood up on all fours just like a dog and barked, "Woof! Woof! Woof!"

Everyone laughed at how Uncle Tompa's trick had worked. In Tibet people think that to bark on New Year's Day is horribly inauspicious. Discreetly, his people called him, "The Barking King."

—RINJING DORJE, *twentieth-century Tibetan storyteller, from his* TALES OF UNCLE TOMPA, THE LEGENDARY RASCAL OF TIBET, *1997*

THE ORIGIN OF BLACK-EYED PEAS

In fact, it is shrouded in mystery. Some claim they began life in China; others, India, others, Africa—and this last claim is the most persuasive, as wild varieties of the plant can still be found there. The confusion arises because this bean was domesticated so early—perhaps by 3000 B.C.E.—and spread across the ancient Afro-European and Asian worlds with early traders over sea routes and the Silk Road. The Spanish finally took it to America in the sixteenth century, but it was more widely introduced and dispersed there by African slaves, who brought with it their enduring tribal associations of good luck.

UNITED STATES

HOPPIN' JOHN SOUP

Serves 6 to 8

THIS "GOOD LUCK SOUP" recipe is adapted from a Junior League of Women cookbook, vintage 1991 Jackson, Mississippi, that was brought to my attention by good friends Maggie and Josie Owens. The soup is excellent: smoky flavor punctuated by smooth beans, okra's silken crunch, and the bite of hot chiles. It's traditional to make it on December 31, so the flavors can blend, then to eat it sometime during the first day of the New Year with lots of hot buttered corn bread.

> *1 pound dried black-eyed peas (they don't need to be soaked)*
> *8 cups (2 quarts) Chicken Stock (page 24)*
> *1 ham hock*
> *1/3 pound smoked ham, cut into 1/2-inch cubes*
> *2 medium yellow onions, chopped*
> *1 green bell pepper, seeded and chopped*
> *1 celery stalk with leaves, chopped*
> *2 garlic cloves, minced*
> *3 dried whole chile peppers, or 1/2 teaspoon cayenne pepper*
> *2 cups sliced fresh okra, or one 10-ounce package of frozen sliced okra, thawed*
> *Salt to taste*

TO PREPARE

Prep the ingredients as directed in the recipe list.

TO COOK

1. Combine the black-eyed peas, stock, ham hock, ham cubes, onions, green pepper, celery, garlic, and chile peppers in a large soup pot. Bring to a boil over high heat, stirring occasionally, then reduce the heat to low, cover the pot, and simmer, stirring occasionally, for 1 hour.

2. When the peas are tender, stir in the okra and salt, bring back to a boil over high heat, then reduce the heat to low again and simmer, covered, for 30 more minutes. The soup should be thickening and you should stir it frequently to prevent scorching. Remove the cover and cook, stirring, until creamy thick — as long as 10 minutes.

To Serve

If you plan to serve the soup immediately, remove the ham hock and chiles and ladle it into bowls. If you are saving it to serve later, let it cool in the pot, then refrigerate it. When you're ready to serve the soup, reheat it carefully, stirring often, then ladle it into bowls, not forgetting to remove the ham hock and chile peppers.

HOW THE BLACK-EYED PEA GOT ITS BLACK EYE

According to the Brothers Grimm, one day a piece of straw, a coal, and a white bean escaped into the wide world from an old woman's hearth. Having escaped an untimely end there, they decided to keep together like good comrades and seek their fortune in another country. Off they went, until they came to a little stream that had neither path nor bridge. Finally the straw had an idea. "I'll throw myself across and you can use me like a bridge, then pull me over too." The coal and the bean congratulated the straw and said it was a fine idea. So the straw threw himself over and the coal, after initial hesitation, began to make his way across. "Oh, oh," he cried when he was halfway over, "I'm so scared, I can't move another step." And he didn't. So he burned right through the straw and they both fell into the water and came to an untimely end after all. The bean, who had remained on the bank, couldn't help laughing over the whole business, and he laughed so hard that he split his side. Fortunately a tenderhearted tailor wandered by. He picked up the bean and mended him with needle and black thread, the only color he had. And there you have it: all black-eyed peas have black markings to this day.

15

St. Tavy's Day

Who is St. Tavy?

St. Tavy, St. David, or Dewi Sant, was a Welsh-born sixth-century saint of the Celtic Church. Rhygyfarch, an eleventh-century Welsh monk, wrote that he was of royal lineage — the product of Prince Sandde's raping Dewi's mother, the saintly niece of King Arthur; that he was consecrated to the church before he was even born; that he performed many miracles while spreading Christianity to the pagan Celtic tribes; and that he became an archbishop before dying on March 1 in A.D. 589. One story tells how when he was preaching to a crowd at Llandewi Brefi and couldn't be heard, he spread a handkerchief on the ground, stepped on it, and was miraculously swept up by earth rising under him into a hill so that all could hear him, with a white dove alighting on his shoulder. Dewi traveled throughout Wales, founding many monasteries that became known for their ascetic practices. He himself drank only water — no beer or wine — and he labored in the fields to sustain the monks and the neighboring poor. After a long and virtuous life, he died a very old man and was buried in what is today St. David's Cathedral in Pembrokeshire.

WALES

LEEK SOUP
CAWN CENNIN
Serves 6 to 8

THIS TRADITIONAL WELSH leek broth is a wonderful way to start a feast on March 1, St. Tavy's day. It is guaranteed to strengthen the heart cords of anyone with Welsh blood, but watch out for the celebration: in Wales, to be "full of loudmouth soup" is to be "drunk as a lord."

> *4 slices bacon*
> *6 thick leeks, trimmed of the roots and dark green, then*
> *chopped*
> *10 cups (2½ quarts) Chicken Stock (page 24)*
> *Salt and pepper to taste*
> *A few circles of sliced leek, for garnish*

TO PREPARE

1. Sauté the bacon in a large soup pot over medium heat until crisp, then remove it from the pan, drain on paper towels, and reserve for the garnish.

2. Prep the remaining ingredients as directed in the recipe list.

TO COOK

1. In the soup pot, reheat the bacon grease over medium heat and stir in the leeks, turning to coat them and sautéing for several minutes, until they take on a little golden color.

2. Pour in the stock, bring to a boil over high heat, then reduce the heat to low and cook, uncovered, for 15 minutes. Remove from the heat. Puree the soup, solids first, then pour back into the pot. Season with salt and pepper.

RIDDLE ME THIS

QUESTION: What am I?
  In the ground my head is
   buried,
  Yet with care I'm never
   harried.
  In my early youth and
   fresh,
  White and tender is my
   flesh,
  Green my tail; of lowly
   plight,
  The rich man's scorn, the
   boor's delight.
  The peasant on me sets
   good store,
  The noble casts me from
   his door.

ANSWER: A leek

TO SERVE

Reheat the soup over medium-high heat, then ladle it into bowls and top with crumbled bacon and circles of leek.

TENDER LEEK MOMENT

Phoenicians introduced the leek to Wales when they were trading for tin in the British Isles, a casual act that would unexpectedly elevate this humble plant to national status. Legend has it that in A.D. 640 the Briton King Cadwallader was sorely pressed by invading Saxons. To distinguish themselves from the enemy, the Welsh wore leeks in their hats, and subsequently gained a great victory over their enemies.

Remember the scene in Shakespeare's *Henry V* when the Welsh Captain Fluellen turns to young King Hal, victorious at Agincourt in France against all odds, and says, "Your majesty says very true: if your majesties is remembered of it, the Welshmen did good service in a garden where leeks did grow, wearing leeks in their Monmouth caps; which, your majesty know, to this hour is an honourable badge of the service; and I do believe your majesty takes no scorn to wear the leek upon Saint Tavy's day" (act IV, scene vii).

I can't help it. It always brings a tear to my eye.

16
EASTERTIDE

AS THE APOSTLES' Creed goes, "Jesus Christ, His only Son, our Lord . . . was conceived of the Holy Spirit, born of the Virgin Mary, suffered under Pontius Pilate, was crucified, died, and was buried. He descended into hell. The third day He rose again from the dead. He ascended into heaven, and sits at the right hand of God the Father almighty."

That matter-of-fact account, however, leaves out all the horror and joy that Christians experienced on that first Easter and have relived each year since as the central mystery of faith.

I can't even imagine the shattering finality of Christ's death to his followers. One day spiritual ecstasy and certainty, hours later and almost out of the blue, the extinction of their leader and with him their hopes, dreams, and faith — "for," as John remarks, "as yet the disciples knew not the scripture, that he must rise again from the dead."

In fact, these disciples — every one of them! — literally disappear from the story for a couple days after Christ's death. Luke says they "stood afar off" during the crucifixion. John notes that they were afraid for their lives and went into hiding; Mark says "they mourned and wept." It was the outsider Joseph of Arimathaea who got Pilate's permission to take the body, wrap it in linen, and seal it in a cave. And come Easter Sunday, it was Mary Magdalene and other women who went to that cave and discovered the stone rolled away, heard the good news from an angel of the Lord, saw the risen Christ himself, and raced off to tell the disciples.

And what did these women say to the disciples? What Christians everywhere say on Easter Sunday: "Alleluia. Christ is risen."

But notice I haven't said one word about Carnival, Cheese Week, Clean Monday, Fat Tuesday/Shrovetide, Ash Wednesday, Lent, *Mezza Quaresima*, Mothering Sunday/Rejoicing Sunday, Palm/Passion/Carlings Sunday, Maundy Thursday, Good Friday, or Holy Saturday? And nothing about Easter being named after a Teutonic goddess, or about Easter eggs and Easter bunnies? Fact is, all these elements came well after the fact. They're all rituals and customs that developed out of old and new beliefs over time so people could understand, remember, and celebrate the central mystery of Jesus' resurrection. And food, as always, plays a huge role in these processes, including soup.

What about the Easter Bunnies and Easter-Egg Customs?

Let's start with Eostre, the Teutonic deity who gave her name to the English holiday. It was the Venerable Bede, of all people, who identified her with the month of April and Christ's passion (*De Temporum Ratione*, eighth-century A.D. England), and she's as good an earth mother as any to sum up man's primeval understanding and mythmaking of earth's natural cycles, and the rebirth of spring—much like Egyptian Isis, Slavic Makosh, Norse Freya, classical Demeter and Ceres, and Aztec Tlazoteotl.

So, when Christ's disciples—now apostles—"went forth, and preached every where" some 2,000 years ago, they were running into heathens who were already pretty comfortable with the main outlines of a death-rebirth story. The apostles said a "son of God" was sacrificed and reborn at the very beginning of spring, and these heathens could relate. The apostles said that this particular sacrifice meant *eternal* joy and salvation. Well, what's not to like? Conversions came pretty easily, all things considered.

Eggs? You bet. They've symbolized rebirth and regeneration

since ancient man first domesticated geese and chickens. Bread? Yep. Sheaves of wheat have been ritually sacrificed on domestic altars from earliest times; also cakes and boiled, salted wheat. Easter bunnies? *Naturellement.* These prolific little critters were big-time sacred to fertility goddesses in general, and to Eostre in particular. Soup? No, not yet.

SHROVE TUESDAY/CARNIVAL

Easter's first custom is Carnival. Think about it. Hints of spring are in the air, you're tired of winter, and now, with Ash Wednesday coming up, you're about to sail into a forty-day season of penitence and fasting. What's a good Christian to do? *Carne vale* — translated, say "goodbye to meat" — in one big blast. Since it's the end of winter, food stocks are way down, but the hens are still laying and the cows are still giving milk for butter and cheese, and if you can't slaughter a pig, you can at least use up the salted meat.

Carnival has always been one big food frenzy: lots of meat everywhere. Sweet eggy breads, like English pancakes, German *kuchen,* Polish *paczki,* Portuguese *sonhos,* Italian omelets and fried dough. Greeks marked this time by methodically progressing from a week of bingeing, to a week of finishing off the meat, to a last week of finishing off the cheese.

Austere soup, understandably, played a minor role in shake-and-shimmy Carnival festivities. But it played a role nonetheless. Northern Italians ate *zuppa alla canavesana,* a thick cabbage soup with cheese, bread, and sausage — also *tofeja,* a very beany soup made in public kettles on the piazza, stuffed with salami and pork fat "priests." Icelanders ate *saltkjöt og baunir,* a thick pea-and-meat soup designed to fill you to bursting on Shrovetide Tuesday so you'd be carried past Ash Wednesday.

Greeks ate *tyrozoumi* on Cheese Sunday, a broth made of wild herbs and the whey of goat cheese, traditionally the first course at the last dinner before Lent. According to George Megas, professor at the University of Athens, families would say a short prayer, lift the entire dinner table with their little fingers three times, and say "Holy broth, cheese-broth—whoever drinks of it and does not laugh shall not be bitten by fleas." Then they would silently drink up three spoonfuls . . . pause . . . then laugh like crazy.

In Basel, Switzerland, *Basler Mehlsuppe*, or "browned-flour soup," was and still is eaten at 3:30 A.M. during Carnival. It's not a rich, luxury soup at all, but excellent for coating the stomach during the three-day celebration, as you're putting on your mask to go out for a romp of marching and drinking.

ICELAND

SALTED LAMB AND PEA SOUP
SALTKJÖT OG BAUNIR
Serves 6 to 8

THIS RICH SOUP recipe was given to me by Nanna Rögnvaldar-dóttir, author of *Matarást (Love of Food)*, a 700-page encyclopedia of Icelandic cooking. Her *saltkjöt og baunir* is what most Icelanders eat on Shrove Tuesday, or *sprengidagur* (literally, "bursting day"). According to Nanna, "Tradition says you should eat as much (especially meat) as you possibly can, until you are about to burst. The reason for this is of course that in the old days, you would have been preparing for seven meatless weeks, so you'd better pig out. The soup is fairly similar to Scandinavian pea soups, except they are usually made with salted pork, not lamb." Salted lamb is not easy to find in many locations, but it is possible to substitute 1 pound of country ham and 2 pounds of fresh lamb for the bacon and salted lamb, below, to get a decent flavor of the dish.

> 1¼ cups yellow split peas
> 12 cups (3 quarts) water
> 1 large onion, chopped
> 2 teaspoons dried thyme, crumbled between the palms of your hands
> ¼ pound bacon, cubed
> 2½ pounds salted lamb shoulder, cut into large chunks
> 1 large rutabaga, peeled and diced
> 2 large potatoes, peeled and thickly sliced
> 4 large carrots, peeled and diced
> Pepper to taste, and salt if it needs it

TO PREPARE
Prep the ingredients as directed in the recipe list.

To Cook

1. Place the peas and water in a large soup pot and bring to a boil over high heat. Skim as needed, then add the onion and thyme. Reduce the heat to low, then simmer, covered, for 45 minutes.

2. Add the bacon and *one piece* of the meat chunks to the soup. (Note: Because of the saltiness of salted lamb, which would seriously oversalt the soup broth, you should boil the rest of the salted lamb chunks in a separate pot of water over medium-low heat, covered, for 1 hour, then drain and add to the soup pot. If you use fresh lamb, you can boil all the meat together in the soup pot.) Bring the soup to a boil over medium heat, then reduce it to low and simmer, covered, for 45 minutes, stirring frequently and adding more water if needed.

3. Add the rutabaga, potatoes, and carrots; cover and simmer for 20 minutes, or until tender. Season with pepper and salt if needed. Remove the meat chunks and cut them into small pieces, discarding any bones, and returning the meat to the soup pot.

To Serve

This pea soup should be very thick. Ladle large portions into big bowls so the "bursting" can begin.

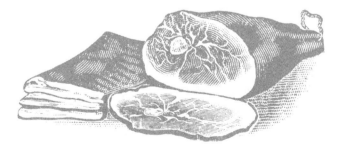

SARCASTIC HALLI BURSTS FROM PORRIDGE SOUP

In the Icelandic "Tale of Sarcastic Halli," which was written in the thirteenth century about events 300 years earlier, King Harald of Norway has competing Icelandic poets at his court: the master poet Thojodolf and the irreverent, not to say outrageous, Halli. Soon after Halli arrives in court, he decides to mock the king for not giving his retainers enough time to eat: after a meager meal, he runs into the kitchen and stuffs himself with porridge. The King is furious and orders Thojodolf to compose a satirical poem on the spot:

> *The handle rattled and Halli*
> *has pigged out on porridge.*
> *A cow's-horn spoon better suits him,*
> *I say, than something fine.*

At the next meal, the King has a trough and spoon brought to Halli in the main hall and orders him to eat until he bursts. He refuses and gets away with it, but the laugh is on him in the end. Back in Iceland, years later, he is served porridge, takes a few bites, and falls backwards, dead. When King Harald learns of it, he says, "The poor devil must have burst eating porridge."

—THE SAGAS OF ICELANDERS, GEORGE CLARK, *translator, 1997*

SWITZERLAND

BROWNED FLOUR SOUP
MEHLSUPPE
Serves 6 to 8

A REAL STOMACH coater, this is actually eaten before dawn, as part of the famous three-day Basel Carnival, right before the first masked parade begins. This traditional *Fastnacht* celebration goes back at least to 1376, when it was first mentioned in city records, but most believe it started as a pre-Christian pagan rite dating back to Roman and old Germanic times.

1/2 cup (1 stick) butter
6 tablespoons flour
8 cups (2 quarts) hot water
2 medium onions, stuck with 3 cloves each
1 bay leaf
Salt to taste
Splashes of dry Madeira wine and/or grated Swiss cheese, for garnish

TO PREPARE
Prep the ingredients as directed in the recipe list.

TO COOK
1. Melt 6 tablespoons of the butter in a large soup pot over medium heat, whisk in the flour, and cook, stirring, until the mixture is smooth and the color of chocolate, about 10 minutes. Be careful that the roux doesn't burn.

2. Remove from the heat and whisk in the water. Add the onions, bay leaf, and salt.

3. Bring to a simmer over medium heat, then reduce the heat to low and simmer the soup, uncovered and stirring occasionally, for at least 1 hour.

4. Remove the onions and bay leaf and whisk in the remaining 2 tablespoons of butter.

To Serve

Ladle the soup into bowls and splash a little Madeira into each one. You can sprinkle a little grated Swiss cheese on each portion, too, or pass a separate bowl for people to serve themselves.

YOU ARE THERE FOR FASTNACHT FOOLERIES

At 2:30 a.m., Marianne, our hostess, knocks on our door, already dressed. "Hurry up, guys. The soup's done." We stagger downstairs, bleary-eyed, and gulp down a big bowl of steaming *Mehlsuppe* to fortify ourselves against the pre-dawn chill. The scene in the street outside could have been painted by Breughel. A middle-aged man rushes by dressed in a bunny suit, a big bunny head firmly cradled under one arm, big bunny ears flopping crazily. A bearded man in a gown of burgundy velvet strides by. A small black and white drum is slung over his shoulder, a froth of white lace cascades over his ample bosom, and his beribboned bustle swishes in time to his steps. As we near the old town, the costumed crowd grows thicker. People rush around resolutely, like characters in a play just before the curtain goes up. We huddle on the sidewalk near the Old Post Office with hundreds of other watchers, and try to stay out of the way. All eyes are on the clock as the minutes tick away to four ... three ... two ... one ... The lights go out. The crowd lets out a huge "Waaaaaah!" and thousands of piccolos and drums strike up a lusty military march. Hundreds of gaudy lanterns light up the darkness. The funny, bustling Basel burghers are gone. In their stead, gnomes, gremlins, witches and sprites loom out of the dark. Every possible figment of the human imagination is there: dinosaurs and chickens, pirates, Indians, trolls, jesters, kings, queens, sheep, monks, Saracens and cavaliers, Pierrots and Columbines, Dalmatians and dwarves. And then the masks begin to move. Marching four abreast, they come from all sides at once. The wail of the piccolos and the rattatat of the drums overtakes us, then fades away, then rises again. A whole platoon of Elvises marches by, followed by 30 or 40 piccolo-playing petticoats. They are huge in the narrow streets, and, suddenly, those outsized *papier-mâché* heads with their grinning mouths and empty eyes are not so funny anymore. They come on in "cliques" of 30 or more. Each follows its own lantern and they wind through the cobbled lanes, crossing paths with other cliques, falling in behind them, then breaking away to rejoin in cacophony on the main square. The pageant goes on until daybreak. Then the phantoms turn back into sleepy people wearing masks, who gradually drift off to bed.

—EVA MUNK, "Waggismania"

LENT

The earliest Christians celebrated a short, tough Lent. Either for one day, or forty hours, or two days — they didn't eat a bite or take a sip of anything. Okay, not exactly uniform. And, in fact, Eusebius reports that St. Irenaeius was annoyed by these variations, urging Pope St. Victor I in A.D. 190 to lay down the law on precisely how long people *should* fast. A couple years later Tertullian echoed the same sentiments, sneering a bit that common Catholic practice was a mere two days (the so-called Passion Feast for "the days on which the bridegroom was taken away") instead of the tougher two-week fast of his own schismatic Montanist sect.

It wasn't until the fourth century that the church declared a much longer, but less severe fast at the Council of Nicea (A.D. 325). It was St. Athanasius who actually set the forty days, when he urged his flock in A.D. 331 to fast for forty full days — to commemorate Jesus' forty days of fasting and temptation in the desert and his forty hours in the tomb. Pope Gregory laid it down as church law in A.D. 604, and by 653 the Council of Toledo was ready to refuse communion to anyone who didn't fast for forty days. Let's not even talk about Charlemagne's ninth-century edict that these recalcitrants be put to death.

By the seventh century, for Catholics, Lent meant no meat, no eggs, no milk nor butter nor cheese, and no sex for forty days. In "Beppo," Lord Byron put it this way:

> *And thus they bid farewell to carnal dishes,*
> *And solid meats, and highly spiced ragouts,*
> *To live for forty days on ill-dress'd fishes,*
> *Because they have no sauces to their stews.*

It was worse if you were Orthodox: all the above plus no fish (except shellfish), no wine, and no olive oil — and for forty-eight days. But the important thing was, now there was a benchmark:

Lent was a fixed star in the constellation of this moveable feast, and Easter-related customs were now free to develop and take root in church calendars.

Needless to say, soup comes into its own during Lent. It may not be the best soup you've ever eaten, but it serves a purpose: austere, thick, filling, hot, often beany — and not highly seasoned as the whole point is penitence and mortification of the flesh.

Cheating during Lent? Oh yes, always. And lots of shady rationalizations, too. The church rule was no "meat" — so fish, mollusks, and crab were okay because they were "cold blooded." Then, upon reflection, cold-blooded turtles and frogs were declared okay, too. Then snails actually began to be raised at convents and monasteries as food for Lent. Iguanas and alligators. Then newborn rabbits, somehow. Creative interpretation reached a new level with eleventh-century aristocratic monks at the St. Gall monastery in Switzerland. These epicures shipped in exotic seafoods for Lent, including a whale; they declared beavers cold-blooded; and they specially reclassified ducks, geese, partridges, and pheasants as "feathered fish" for the duration of the Lenten season.

- To this day, Mexicans dote on sea turtle soup for Lent, fishing some 35,000 of them annually and prompting conservationists to publicly beg the Pope to rewrite the rules and declare these endangered creatures "meat."
- Nicaraguans, likewise, traditionally make *sopa de garrobo* of iguanas, rice, and vegetables their primary Lenten diet.

Over time, too, some cultures just changed the Lenten rules.

- The Swiss, with their dairy culture, traditionally eat *Käsesuppe und Fastenspeise,* a thick soup made of water-soaked bread that is cooked in butter and sprinkled with cheese and onions.
- Romanians can't resist a dollop of sour cream on *supa de fasole,* dried bean soup.

• Mexico's *caldo de vigilia,* a soup of dried fish, tomatoes, cactus, string beans, and potatoes, ends up with creamy eggs stirred in to curd and thicken the soup.

So let's take a look at a sampling of Lenten soups, the ones I think are delicious in spite of the austerity message they are trying to send. I've offered them in portions for six to eight people, to suit a family dinner with possible leftovers, since most just get better by the second day. They can, however, be halved — or doubled — as appropriate.

ALBANIA

BEAN SOUP
JANI ME FASULE
Serves 6 to 8

THE ORIGINAL RECIPE calls for a full cup of olive oil. I've halved that, and I think it's still plenty rich and fruity. All in all, this is a delicious and unexpectedly interesting dish: the creaminess of bean soup accented by a concentrated, savory tomato sauce that is cooled by the dash of fresh minty yogurt. Okay, the yogurt seems to be breaking the dairy rules, but traditions evolve and this is a superb crown for the soup.

>*2 cups dried white beans*
>*8 cups (2 quarts) water or Vegetable Stock (page 23)*
>*½ cup olive oil*
>*2 large onions, chopped*
>*4 tablespoons tomato paste*
>*1 generous tablespoon minced fresh parsley*
>*1 teaspoon chili powder*
>*Salt to taste*
>*2 generous tablespoons minced fresh mint*
>*Whipped yogurt and minced fresh mint, for garnish*

TO PREPARE
1. The night before, soak the beans in plenty of water.
2. Prep the remaining ingredients as directed in the recipe list.

TO COOK
1. Drain the beans and rinse them. In a large soup pot, bring the water to a boil over high heat, add the beans, then reduce the heat to low, cover, and begin simmering.

2. Heat the oil in a skillet over medium heat and sauté the onions until they turn yellow and a little transparent, just a few minutes. Reduce the heat to very low, then stir in ¼ cup of the sim-

RIDDLE ME THIS

QUESTION: What am I?
   There is a white egg in a
      green house,
   And if you break open the
      house you can take the
      egg out.
   But I tell you to a man, no
      bird ever laid it.

ANSWER: A bean

mering bean stock, the tomato paste, parsley, chili powder, and salt. Cook for 10 minutes, or until a thick sauce forms. Scrape the sauce into the soup pot, rinsing the skillet with broth and pouring it back into the soup to get every scrap of goodness.

3. Stir in the mint, cover, and simmer for 2 hours, or until the beans are very soft. Season with salt.

TO SERVE

Ladle the soup into bowls and top each portion with a dollop of whipped yogurt and a sprinkle of mint.

MOTHER TERESA, BORN AGNES BOJAXHIU, ON "SHARING CHRIST'S PASSION"

There is hunger for ordinary bread, and there is hunger for love, for kindness, for thoughtfulness; and this is the great poverty that makes people suffer so much.

Suffering in itself is nothing: but suffering shared with Christ's passion is a wonderful gift. Man's most beautiful gift is that he can share in the passion of Christ. Yes, a gift and a sign of His love—by giving his Son to die for us.

And so in Christ it was proved that the greatest gift is love: without Him we could do nothing. And it is at the altar that we meet our suffering poor. And in Him that we see that suffering can become a means to greater love, and greater generosity.

—*DAILY READINGS WITH MOTHER TERESA, 1993.*

Mother Teresa was born into an Albanian family of deep nationalistic pride and profound faith. When her father died and left the family in poverty in Skopje, she followed her calling as a postulant to Ireland, taking the name of Teresa, after the nineteenth-century French Carmelite nun, then beginning her life of compassion and faith in Calcutta in 1929.

GREECE

TAHINI SOUP
TAHINOSOUPA
Serves 6 to 8

IF YOU LIKE hummus—that fabulous chickpea-tahini dip for crispy pita bread—you'll like this soup. It's creamy looking, tart, and earthy with a nice pasta bite for texture; very pretty in soup plates with that sprinkling of minced parsley, stimulating the appetite but also filling the belly. Many thanks for this recipe to my friend Vivian Efthymiopoulou in Athens, a lawyer and speechwriter by profession, and a food lover and food writer in her heart.

> *8 cups (2 quarts) water*
> *1 tablespoon salt*
> *2 garlic cloves, crushed or pressed*
> *2 cups soup pasta (any small pasta is fine—noodles, pastina, etc.)*
> *½ cup tahini (a paste of sesame seeds, with the consistency of peanut butter)*
> *1 lemon, juiced*
> *A sprinkling of minced parsley and thin lemon slices, for garnish*

TO PREPARE
Prep the ingredients as directed in the recipe list.

TO COOK
1. Bring the water to a boil in a large soup pot over high heat, salt the water, then add the garlic and pasta, and cook until tender. Remove from the heat, but do not drain.

2. In a large bowl, whisk the tahini until it's creamy, then beat in the lemon juice, which will make it clot. Slowly beat 1 cup of the hot pasta water into the tahini, then another cup—it will turn

A LESSON IN THREE MILLENNIA OF GREEK HISTORY

Greece is a small ship beaten by North winds and South winds and winds from the East and West.

—NIKOS KAZANTZAKIS, *twentieth-century Greek novelist*

"IN CHURCH"

*I love the church — its
    hexapteriga,
the silver of its sacred vessels,
    its candlesticks,
the lights, its icons, its pulpit.*

*When I enter a church of the
    Greeks,
with its fragrances of incense,
with its voices and liturgical
    choirs,
the stately presence of the
    priests
and the solemn rhythm of
    each of their movements —
most resplendent in the
    adornment of their vest-
    ments
my mind goes to the high
    honors of our race,
to the glory of our Byzantine
    tradition.*

–C. P. CAVAFY, *twentieth-century
Greek poet*

white — then pour the tahini mixture back into the soup pot. Be careful not to reheat the soup — it will be spoiled.

TO SERVE

Serve the soup immediately, ladling it into bowls, sprinkling with parsley, and serving lemon slices on the side.

ITALY

LENTEN BEAN AND VEGETABLE SOUP
MINESTRONE DI MAGRO
Serves 6 to 8

EVEN THIS "MEAGER" Italian soup is wonderful—very filling, very nutritious, very good for dieting, and perfect for Lent. This one from Tuscany is absolutely stuffed with colors, textures, and flavors—a true vegetarian dream—and has a nice finish with the crisped garlicky toast soaking up the broth.

> *2 cups small dried white beans*
> *10 cups (2½ quarts) water*
> *½ cup plus 1 tablespoon olive oil*
> *4 garlic cloves, 2 pressed and 2 chopped*
> *1 large onion, chopped*
> *4 celery stalks with leaves, chopped*
> *2 carrots, peeled and diced*
> *2 potatoes, peeled and diced*
> *4 tablespoons tomato paste*
> *¼ head cabbage, finely shredded*
> *2 cups washed, stemmed, stacked, and finely sliced spinach*
> *2 tablespoons pesto (see sidebar)*
> *¼ cup finely chopped fresh parsley*
> *½ teaspoon dried rosemary, crumbled between your palms, or*
>   *1 teaspoon fresh rosemary, finely minced*
> *Salt and pepper to taste*

> GARNISH
> *6 to 8 thick slices stale Italian bread*
> *Olive oil*
> *1 garlic clove*
> *Freshly ground black pepper*

PRESTO PESTO

You can buy pesto already prepared in most supermarkets—it lasts a long time in the refrigerator, longer if you freeze it and chip it out as needed.

You can also make it from scratch: Put 1 cup fresh basil leaves in a blender or processor with ½ cup pine nuts or walnuts, 2 garlic cloves, and ¾ cup grated Parmesan cheese. Process until thoroughly mixed, then gradually pour in ½ cup olive oil until the sauce is thick and completely pureed.

Are you thinking that *pesto* sounds a lot like the French *pistou*? You'd be right. *Soupe au pistou* is a marvelous French springtime vegetable soup, also appropriate for Lent, that makes a *pistou* with basil, tomato paste, garlic, and oil— *magnifique!*

"CANTICLE OF CREATED THINGS"

*Be praised, my Lord, for our
    sister bodily death,
from whom no living man
    escapes;
woe unto those who die in
    mortal sin,
but blessed be those whom
    death shall find
living by thy most sacred
    wishes,
for through the second death
    no harm
shall come to them.*

—ST. FRANCIS OF ASSISI, *POEMS
FROM ITALY, 1972*

TO PREPARE

1. The night before, soak the beans in plenty of water.

2. Prep the remaining ingredients as directed in the recipe list.

TO COOK

1. Drain the beans, rinse them, and put them in a large soup pot with the water, 1 tablespoon olive oil, and pressed garlic. Bring to a boil over high heat, then reduce to low, cover, and simmer for 1 to 2 hours, until the beans are tender.

2. Heat the ½ cup olive oil in a skillet over medium-low heat, then sauté the onion, chopped garlic, celery, and carrots for about 5 minutes, until they are translucent and beginning to take on color.

3. When the beans are tender, scrape the vegetables into the broth, rinsing the vegetable pan with a little soup broth to get every scrap of goodness. Then stir into the soup the potatoes, tomato paste, cabbage, spinach, pesto, parsley, rosemary, and salt and pepper. Add water as needed to keep the soup brothy. Bring to a boil over high heat, then reduce the heat to low again, cover, and simmer for 30 minutes.

4. Meanwhile, make the toast garnish. Brush each bread slice with olive oil, then dry and crisp the slices in a 325°F. oven until dry, about 15 minutes. Rub each slice with raw garlic and set aside.

TO SERVE

Place a slice of toasted bread in the bottom of each bowl, ladle hot soup over it, then drizzle each portion with a little olive oil, followed by a grinding of black pepper.

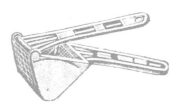

MEXICO

VIGIL SOUP
CALDO DE VIGILIA
Serves 6 to 8

THIS UNUSUAL SOUP springs from Mexico's bounty of coastline and seafood, making fresh and dried fish especially appealing during the "no meat" season of *Vigilia,* when many Catholics observe its forty days by eschewing meat on Fridays and during Holy Week. The soup is festive looking—it even resembles the Mexican flag with all those greens nestled in a red broth, creamy eggs mounding across the soup surface. And it's tasty—savory, rich, full of contrasting textures, and filling.

1 pound tomatoes, fresh or canned

1 large onion

4 garlic cloves

*1 cup prepared nopales (using 2 to 4 prickly pear cactus pads),
    or substitute more green beans or sliced okra*

3 tablespoons corn oil

16 cups (4 quarts) water

*½ pound (1 cup) topote (traditional dried fish, sold in most
    Mexican markets), or any dried or dry-smoked fish,
    washed, skin, scales, bones, or fins removed, and cut into
    bite-size pieces*

1 cup diced waxy potatoes, unpeeled

1 cup trimmed green beans, in 1-inch pieces

1 cup peas, fresh or frozen

*1 tablespoon fresh epazote leaves, or 1 teaspoon dried epazote,
    hydrated in hot water for 10 minutes*

Salt and pepper to taste

2 eggs, beaten

"TARAHUMARA HERBS"

Into Catholics
by the New Spain missionar-
ies they were turned
—these lion-hearted lambs.
And, without bread or wine,
they celebrate the Christian
ceremony
with their chicha beer and
their pinole
which is a powder of univer-
sal flavour.

They drink spirits of maize
and peyote,
herb of portents,
symphony of positive esthetics
whereby into colours forms
are changed;
and ample metaphysical
ebriety
consoles them for their hav-
ing to tread the earth,
which is, all said and done,
the common affliction of all
humankind.

*—*ALFONSO REYES, *twentieth-*
century Mexican poet

TO PREPARE

1. Heat a skillet over medium-high heat, toss in the tomatoes, and roast them for 5 to 10 minutes, turning frequently, until they are fragrant and soft. (If they are fresh, peel them at this point.) Chop the onion and garlic until fine in a blender, then add the tomatoes and puree the mixture.

2. Prepare the nopales: with a knife or potato peeler, carefully scrape away all the spines, then trim all the sides. Rinse well, checking to make sure you have all the spines out. Cut into 1-inch square pieces. Bring 2 cups of water to boil in a small saucepan, salting it well, then add the nopales pieces, lower the heat to medium-high, and cook, partially covered, for 10 minutes. When they are done, drain them, rinse them in cold water, and drain them again, then rinse and drain them one more time.

3. Prep the remaining ingredients as directed in the recipe list.

TO COOK

1. In a large, attractive soup pot or Dutch oven, heat the corn oil over medium heat, then add the tomato mixture. Fry for 5 to 10 minutes, until the tomato cooks down and thickens. Pour in the water, bring to a boil, then add the fish, potatoes, green beans, and peas. Reduce the heat to low, cover, and simmer for 15 to 20 minutes. (If you are substituting green beans or okra for the nopales, put them in with the main soup at this point.)

2. Add the nopales and the epazote leaves, cover, and cook 5 more minutes. Season with salt and pepper.

> ## "PROVINCIAL SUNDAYS"
>
> *On Sundays when the weather's good, traditionally*
> *in my home town, young ladies show their pretty heads*
> *in the main square, their eyes reflecting sweetness*
> *and the town band playing languid melodies.*
>
> *And when the dreamy night descends on the town,*
> *the lovers look at one another with fine expressions*
> *in their eyes, the orchestra's flutes and violins*
> *coin a thousand romantic sounds in the festive night.*
>
> *In provincial towns at dawn, holidays*
> *offer visitors a lovely scene:*
> *with their fresh faces, their missals in their hands,*
>
> *young ladies on the way to church —*
> *because on a holiday, among them there is not one,*
> *not one beauty, who would miss Mass.*
>
> —RAMÓN LÓPEZ VELARDE, *twentieth-century Mexican poet*

TO SERVE

Raise the heat to medium-high, take the cover off the soup, and when it is at a medium boil, pour in the beaten egg all around the surface in a smooth motion. When the egg curdles, take the soup off the heat immediately and serve.

ROMANIA

CHILLED GARLIC-BEAN SOUP
SUPA DE FASOLE
Serves 6 to 8

EXTREMELY THICK, TO fill the Lenten belly, this soup is popular in the Orthodox part of Romania. It's unusual—eaten cold, dressed with walnut oil, and many think the garlic should be chopped raw and sprinkled on top. Hope you don't mind (I know your honey won't), this recipe tames the garlic a bit. In the end, the soup is totally surprising in its sweet nuttiness and beauty: an orange and white mosaic in a tan broth. And the crunch of salt crystals in those tender beany-carrot spoonfuls is wonderfully decadent in today's age of undersalting.

2 cups small dried white beans
8 cups (2 quarts) water or Vegetable Stock (page 23)
6 carrots, peeled and diced
Salt and pepper to taste
4 garlic cloves, pressed
Walnut oil
Sprinkling of coarse sea salt and coarsely ground black pepper

TO PREPARE
1. The night before, soak the beans in plenty of water.
2. Prep the remaining ingredients as directed in the recipe list.

TO COOK
1. Drain and rinse the beans, then put them in a large soup pot with the water and carrots, and bring to a boil over high heat. Reduce the heat to low, cover, and simmer over a very low heat for 4 hours, until the beans are very soft. Add water as necessary.
2. Pour the soup into a large serving bowl, season with salt and pepper, and stir in the garlic. Let cool to room temperature. (You may refrigerate if you'd like the soup cold.)

To Serve

Stir the soup and reseason, heavy on the pepper, then pour walnut oil over the top, sprinkle with coarse sea salt and more black pepper, and take to the table with a large serving spoon for people to help themselves.

"Mount of Olives"

Mount with heaven-pointed
   peak,
Steady in blue dream.
Beaten by ancient hate
With chain whips
The flattened plain, hungry
   for height,
Watches its chance to rise
   above you,
Bring you the dust
Roused by flocks and clumps
   of men.
Mount, censers of springs,
Altar of hawks, house of suns,
Denying the brief flower
Drunk with its fragrance—
You at the margin of great
   mysteries
Are a sign of lasting power,
Irremedial life,
Most hemmed-in of stars!
Our soul, flimsy and poor,
Knows nothing of springs and
   harvests.
Our hope wanders among us,
Leaves its faint track in the
   mud,
A wheel with gold spokes.

—TUDOR ARGHEZI, *twentieth-century Romanian poet*

RUSSIA

ICED SOUR FRUIT AND VEGETABLE SOUP

OKROSHKA POSTNAYA
Serves 6 to 8

THIS GLORIOUS "LEFTOVER" cold soup is startlingly good for
Lenten fare, using mostly dried fruits and vegetables from winter
storage and the brand-new shoots of spring—no meat, no sour
cream, no eggs, of course, as in non-Lenten variations of *okroshka*.
But it sure makes you plan ahead. If you're going to make homemade *kvass* (see the sidebar recipe), you're going to have to start
about five days ahead. At the very least, you've got to start two days
before to make the marinated mushrooms and start the beans, or
the day before to make all the fruits and vegetables so they can chill
overnight in separate plastic baggies. Or, you could get into the
spirit of the thing: just use up your leftovers and use a substitute for
the *kvass*. Your choice, but here's an elegant version that has you
preparing seemingly endless dishes all separately, then assembling at
the last minute in the most textured soup you may ever eat: sweet
and sour, spongy and crisp, all different colors, all different tastes,
all different temperatures, all in a delicate, effervescent, tart, and
rosy pink broth.

> 9 cups kvass (see sidebar recipe or substitute 6 cups wheat beer
> mixed with 3 cups dry white wine; I kitchen-tested
> Dundees Honey Brown lager and an inexpensive Pinot
> Grigio against my homemade brew and was amazed at
> how close they were)
> 1 cup dried red kidney beans

FOR THE MUSHROOMS
> 1 pound fresh mushrooms (boletes, oysters, or any you can find
> or buy), wiped, trimmed, and quartered
> 1/2 cup fresh lemon juice

¹/₂ cup safflower oil
1 medium onion, quartered and thinly sliced
1 clove garlic, pressed
3 bay leaves
Salt and pepper to taste

FOR THE SOUP
   2 red beets, peeled and diced
   2 potatoes, peeled and diced
   ¹/₂ pound (about 1¹/₂ cups) assorted dried fruit (apples, prunes,
      peaches, apricots, cherries, or a package of "assorted" fruits)
   2 large cucumbers, peeled and diced

FOR THE THICKENER
   2 tablespoons olive oil
   1 tablespoon Russian (or Dijon) mustard
   Salt and white pepper to taste

GARNISH
   ¹/₂ cup chopped fresh parsley
   ¹/₂ cup chopped fresh dill
   1 cup chopped green onions

TO PREPARE

You should start this soup six days ahead if you plan to make your own *kvass* (see sidebar recipe), two days before if not.

1. Two days ahead, soak the beans for the soup in plenty of water.

2. The day before, prepare the mushrooms. In a plastic container, mix the mushrooms with the lemon juice, safflower oil, onion, garlic, bay leaves, salt, and pepper. Give them a shake every couple of hours at room temperature to mix well, then leave overnight in the refrigerator.

3. Also the day before, prepare all the remaining soup ingredients:

   • Drain and rinse the beans: put them in a pot with about 6

"SPRING"

Ah, Spring, sweet Spring,
chief pride of Nature!
The air is foul, the ground is
sludge;
Men curse the mud when
they go walking,
And plunged in muck, a horse
can't budge.

The cab breaks down, so does
the carriage;
Season of colds in chest and
nose,
To you, fair Spring, is rever-
ence tendered
By cartwrights and by
medicos.

—PYOTR VYAZEMSKY, *nineteenth-century Russian poet*

cups water, bring to a boil, reduce the heat, cover, and cook for 1 to 2 hours, until they are very tender. Drain, discarding the water, and chill.

- Cook the beets in a little salted water until just tender, 30 to 45 minutes. Drain, discarding the broth, peel, dice, and chill in a plastic bag.
- Cook the potatoes in a little salted water until just tender, about 15 minutes. Drain, discarding the broth, peel, dice, and chill in a plastic bag.
- Stew the fruit in a little water until tender. Let cool, then store in a plastic bag and refrigerate.
- Store the diced cucumber in a plastic bag and chill until ready to use.

TO SERVE

1. Drain the mushrooms, discarding the bay leaves, and place them in a large tureen with the beans, beets, potatoes, fruit, and cucumbers.

2. In a separate large bowl, whisk the olive oil, drop by drop, into the mustard, until it forms a thick sauce, then slowly whisk in the *kvass* (or your easy mixture of wheat beer and wine), and season with salt and white pepper. Pour over the fruit and vegetables in the tureen.

3. Top the soup with the chopped parsley, dill, and green onion and carry it, resplendent, to the table for ladling into individual bowls.

THE MAKING OF KVASS

So many kinds of *kvass!* And some more an acquired taste than others. I really like this recipe as a base for *Okroshka postnaya,* and pleased with myself on how easily this is made and how good, I even like taking swigs from it in the gallon water jug in the fridge.

1 pound day-old black or pumpernickel bread, sliced and dried in a slow oven until crisp, then cut into cubes
24 cups (6 quarts) boiling water
¼ cup lukewarm water (110–115° F.)
2 packages (or 2 tablespoons) active dry yeast
1 cup sugar
¼ cup whole fresh mint leaves, lightly packed
2 tablespoons raisins

1. Sometime before you go to bed one night, put the bread cubes in a large soup pot and pour the boiling water over them. Cover with a towel, put in an unheated oven, and let sit, while you're sleeping, for at least 8 hours.

2. Get up in the morning, 20 minutes early if you're going to work, and strain the mixture through a cheesecloth-lined sieve, stirring the soaked bread and pressing on it to get as much liquid as possible out of it. Reserve the liquid and discard the bread. Get the ¼ cup water to the right lukewarm temperature (spigot warm is okay; or use the microwave temperature probe if you're nervous), stir in the yeast and ¼ teaspoon sugar, and let sit for 10 minutes, until it's nicely frothy (go brush your teeth). Scrape the yeast mixture into the reserved bread-broth with the rest of the sugar and the mint leaves, give it a stir, cover with a towel, and stick the pot in the oven, forgetting completely about it till you get home that night.

3. At least 8 hours later (you're home from work; pour yourself a glass of wine), strain the broth through a cheesecloth-lined sieve again, then go looking for that clean gallon jug you've got stuck somewhere. Pour the strained liquid into the jug and plop in the raisins. Loosely rubberband a piece of plastic wrap over the top, and let sit for 3 to 5 days in a cool spot. You'll see the sediments sink to the bottom, the raisins rise to the top, and the liquid on top turn golden brown and pretty clear. It will smell sharp and yeasty.

4. At this point, pour the amber liquid off the top, discarding the sediments. Rebottle the kvass and refrigerate it until you are ready to use it—for the soup or just for a quick pick-me-up.

HOLY WEEK

PALM SUNDAY/CARLINGS SUNDAY

Palm Sunday begins Holy Week, the last week of Lent. It commemorates the day Christ arrived in Jerusalem for Passover week, when people strewed palms in his path to welcome him. Also called Passion Sunday, it is the time when Christians begin to turn their thoughts away from their own sins and toward Christ's suffering on the cross.

- The English think of . . . peas. Why peas? Likely by accident, because "Passion" sounded like Middle English *Peason.* So in northern England and Scotland, dried peas became associated with the day and came to be called "carlings," after the purple mourning draperies — *care* in Middle English — that were placed on church altars that day. In any event, these dried carlings are still sold in packages, and steeped in water over Friday night, then boiled with fat bacon on Saturday evening, and served hot or cold in pubs and hospitals on Sunday with salt and vinegar.
- In the South of France, people serve chickpea soup, recalling the tradition of Christ's walking through fields of chickpeas on Palm Sunday.

MAUNDY THURSDAY/GREEN THURSDAY

Maundy Thursday recalls the Last Supper and Christ washing the feet of his disciples. It's called Maundy Thursday from the "mandate" (Latin *mandatum*) of humility Christ laid down after the foot washing. It's called Green Thursday from the Germanic word *grunen* ("to mourn") and also, likely, from the green bitter herbs that were part of the traditional Jewish Passover dinner. Accordingly, many people still eat green soups of these herbs in honor of the day.

- The French serve a potato soup with bitter greens — some combination of dandelion greens; beet, carrot, or radish tops; watercress, spinach, arugula, Swiss chard, escarole, chicory, green onions, collards, mustard or turnip greens.
- Chervil soup is eaten throughout Europe because it's green and because it tastes like myrrh, which flavored the wine offered to Christ while he hung on the cross.

GOOD FRIDAY

On this day of Christ's crucifixion, many people by tradition would eat nothing at all. Those who did would remember the vinegar: "Now there was set a vessel full of vinegar: and they filled a sponge with vinegar, and put it upon hyssop, and put it to his mouth." It was the last ministration. "When Jesus therefore had received the vinegar, he said, It is finished: and he bowed his head, and gave up the ghost" (John 19:30). As a consequence, and in honor:

- In Greece, lentil soup is dosed with vinegar and eaten.
- In Poland, *zur* is served, a very sour rye soup.
- In New Orleans, Cajun cooks make *Gumbo z'herbes* with seven bitter greens and vinegar to flavor the oyster and okra soup.

In the Swabian district of Germany, however, people traditionally made a clear soup with *Maultaschen,* or "snout pockets" — wonderfully fat stuffed noodles. And the stuffing? Since medieval times, it has been meat — prompting critics to ask, "Do you think God is so dumb that he can't see through the noodle dough?"

CORSICA

"SOUP OF THE LORD"
MINESTRA DI FASCIOLU SECCU
Serves 6 to 8

THIS IS A basic soup, solid fare appropriate for such a serious occasion. And yet, it's a lovely soup—pretty to see with red beans cuddled by elbow macaroni, fragrant with rosemary, and set off by a generous garnish of fresh minced greens, all mouthwarming in its pepperiness.

> *2¹/₂ cups (1 pound) dried red beans*
> *2 tablespoons olive oil*
> *1 medium onion, chopped*
> *2 garlic cloves, chopped*
> *2 fresh tomatoes, peeled and chopped, or 4 canned tomatoes*
> *8 cups (2 quarts) water*
> *A large sprig fresh rosemary, or 1 teaspoon dried rosemary,*
>   *crumbled between your palms into the soup*
> *Salt and pepper generously to taste*
> *¹/₂ pound elbow macaroni or ziti (about 3 cups)*
> *Minced bitter green (dandelion, arugula, etc.) or green onions,*
>   *for garnish*

PENITENTIAL CUSTOMS

Since the Middle Ages, Corsican penitents who wish to expiate their sins join their village's Procession du Catenacciu on Maundy Thursday or Good Friday, traversing the Way of the Cross in bare feet and draped with a cowl. It's solemn and deadly serious, but that doesn't prevent fellow parishioners from collecting wild rosemary along the way to flavor the traditional bean and pasta soup they are preparing to eat on Good Friday. The most famous (and tourist attracted) procession takes place in the town of Sartene, where the parish priest selects one anonymous penitent, covered from head to foot in a red robe and cowl, to carry a seventy-pound oak cross through the town while dragging a thirty-pound chain behind him.

To Prepare

1. The night before, soak the beans in plenty of water.
2. Prep the remaining ingredients as directed in the recipe list.

To Cook

1. Heat the oil in a large soup pot over medium heat and sauté the onion and garlic in it for 5 minutes. Add the tomato and cook down for a minute or two, then pour in the water, add the rosemary, and bring to a boil.

2. Drain the beans and rinse them. Add them to the soup, bring back to a boil over high heat, then reduce the heat to low, cover, and simmer for about 1 hour, until the beans are soft.

3. Season the soup generously with salt and pepper, then add the pasta and cook over medium heat until tender, 20 to 30 minutes, stirring from time to time and adding water to this thick soup as needed. You want the soup soft and well cooked.

To Serve

Remove the rosemary sprig, ladle the soup into bowls, and top with minced bitter greens, to recall the bitterness of the season.

ROMAN SENECA NEEDS STOICISM TO ENDURE EXILE IN CORSICA

Banished to Corsica for eight years by Roman Emperor Claudius for alleged relations with the emperor's niece Julia Livillia, Seneca lamented in his *Epigram II*:

Corsica, land peopled by
*   Ionian settlers,*
Corsica, once called Cyrnos
*   by the Greeks,*
Corsica, smaller than
*   Sardinia and bigger than*
*   Elba,*
Corsica, rivers bursting with
*   fish,*
Corsica, scorching hot as soon
*   as early summer starts*
*   And deadlier yet when the*
*   dog days patter in,*
You're the same to jailed and
*   free people alike:*
The ashes of the living en-
*   dure on your light earth.*

UNITED STATES

NEW ORLEANS GUMBO
CAJUN GUMBO Z'HERBES
Serves 6 to 8

TUSKEGEE VOODOO

Leah Chase, a New Orleans restaurateur, tells the story from back in the 1940s when members of the Tuskegee Airmen came to eat gumbo. When they saw her add filé powder (from sassafras) into the soup, one of them warned the others that it might be voodoo powder and if they ate it, they'd never leave New Orleans alive.

THIS IS AN extraordinary soup, and boy is it ever *green*. It's pronounced "gumbo zarb," a corruption of the French *gumbo aux herbes,* and is served both on Good Friday and on New Year's Day in New Orleans, often made by the kettleful. Some say it started out as a variation of bouillabaisse, from early French Acadian cooks making do with local ingredients, but those Acadians were generally from the North of France, not Marseilles where bouillabaisse originated. In any event, at Easter, those greens conjure up the bitter herbs of a traditional Passover "Last Supper" on the Mount of Olives, while at New Year's, they're said to conjure a steady flow of "greenback" dollars in the coming year. Not only that, natives in New Orleans swear that for each different green you use in the soup, you'll make a new friend. Me? I like to make life easy and pick up fresh mesclun greens at the grocery, assuring many friends in my future. The soup is hugely tasty, especially with the sassafras tang of the filé powder and with the universe of textures, oysters and okra slices swimming through that Sargasso sea of green.

1½ pounds greens—at least 3 kinds, but ideally 7 of the following: spinach, arugula, escarole, endive, watercress, Swiss chard, mustard greens, turnip greens, radish greens, carrot tops; for a lovely shortcut, measure out your greens from the mesclun mixes at the grocery, truly in the spirit of early spring greens

½ cup peanut oil

½ cup all-purpose flour

2 medium onions, diced

2 hot green chile peppers, seeded and minced

4 celery stalks with leaves, diced

2 turnips, peeled and diced

4 garlic cloves, chopped
8 cups (2 quarts) water
2 bay leaves
1 teaspoon dried thyme, crumbled between your palms
½ teaspoon allspice
1 cup sliced okra
2 teaspoons filé powder (optional)
3 tablespoons vinegar
Salt and pepper to taste
4 cups shucked oysters, with their liquor

To Prepare

1. Wash the greens thoroughly, remove their stems and hard centers, stack, and chop fine. Set aside.

2. Prep the remaining ingredients as directed in the recipe list.

To Cook

1. Heat the oil over medium-high heat in a heavy pot (preferably iron), then sprinkle the flour on it, whisking like crazy as it cooks to a dark milk-chocolate color. (See page 337 for tips on making excellent, and easy, roux.)

2. As the roux approaches the proper color, reduce the heat to medium and start adding the vegetables — the onions, chile peppers, celery, turnips, and garlic — stirring hard with a wooden spoon. Then add all the chopped greens.

3. Let cook, stirring, for about 10 minutes, until the vegetables are tender and the greens have wilted, then pour in the water. Bring

to a boil over high heat, then season with the bay leaves, thyme, and allspice, and stir until the roux is dissolved. Reduce the heat to low, cover, and let simmer for about 45 minutes.

4. Stir in the okra, filé powder (if using), and vinegar. Season with salt and pepper. Let cook for 10 more minutes, until the okra is tender.

5. Remove the bay leaves and add the oysters with their liquor. Cook briefly, just until their edges curl, then remove from heat immediately.

TO SERVE

Ladle the soup into big bowls and serve immediately.

EASTER

Alleluia! This culmination of the Easter season, when Christ rose from the dead, is full of joy and is celebrated at a table now cleared of Lenten austerities. No surprise, then, that Easter soup is positively bristling with all the forbidden foods — and often serves to break the Lenten fast while preparations are under way for the really extravagant Easter feast that follows, with its platefuls of meat roasts, egg and cheese dishes, creamy concoctions, sweet buns, and fabulous cakes.

In Greece, Albania, and Cyprus, *mayeritsa* traditionally breaks the Lenten fast — made with rice, egg yolks, milk, and the innards of a lamb that has been slaughtered for the approaching feast.

In Romania, *bors de miel* is eaten, a sour soup made with lamb's head and enriched with eggs and sour cream, and in Poland *barscz* is served first thing on Easter morning, a sour milky soup thick with sausages and chopped eggs.

Egyptian Copts break the Lenten fast with *fatta*, a soup of lamb, bread, and rice in a meat broth enriched with butter and soured with vinegar and garlic, and Russians celebrate with a thick, red borshch — beets, beef, ham, and hard-boiled eggs thickened with sour cream.

Italians gorge on *benedetta* ("blessed"), with its meatballs, eggs, cheese, and holy water that was blessed in church the day before, or on *brodetta pasquale*, made with beef and lamb broth, eggs, lemon, and cheese. Bulgarians, by contrast, start the Easter meal with *tarator*, a cold, tangy yogurt soup that piques and prepares the appetite for the feast to come.

BREAKING THE EASTER FAST

Talk about a late-night snack. *Mayeritsa* is traditionally left bubbling on the stove while you go off to your Saturday midnight church service. When you get home, it takes just five minutes to finalize the soup and you break the Easter fast on the spot, serving it with feta cheese and bright-red hard-boiled eggs, and often lighting the meal with the "Resurrection candles" you brought home from the midnight service.

ALBANIA, GREECE, AND CYPRUS

LAMB AND RICE SOUP
MAYERITSA
Serves 6 to 8

THIS SOUP IS traditional and ritualistic: while a freshly slaughtered spring lamb will be roasted for the main course of the Easter feast, a soup is supposed to be made from the remaining parts — the lungs, liver, heart, and intestines, all cooked in a broth made from the lamb's head. Well, this recipe just isn't that pure. On the other hand, it really is lovely — like a savory rice pudding with little bits of lamb and parsley and a lemony tang. Just ignore the fact that you're using cornstarch to approximate the thickening you would have gotten from the entrails. This is a soup that is all about the joy of redemption, the richness of Christian living in Mediterranean communities, and just plain good eating. It's also wonderful reheated, so long as you reheat carefully and don't curdle it.

2 pounds lamb on the bone (shank is excellent)
2 medium onions, finely chopped
4 celery stalks with leaves, finely chopped
12 cups (3 quarts) cold water
¾ cup raw rice
½ cup parsley, finely chopped
4 egg yolks, beaten
2 tablespoons cornstarch
1 cup milk
1 lemon, juiced
Salt and pepper to taste

TO PREPARE
Cut the lamb off the bone and chop it coarsely, then prep the remaining ingredients as directed in the recipe list.

To Cook

1. Place the meat, bones, onions, and celery into a large soup pot and cover with the water. Bring to a boil over medium-low heat, then reduce to a simmer. Skim any foam, discarding it. Cover the pot and cook for about 1 hour.

2. Stir in the rice and parsley, cover, and cook for about 25 more minutes, until the rice is very tender. Remove the lamb bones and discard them.

3. When you are ready to finalize the soup, whisk the egg yolks, cornstarch, and milk together until smooth, then whisk them slowly into the broth. Let the soup cook over low heat, uncovered, for about 5 minutes. Remove from the heat, stir in the lemon juice, and season with salt and pepper.

To Serve

Whether you are serving it after the midnight service or not, ladle the soup into bowls and serve immediately with feta cheese and hard-boiled eggs.

"A Great Procession of Priests and Laymen"

A procession of priests and laymen,
all the professions represented,
goes through the streets, the squares, and portals
of the celebrated city of Antioch.
At the head of the impressive, great procession,
a handsome young man, dressed all in white, carries
in hands uplifted the Cross,
the power and our hope, the Holy Cross.
The pagans who were formerly so arrogant,
now diffident and timid, hastily
draw away from the procession.
Far from us, let them always remain far from us
(as long as they do not renounce their error).
The Holy Cross advances. In every neighborhood
of the city where Christians live in piety
it carries consolation and joy.
They come out, the pious ones, to the doors of their houses
and full of exultation they worship it—
the power, and the salvation of the universe, the Cross.—

It is an annual Christian festival.
But today, see, it is celebrated more brilliantly.
The state has finally been delivered.
The most wicked, the detestable
Julian reigns no more.

Let us pray for the most pious Jovian.

—C. P. CAVAFY, twentieth-century Greek poet

BULGARIA

ICED CUCUMBER SOUP
TARATOR
Serves 6 to 8

COLD, SHARP, AND tart—this soup is a glorious way to celebrate Easter and a superb summer first course that refreshes while it stimulates the palate. It's easy and fast to make and very low calorie.

> 4 cucumbers, peeled and chopped
> 2 garlic cloves, minced
> 4 tablespoons fresh dill, chopped
> 1/2 teaspoon salt
> 1 cup water
> 8 cups plain yogurt
> Toasted almond slices, for garnish

TO PREPARE
1. Prep the ingredients as directed in the recipe list, including toasting the almonds for the garnish.

2. In a blender, puree the cucumbers and garlic, pulsing the blades to liquify the mixture. Toss in the dill, salt, water, and yogurt and mix well. Refrigerate for at least 2 hours.

TO SERVE
Ladle the soup into bowls and sprinkle with toasted almonds.

MUSICAL INSPIRATION

Tarator is a favorite recipe of Maestro Kurt Masur, former conductor of the New York Philharmonic. Mr. Masur, a Silesian by birth (over the centuries, that's meant German, Polish, and Czech, depending on the year and torn history of central Europe), makes the soup himself, describing it as simple and delicious—both of which are true.

THE EASTER SERMON OF ST. JOHN CHRYSOSTUM

Let us all enter into the joy of the Lord!
First and last alike receive your reward;
rich and poor, rejoice together!
Sober and slothful, celebrate the day!

You that have kept the fast, and you that have not,
rejoice today for the Table is richly laden!
Feast royally on it, the calf is a fatted one.
Let no one go away hungry. Partake, all, of the cup of faith.
Enjoy all the riches of His goodness!

—ST. JOHN CHRYSOSTUM, *fourth-century priest who preached so persuasively that he earned the name Chrysostum, or "golden mouthed." He was born in Antioch and served as Patriarch in Constantinople until he was banished to the shores of the Black Sea for his zeal in preaching against worldliness*

THE STORY OF *FATTA*

Throughout the Mideast, *fatta* describes a way of breaking crisped pitas into a dish before ladling the soup or whatever on top. *Shorbet el Fata,* for example, describes an Islamic feast day soup that is eaten seventy days after Ramadan and is made from the leftover meat and bones of the Eid al Adha sacrificial lamb. It's a soured, spiced lamb broth, ladled over pita crisps, then topped with yogurt. *Fatta* is also eaten in Yemen as crisped pieces of pita in a lentil salad.

EGYPT

LAMB AND GARLICKY RICE SOUP
FATTA
Serves 6 to 8

IT'S SO OBVIOUS, this ceremonious serving of the lamb on a side plate — like a communion, spooning small bits of the Lamb of God into a spare, garlicky bread soup. The bread symbolizes the body of Christ. The touch of vinegar recalls the passion. And the rice is white, like the Lamb before the sacrifice, but of course it is also nicely filling and helps get you through all the services and Easter prayers until the proper feast is laid on the table later in the day.

Certainly this soup, served by Egyptian Christians as the very first meal after the Lenten fast, is deeply satisfying, a jolt of meat and protein after weeks of deprivation, but it also clearly marks as a halfway point the transition from sorrow and spareness to joy and appetite.

> *10 cups (2½ quarts) cold water*
> *2 pounds lean boneless lamb, cut into small pieces*
> *2 medium onions, left whole*
> *1 dried hot chile pepper*
> *Salt and pepper to taste*
> *1 cup raw rice*
> *2 cups boiling water*
> *4 tablespoons (½ stick) butter*
> *8 garlic cloves, pressed*
> *1 tablespoon vinegar*
> *4 pita breads, crisped in the oven*

TO PREPARE

1. Prep the ingredients as directed in the recipe list, including crisping the pita breads.

2. Place the cold water, lamb, onions, chile pepper, salt, and

pepper in a soup pot and slowly bring to a boil over medium heat, skimming as necessary. Reduce the heat to low, partially cover, and let the soup cook until the meat is tender, about 1 hour.

3. Meanwhile, in a separate saucepan, cook the rice over low heat in the 2 cups boiling water, covered, until tender, about 20 minutes; spoon into a serving bowl and set aside, keeping warm.

TO COOK

1. When the meat has finished cooking in the broth, discard the onions and chile pepper, then remove the meat from the soup and reserve. Keep the soup on a low simmer.

2. Melt the butter in a frying pan over medium-high heat and toss in the reserved meat, stirring until it is evenly browned. Remove the meat to a serving dish and keep warm.

3. Toss the garlic into the remaining butter and sauté over medium heat until golden brown, then scrape it into the soup and stir in the vinegar.

TO SERVE

Bring the soup to a high boil. Break the crisped breads into individual bowls and ladle the soup over them, passing the meat and rice separately.

THE "STINKING ROSE" THROUGH THE AGES

- Virgil (first century B.C.E.) avowed garlic would restore the strength of reapers against the heat, and the poet Macer (ditto) said it was helpful in keeping people who were threatened by the possible attack of snakes from falling asleep.
- Horace (first century B.C.E., five years younger than Virgil) suffered indigestion on the very day of his arrival at Rome from eating a sheep's head laced with garlic and so had a horror of it.
- Pliny the Elder (first century A.D.) said garlic was good for toothache, ulcer, and asthma, not to mention stimulating sexual and gustatory appetites.
- Galen (second century A.D.) used it as an antidote to poisons.
- Athenaeus (second century A.D.) forbade anyone who had eaten garlic to enter the sacred temple of Cybele.
- Mohammed (sixth century A.D.), prophet of Islam, extolled its use for scorpion and snake bites.
- During the Dark Ages (ninth–fifteenth centuries A.D.), Europeans believed garlic could ward off the plague and wore garlands of it as protection; to this day they recall folklore traditions that it protects against the "evil eye" and can make witches and vampires disappear at its very sight.
- Richard Folkard, in *Plant Lore* (1884), advises, "To dream that you are eating garlic denotes that you will discover hidden secrets and meet with some domestic jar. To dream that there is garlic in the house is lucky."
- As recently as 1917 and 1918, Americans wore garlic garlands in public during influenza epidemics, and Eleanor Roosevelt was said to take three chocolate-covered garlic pills each morning, on the advice of her doctor, to improve her memory.

THEOCRITUS ON BEAUTY AND RICOTTA

In Idyll 11, this ancient poet from Syracuse (third century B.C.E.) depicts the hopeless yearning of dopey Cyclops Polyphemus for the fair nymph Galatea, who was to his one eye "whiter than ricotta, gentler than a lamb, livelier than a calf, firmer than an unripe grape."

It was one-eyed Polyphemus in Homer's epic, of course, who gobbled up six of Odysseus's men before being easily fooled, intoxicated, and blinded so that Odysseus could escape to return to Ithica and his faithful Penelope.

And what's ricotta, anyway? Very white, for one. But also a very famous Italian "whey cheese"—that is, a cheese made of what's leftover from, say, provolone cheese production. It means "twice cooked" because it's coagulated into a fine grain, spoonable cheese from the uncoagulated liquid that's left from the first milk separation. You'll find mostly cow ricotta at the store, but it's also made from sheep, goat, and buffalo milk.

ITALY

MEATBALL AND CHEESE DUMPLING SOUP
BENNEDETTO
Serves 6 to 8

INCREDIBLY, *EVERYTHING* YOU'VE missed during Lent appears in this soup: creamy egg and ricotta-cheese dumplings, chicken, and tender meatballs all in a rich chicken broth with light globules of fat. Heaven! And, in fact, *bennedetto* means "The Blessed."

FOR THE BROTH
  9 cups Chicken Stock (page 24)
  1 large carrot, peeled and minced
  1 large onion, minced
  2 celery stalks with leaves, minced
  2 garlic cloves, minced
  1 cup shredded cooked chicken meat

FOR THE MEATBALLS
  3/4 pound lean ground beef or lamb
  1 tablespoon minced fresh parsley
  Salt and pepper to taste

FOR THE DUMPLINGS
  1 cup ricotta cheese
  1 large egg
  1/2 tablespoon minced fresh parsley
  Salt and pepper to taste

  Minced fresh parsley, for garnish

TO PREPARE
  1. Start the soup: Heat the stock over medium-high heat in a Dutch oven (room to cook the meatballs and dumplings) and stir in

the carrot, onion, celery, and garlic. Reduce the heat to medium-low and simmer, covered, for 30 minutes. You should add the shredded chicken at this point.

2. Prepare the meatballs: Hand-mix the ground meat with the parsley, salt, and pepper, then form into small meatballs the size of large marbles. (You may store them in the refrigerator until you are ready to cook them.)

3. Prepare the dumplings: Mix the ricotta cheese with the egg, parsley, salt, and pepper. Stir well. Refrigerate the dumplings until you are ready to cook them.

To Cook

1. When the soup has cooked for 30 minutes, and you have added the shredded chicken, taste carefully for seasoning — this is the last time you will be able to stir in salt and pepper, as you're about to make the soup very crowded with fragile meatballs and dumplings. Slide the meatballs into the soup and cook gently for 5 minutes without touching them.

2. Cover the pot and build up a head of steam in it over medium heat. Then, using a teaspoon, slide spoonfuls of the cheese dumpling mixture into the lightly bubbling broth. Be careful here. The dumplings are delicate and you don't want them to break up in the broth. Don't touch them or stir them around. Cook, covered, until the dumplings are set, 6 to 8 minutes. No peeking!

To Serve

Evenly distribute the meatballs and dumplings among the bowls, then ladle in the broth and garnish each portion with minced parsley.

DEEPLY REPENTANT

Deeply repentant of my sinful ways
And of my trivial, manifold desires,
Of squandering, alas, these few brief days
Of fugitive life in tending love's vain fires,
To Thee, Lord, Who dost move hard hearts again,
And render warmth unto the frozen snow,
And lighten every bitter load of pain
For those who with Thy Sacred ardours glow,
To Thee I turn, O stretch forth Thy right hand
And from this whirlpool rescue me, for I
Without Thine aid could never reach the land;
O willingly for us didst suffer loss,
And to redeem mankind hung on the Cross,
O gentle Saviour, leave me not to die.

—GASPARA STAMPA, sixteenth-century Italian poet

POLAND

SOUR RYE AND SAUSAGE SOUP
BARSCZ
Serves 6 to 8

THIS AUTHENTIC POLISH recipe was brought to the United States from Kraków in the early 1900s by Agnes Kravitz, who settled in northeastern Pennsylvania and passed the "little bit of this, little bit of that" recipe to her daughter Theodosia (Tess) Burke, who in turn passed the love of it on to her own daughter-in-law, Maria Burke. Maria sent it to me, for which I shall always be grateful. It's a rich and unusual soup—thickly white from milk and dark rye flour, sour from fermenting the flour into traditional *barscz kwaszony zytni* (similar to the Russian *kvass*, page 235), tart from freshly grated horseradish, and highly textured from chopped egg, smoked kielbasa, and rye bread. As Maria says, "it's something you have to acquire a taste for, but once you do, there's no substitute for it." As a convert, I agree. *Barcsz* is excellent for Easter morning, or for any time the mood strikes you.

FOR THE *BARSCZ*
¼ pound dark rye flour
4 cups warm water

FOR THE CONDIMENTS
6 to 8 slices rye bread (1 slice per person), torn into bits
1 pound smoked kielbasa (Polish sausage), chopped
6 to 8 hard-boiled eggs (1 egg per person), chopped
Horseradish, freshly grated and mixed with a little vinegar

FOR THE SOUP
8 cups (2 quarts) water
2 eggs
2 cups milk or buttermilk
Salt and pepper to taste

To Prepare

1. Six days ahead, begin the *barscz:* Stir together the rye flour and warm water in an ample container (ceramic is good) and set it aside in a warm place, covered with a towel. (I made mine in a big plastic container, covered it with a potholder, and put it on the back of the stove. The kitchen counter is also fine.) Stir once a day. The fermentation and sour smell is a sign that it's getting good. Measure out 2 cups of the *barscz.* You can save the *barscz* you don't use, let it settle again, then decant the clear liquid, refrigerate, and use as a flavoring in other soups (for example, the Lenten *Okroshka postnaya* on page 232).

2. Prep the condiments as directed in the recipe list.

To Cook

Bring the water to a simmer in a large soup pot on the stove. Beat together the eggs and milk, then slowly stir them into the simmering water. Turn up the heat a bit, let the broth thicken, then slowly pour in reserved *barscz.* Stir with a wooden spoon until the broth thickens to the consistency of watery oatmeal or runny pea soup. Season well with salt and pepper. It should smell sour.

To Serve

Place some of the bread bits, chopped sausage, and chopped egg into each bowl. Ladle the soup over each portion, then stir in horseradish to taste.

"A Skull"

*Before Mary Magdalen,
  albescent in the dusk,
A skull. The candle flickers.
  Which of her lovers
Is this dried-up bone, she
  does not try to guess.
She remains like that, for an
  age or two
In meditation, while sand in
  the hourglass
Has fallen asleep — because
  once she saw,
And felt on her shoulder the
  touch of His hand,
Then, at daybreak, when she
  exclaimed: "Rabboni!"
I gather dreams of the skull
  for I am it,
Impetuous, enamored, suffer-
  ing in the gardens
Under a dark window, un-
  certain whether it's mine
And for no one else, the secret
  of her pleasure.
Raptures, solemn oaths. She
  does not quite remember.
And only that moment per-
  sists, unrevoked,
When she was almost on the
  other side.*

—Czeslaw Milosz, twentieth-century Polish poet

BEET SOUP
BORSHCH
Serves 6 to 8

THIS RECIPE WAS given to me by Andrei Radchenko of Miami, Florida, who grew up and spent most of his young adult life in Kiev. He cautions that it's important to locate true "borshch beets," which have whitish stripes inside when you cut them in half. Alas, there is no way to tell if you have the right ones before you get them home, so you might want to ask your grocer or shop at a farmer's market and ask for a look. Andy says he's generally lucky four out of five times, which isn't bad. Also please note the spelling of the soup: Americans commonly see it spelled *borscht,* but that's like pronouncing *whiskey* "viskey."

As for the soup making, start early and plan to be home pretty much all day, while you keep feeding the pot. Serve this soup as a first course at Easter dinner, or at Christmas dinner, or as a meal in its own right, anytime of the year, with sourdough buns *(pampoosh-kee)* sauced with garlic oil and served with side dishes.

FOR THE BROTH
½ cup dried red beans
2 to 3 pounds pork ribs
12 cups (3 quarts) cold water
1 medium onion
1 carrot, scrubbed and trimmed
1 celery stalk with leaves, cut in half
1 large or 2 medium beets, peeled and julienned

FOR THE SOUP
2 tablespoons vegetable oil
1 medium onion, diced
1 celery stalk with leaves, diced
2 carrots, peeled and diced

2 green bell peppers, cored, seeded, and diced
2 fresh tomatoes, peeled and diced, or 4 canned tomatoes,
    diced
2 potatoes, peeled and cut into thick slices
Herbs and spices to taste, to include salt, bay leaf, black
    pepper, piece of dried red chile pepper, and thyme
½ small cabbage, thinly sliced

FOR THE SOUP SEASONING
3 ounces salt pork fat or bacon, chopped
2 garlic cloves
2 tablespoons chopped fresh dill
½ cup yogurt
⅓ to ½ cup tomato paste

Sour cream, fresh dill, and parsley, for garnish

A SHORT HISTORY OF BORSHCH

Borshch, a Ukrainian specialty well loved by Russians, was originally named after a weed—the *borshchevik*—a universal ingredient in the earliest days of soup making. It was only later, in
the tenth and eleventh centuries, that peasants starting adding
beetroot to the soup, when it was imported from Europe into
the Ukraine. It was love at first bite: the Ukraine soon became
the main beet-growing region in Russia. In fact, the classic
Russian *borshch*, as noted, is called *malorossisky borshch*, from
the Old Russian name for Ukraine. While Ukrainians used their
abundant beets for everyday soup, in the less fertile north,
borshch was a special treat to be cooked only for festivals.

Yuri Olesha, Soviet writer, evokes the power and mythic sug-
gestiveness *borshch* holds for Russians and Ukrainians in *No
Day Without a Line:* "With what gusto I ate! How delicious it
was. It was Greek, southern fare. Powerfully, like the body of a
bull, a whole green pepper lay in the borshch, displaying its
side like the bull that abducted Europa."

"EASTER SUNDAY"

*In the Russian there is a spe-
cial feeling for the feast of
Easter Sunday. He feels this
kinship more keenly if he
happens to be in a foreign
country. . . . It seems to him
that in Russia people somehow celebrate this day
better, and the people themselves are more joyful and
better than on other days,
and life itself is somehow
different, not ordinary everyday. Suddenly it seems to
him that this solemn mid-
night, this ubiquitous ringing
of bells, which seems to fuse
all the earth into one sound,
all the cries, Christ has risen!*

—NIKOLAI GOGOL, *nineteenth-
century Ukrainian satirist, from
*LETTER 32

TO PREPARE

1. The night before, soak the beans in plenty of water.

2. Prep the remaining ingredients as directed in the recipe list.

TO COOK

1. Place the pork ribs in a large soup pot with the cold water. Bring to a boil slowly over medium-high heat and remove the scum as necessary. Add the onion, carrot, and celery, reduce to a simmer, partially cover the pot, and cook for about 2 hours. When done, strain the broth, cut the meat off the bones (reserving it), and discard the bones and vegetables.

2. Drain the beans and rinse. Add them and the beets to the strained broth, bring to a boil over high heat, then reduce the heat to low, cover, and simmer until the beets are white and the beans tender, about 1 hour.

3. In a skillet, heat the vegetable oil over low heat, then add the onion, celery, carrots, and green pepper and sweat, covered, until the onions are yellow, 5 to 10 minutes. Scrape into the soup pot, simmer for a few minutes, then add the tomatoes, potatoes, herbs, and spices, and simmer until the potatoes are tender, about 20 minutes.

4. Add the cabbage and simmer until it's the consistency you like — crunchy or soft.

5. In the meantime, chop the pork fat (or bacon), garlic, and dill in the food processor, processing in the yogurt at the end.

6. When the cabbage is the way you like it, remove the chile pepper and bay leaf from the soup and stir in the reserved pork, the tomato paste, and the garlic-dill-fat mixture. Return the pot to a simmer over medium-high heat, then cover the pot, turn the heat off, and let the flavors mingle for at least 30 minutes.

TO SERVE

Ladle the soup into bowls and top each portion with a dollop of sour cream, sprinkled with a little fresh dill and parsley.

17

JEWISH HISTORY AND
FESTIVALS

ONCE UPON A time, the Jewish people made a covenant with God that included specific dietary laws. Likely Abraham had no inkling of their unforeseen consequences, but they turned out to be profound.

There were three big items right from the start, and these were:

1. Meat and dairy products can never be eaten at the same time ("You shall not boil a kid in its mother's milk"—Deuteronomy 14:21).
2. Meat must be drained of all blood before being eaten ("You [Noah] shall not eat flesh with its life, that is, its blood"—Genesis 9:4).
3. People are not permitted, by God's law, to work on the Sabbath, from sunset Friday until Saturday evening "when 3 stars are seen" ("Remember the Sabbath day, to keep it holy . . . in it, you shall not do any work"—Genesis 20:8–10, the fourth of the Ten Commandments that God gave Moses on Mount Sinai, coming out of Egypt).

Right from the start, then, Jewish people could not, realistically, go to a non-Jew's tent and have a casual dinner without breaking God's law, creating inevitable distance from any neighbors. Accordingly, over the millennia and with all the refinements imposed by Talmudic interpretations, these restrictions dramatically shaped the history of the Jewish people. In fact, I don't think there's any earthly way to understand the development of Jewish cuisines, festival traditions, rhythms of life, and ways of interacting with other cultures and societies without a thumbnail sketch of that history.

A THUMBNAIL SKETCH OF THE "SEPHARDIC" MIGRATIONS

When Nebuchadnezzar, King of Babylon, destroyed Jerusalem's First Temple in 586 B.C.E. and deported the population to present-day Iraq, it was a sign of things to come. Although Persian King Cyrus later allowed the Jews to return and rebuild, in A.D. 70 the Roman general Titus destroyed the Second Temple and ruled that no Jews could live in Jerusalem henceforth. The Diaspora was on.

The first migration wave fanned out from Jerusalem throughout the Mediterranean and into Central Asia along established trade routes, to Syria, Iraq, Iran, and India; to Egypt and along the North African coast to Morocco; to Greece, Italy, France; and ultimately to what is now Spain and Portugal.

These peoples eventually became known as the *Sephardi,* meaning "from Spain," all jostling for a living, shoulder to shoulder, in strange climes with peoples of many different faiths — animist, pantheistic, Christian, Zoroastrian, you name it. But when the Arab tribes rose in the seventh century to spread Islam across the world, the *Sephardi* rather suddenly found themselves in a uniformly Islamic world. And, for the most part, they were actually pretty comfortable in it for some eight hundred years, as Islamic rulers in all these different places practiced religious toleration.

It wasn't until 1492, with the fall of Granada and the ferocious beginning of Grand Inquisitor Torquemada's Spanish Inquisition that a reverse migration occurred that would take most of the *Sephardi* — those who refused to convert to Christianity or pretend to — back to the Ottoman Empire.

Accordingly, the Sephardic cuisine developed as diversely as their countries of settlement. Claudia Roden, in her superb *The Book of Jewish Food,* describes it as "sensual, aromatic, and colorful"—and she shows how it successfully integrated a Spanish style with Turkish, North African, Arabic, and Persian styles, all within the restrictions of Jewish dietary laws. Across the Sephardic Jewish world, annual festivals were celebrated with all sorts of foods and seasonings, including soups with beef and pomegranate, pumpkin and chickpeas, favas and peas, rice and cilantro, eggs and lemon, walnuts, cinnamon, cloves, saffron, and hot chiles.

THE RISE OF THE ASHKENAZIS

At the same time, and over time, as the Roman Empire disintegrated and northern Europe began to develop, Jews in southern Europe extended their trade routes northward, and sparse Jewish communities in France, Italy, and Germany began to grow up. The Yiddish language was born by the thirteenth century as a dialect of German, and so were the identities of today's Ashkenazi Jews, who by the way had dramatically different lifestyles and cuisines from their southern cousins. Again I cite Claudia Roden: "There was a strong ascetic streak in German Jews, and their lives were inclined to spirituality rather than sensual expression. . . . They ate like the Germans—substantial foods, warming soups thick with oats, barley, groats, and dumplings. . . ." For Sabbath and for festivals, they pulled out all the stops and killed a chicken.

These communities, living entirely within the Christian world, began to move east along northern routes in the thirteenth century to escape persecution at the time of the Crusades, and they began to flood east by the sixteenth and seventeenth centuries, when those persecutions became unbearable. Instead of returning to the Mideast, these Jews moved east across Europe and ended up in cities and tiny villages throughout eastern and central Europe, the Balkans, the Baltics, Ukraine, and Russia.

In terms of soup traditions, there is a great and uniform sameness to the Ashkenazi soup menu. For weddings, chicken soup (*goldene yoich*—just the broth, but "golden" because of the fat globules on top). For sickness and convalescence, chicken soup. For the Sabbath, chicken soup. For the New Year at Rosh Hashanah,

PREMIUM CHICKEN SOUP

The fabulously wealthy banker Baron von Rothschild was traveling through the Austrian countryside and stopped for lunch at a little deli. The soup was absolutely delicious. When he finished, the waiter brought him the bill. Rothschild was stunned: "10,000 kreutzers for a bowl of chicken soup!" he exclaimed. "That's impossible. Is chicken soup so rare in these parts?" "No," replied the waiter, "but Rothschilds are."

chicken soup with round pasta. For Yom Kippur, chicken soup, but with dumplings *(kreplach)*, where the dough covers the filling as we all hope kindness will cover our sins on this Day of Atonement. The seventh day of Sukkot? Chicken soup with *kreplach,* same reason. Chanukah, chicken soup. Passover, chicken soup—this time with matzo balls *(knaidlach)* because not a speck of leaven should be in the house, much less in the soup.

ROSH HASHANAH

Rosh Hashanah, the first holiday of the Jewish New Year, celebrates the actual creation of the world (generally pinpointed by medieval scholars as October 13). It is a movable feast, based on the lunar calendar and falling in September or October, and it begins with a feast — a traditionally "sweet" feast that launches a ten-day period of reflection and prayer, ending with the celebration of Yom Kippur, the Day of Atonement. It is believed that during this start to the New Year all mankind passes before God, who looks into their deeds and hearts . . . and then passes judgment on them on Yom Kippur. Rosh Hashanah's opening feast thus — optimistically — rolls out foods that symbolize hope and sweetness (raisins in challah; honey, apples, figs, sweet potatoes, squashes, and carrots), fertility and abundance (pomegranates, eggs, and rice), or that signify the eradication of one's sins and enemies (leeks, called *karti*, or "cut off" in Hebrew, can help you cut off *all* those bad things).

Soup shows up at most traditional Rosh Hashanah feasts throughout the Jewish world. Chicken soup with *kreplach* is popular everywhere because of the pious hope factor (see above). Leek soup is traditional in Sephardic traditions because of its apparent potential for getting rid of enemies — and also sweet pumpkin and chickpea soup. Moroccan Jews substitute yellow split peas for the chickpeas and add saffron, ginger, cinnamon, and cloves to make *l'hamaak dil gar'a.* Many Iranians eat a hearty chicken soup with rice after carrying out *"simana milta,"* which itemizes each of the symbolic foods before consuming them. Iraqis dine on lemony *hammoud* soup with *kibbe* meatballs and cucumber.

"A STORY ABOUT
CHICKEN SOUP"

*In my grandmother's house
there was always chicken
soup
And talk of the old country —
mud and boards,
Poverty,
The snow falling down the
necks of lovers.*

*Now and then, out of her
savings
She sent them a dowry.
Imagine
The rice-powdered faces!
And the smell of the bride,
like chicken soup.*

—LOUIS SIMPSON, contemporary
American poet

WORLDWIDE

CHICKEN SOUP WITH DUMPLINGS
GOLDENE YOICH MIT KREPLACH
Serves 6 to 8

WHAT'S NOT TO like about this soup? It's wonderfully rich and
aromatic with its double chicken consommé, flavored with root
vegetables and set off with dumplings. Guaranteed to lift spirits and
hearts on any occasion, it will certainly start the New Year right.
It's a good idea to make the soup the day before you'll be serving it
so the flavors can blend and so you can easily remove all the congealed chicken fat from the top.

> *16 cups (4 quarts) Chicken Stock (page 24), cold or at room
>   temperature (you may also use cold water, but the soup will
>   not be as rich)*
> *4 to 5 pounds chicken, cut up (a stewing hen is traditional, but
>   any chicken parts are fine; be sure to reserve the liver if
>   you'd like to make a liver paste filling for the kreplach)*
> *4 celery stalks with leaves, chopped*
> *4 parsley roots, peeled and chopped (if not available, add more
>   parsley)*
> *2 large onions, chopped*
> *6 carrots, peeled and chopped*
> *4 to 6 parsnips, peeled and chopped*
> *1 celery root, peeled and chopped (if not available, add more
>   celery)*
> *1 bunch fresh parsley, finely chopped*
> *¼ cup finely chopped fresh dill*
> *Salt and pepper to taste*
>
> *Kreplach (see sidebar)*

TO PREPARE

1. Prep the ingredients as directed in the recipe list.
2. Make the dumplings (see sidebar).

TO COOK

1. Put all the ingredients except the salt and pepper and the kreplach in a large soup pot with the chicken stock, cover, and bring to a boil over medium heat. Reduce the heat to low and simmer, lightly covered, for 2 hours, until everything is tender and soft. Skim off the foam from time to time if needed.

2. After 2 hours, remove the chicken and pick its meat, discarding the skin and bones. Cut the meat into bite-size pieces and set aside, reserving some to fill the *kreplach.*

3. Strain the stock, pressing on the vegetables to extract all the flavor and goodness before discarding them. Stir in the chicken and season with salt and pepper. At this point, you can cool the soup, uncovered, and refrigerate overnight so the flavors can blend, then easily skim as much of the congealed fat as you want before reheating.

4. When making the final preparations, return the soup to a simmer, and let the steam build under a cover. Add the *kreplach,* cover the pot quickly, and simmer for 20 minutes. Don't lift the lid!

TO SERVE

Ladle the soup into bowls and start thinking about your deeds over the past year and your hopes for the coming one.

KREPLACH (MAKES ABOUT 18 TRIANGLES)

1 cup all-purpose flour
½ teaspoon salt
1 egg
⅓ cup ice water
3 to 4 tablespoons chopped liver paste or minced chicken, for filling

Mix the flour, salt, egg, and ice water, then knead until smooth, about 5 minutes. Shape into a ball and let rest 30 minutes. Flatten the ball and roll it out ⅛ inch thick, then cut into 18 squares, each 2½ inches square. Drop ½ teaspoon of filling onto each square, moisten the edges, then fold into a triangle. Press the tines of a fork all along the edges to seal. Let rest 20 minutes on one side, then 20 minutes on the other. Refrigerate until ready to cook.

AIRY THOUGHTS

"The smell of a chicken soup fart with noodles is absolutely one hundred per cent unmistakably Jewish."

—BRYCE COURTENAY,
*contemporary Australian novelist,
from THE POTATO FACTORY*

GEORGIA

BEEF AND POMEGRANATE SOUP
KALIA
Serves 6 to 8

ANDRÉ GIDE TELLS YOUNG
NATHANAËL OF FRUITS
"WHOSE MEMORY, ONCE
YOU CAN NO LONGER PICK
THEM, INCITES YOU TO NEW
THIRSTS"

*Let me tell you of the pome-
    granate; of its juice,
Sourish like the juice of green
    raspberries;
Its wax-like flower the color
    of fruit;
Its closely guarded treasure;
Its partitions in the hive;
Its abundance of flavor;
Its pentagonal architecture;
Its skin giving in;
Its grains bursting;
Grains of blood dripping into
    azure cups;
Drops of gold falling into
    plates of enameled bronze.*

—ANDRÉ GIDE, *twentieth-century
French writer, posing as the
prophet Ménalque, in LES NOURRI-
TURES TERRESTRES*

THIS IS AN EXOTIC AND beautiful soup—bright red chunks of pepper, melt-in-your-mouth beef, sweet onions, crunchy walnuts, all in
a sweet-tart and intensely beef and pomegranate broth. Trust me on
this: you carnivores will love this soup (and you know who you are).

    2 pounds lean boneless beef, in 1 piece
    *8 cups (2 quarts) Beef Stock (page 26), cold or at room
        temperature*
    2 tablespoons butter
    2 medium onions, chopped
    1 red bell pepper, seeded and diced
    4 garlic cloves, chopped
    1 teaspoon ground coriander
    1 teaspoon dried oregano, rubbed between your palms
    1/4 teaspoon ground fenugreek (or curry powder, in a pinch)
    1/4 teaspoon dried mint, rubbed between your palms
    *3/4 cup pomegranate juice (juice pomegranates by rolling them
        hard on the floor under your foot, then squeezing them in
        an orange juicer, or you may also dilute pomegranate paste
        half and half with water)*
    Pomegranate seeds and toasted walnut pieces, for garnish

TO PREPARE
    Prep the ingredients as directed in the recipe list, to include
toasting the walnuts and reserving the pomegranate seeds for the
garnish.

TO COOK
    1. In a large soup pot, immerse the beef in the stock and bring
it to a boil over medium heat. Reduce the heat to low, cover, and

PASSIONATELY POMEGRANATE

Not surprisingly, the word *pomegranate*, from the Latin *pomum granatum*, means "apple of many seeds." But if you can't bring yourself to chew and swallow those many seeds, you probably aren't interested in buying the fresh fruit, with its leathery red skin, regardless of its seductive flavor. And seductive it has always been.

In the Old Testament Song of Songs, Solomon describes Sheba as a garden whose "plants are an orchard of pomegranates"; he says, "As a piece of a pomegranate are thy temples within thy locks." She then says she wants him to drink "the spiced wine of the juice of my pomegranate"—whew! this is suggestive courtship at its best.

The ancient Greeks associated pomegranates with the story of Persephone. When inflamed Pluto abducted Persephone to the underworld to set her on his throne, her mother, Demeter—goddess of nature—was not happy. She grieved the world into famine so that Zeus was forced to intervene, requiring Pluto to restore Persephone to earth, so long as she had eaten no food in the interim. Alas, unhappy as she was, Persephone had eaten six pomegranate seeds to quench her thirst. The compromise? She would return to earth for six months—and return to Hades for the other six. Demeter, with a mother's sense of fairness, obliged with weather to match: summer when Persephone was home, winter when she wasn't. It's this association of pomegranate with death and rebirth that later made it a Christian symbol of the Resurrection.

In the meantime, Romans imported the pomegranate from North Africa, calling it *malum punicum,* or "apple of Carthage." In Arabic folklore and poetry, it is a symbol for the female breast. In Judaism, the pomegranate symbolizes fertility—all those seeds—and relates to the first commandment of the Torah: to be fruitful and multiply.

simmer until nearly tender, about 2 hours. Remove the meat, let cool, and reserve.

2. Heat the butter in a skillet and sauté the onions until golden. Add the red pepper, garlic, coriander, oregano, and fenugreek, stirring for another few minutes, then scrape into the soup pot. Wash the skillet out with broth to extract every bit of flavor.

3. Cut the meat into small dice and scrape it into the soup pot. Simmer for 30 more minutes.

4. Crumble the dried mint into the soup, then stir in the pomegranate juice and simmer for 10 minutes.

To Serve

Ladle the soup into bowls and garnish each portion with a sprinkling of pomegranate seeds and toasted walnuts.

IRAN

VEGETABLE AND RICE SOUP
ÂSH-E KALAM-O HAVEEJ
Serves 6 to 8

CLASSICALLY PERSIAN, WITH all the sophistication that implies, this soup is thick; it is colorful with bright orange bits of carrot and slivers of dark green spinach. It is subtle in flavor—all in a rice-thickened broth that soothes and excites the palate at the same time.

2 tablespoons chicken fat
2 medium onions, halved (root to stem), then sliced into half-
    moons
²/₃ cup raw short-grain, starchy rice
3 tablespoons tomato paste
½ teaspoon freshly ground black pepper
10 cups rich Chicken Stock (page 24)
5 carrots, peeled and diced
2 cups finely chopped cabbage
3 cups washed, stemmed, stacked, and thinly sliced spinach
1 cup finely chopped fresh parsley
½ cup finely chopped fresh cilantro
Salt to taste
2 cups diced cooked chicken

TO PREPARE
Prep the ingredients as directed in the recipe list.

TO COOK
1. Heat the chicken fat in a large soup pot over medium heat and stir in the onions. Cook until golden, then stir in the rice and cook until it is opaque.

2. Stir in the tomato paste and pepper, then pour in the stock and bring to a boil over high heat, stirring. Reduce the heat to low and simmer, covered, for 30 minutes.

PERSIAN RICE

Ah, Persian rice—the most prized delicacy of one of the world's most delicate cuisines. How did it get to Persia in the first place? One myth has it that King Tahmures, of the legendary Pishdadian dynasty in ancient Persia, brought it straight from China in 835 B.C.E. At 3,500 miles, as the crow flies, over some of the roughest terrain on earth, that would have been an unusually long military campaign. More likely it found its way gradually over the Silk Road, arriving in Persia with Turkic tribes via northern India some 2,000 years ago. Today five microvarieties are grown and produced in Iran, in small quantities, alas, rarely exported. Four are for high holidays, all very long-grained, hard, and fragrant: *Ambar-boo* (amber scented), *Darbâri* (imperial court), *Dom Siâh* ("black tailed" variety of basmati rice), and *Sadri* (for the poor). *Gerdeh*, a round and starchy rice, is used for desserts, stuffings, meatballs, and soups like this one.

A TALE OF BINYAMIN
KASKODA, PERSIAN JEWISH
DETECTIVE

Pinhas Sadeh, in his mar-
velous collection of Jewish
folktales, tells the story of a
clever Jew in Teheran,
Binyamin Kaskoda, gumshoe
extraordinaire for the Shah.
When a thief broke into the
Shah's treasury, Binyamin
was put on the case. "Your
majesty, have all the known
thieves in Teheran lined up,"
he said, "and I will tell you
which one robbed you."
When they were all gath-
ered, Binyamin gravely
looked deep into each of the
suspects' eyes. "I now know
who the thief is," he ex-
claimed. "Everyone else can
go home." When they all
turned to go, Binyamin
angrily shouted, "Hey, you
thief! Who said you could go
too?" Involutarily the true
thief turned around, and that
was it for him. Binyamin,
rewarded by the Shah, no
doubt went home to cele-
brate with a bowl of *Âsh-e
kalam-o haveej.*

3. Add the diced carrots, cabbage, spinach, and herbs; return
to a boil over high heat, then reduce heat to medium-low, cover, and
cook 20 more minutes, or until the cabbage is just tender. Season
with salt. Stir in the chicken and let it heat through for another 5 to
10 minutes.

TO SERVE

Ladle the soup into bowls and serve immediately.

Iraq

LEMONY LAMB SOUP
Kibbe hammoud
Serves 6 to 8

OKAY, I AGREE: this recipe looks impossible. Who can even think of making meat paste torpedoes and then stuffing them with exotic spiced meat? Trust me, it's worth it. And if you have a food processor and just take the *kibbe*-making one step at a time, you will end up with one of the most extraordinary soups you could ever imagine. A deep tomato-red lemony broth populated with meat-on-meat *kibbes* (more on them in a minute) and sprinkled at the last minute with spicings of fragrant mint. Swoon. And what about those *kibbes*? Imagine a ground meat shell, then imagine biting into it: your teeth press on a thin crust of beef and rice, then you breach the shell and juicy lamb and spices explode on your teeth into your mouth, sending up semaphores of saffron, rosewater, and deep spices.

FOR THE *KIBBE* FILLING

*1½ pounds boneless lamb, with fat, finely minced (freeze the
    meat and fat first, then thaw just enough to cut it into cubes
    and process in a food processor)*

1 medium onion, finely chopped

*A pinch of saffron threads, ground to a powder and dissolved
    in 2 tablespoons hot water*

5 drops rosewater (see sidebar)

*1 teaspoon baharat spice (mix ¼ teaspoon black pepper; ¼
    teaspoon cumin; ⅛ teaspoon ground cloves; ⅛ teaspoon
    ground coriander; pinch of ground cardamom; pinch of
    nutmeg; and pinch of ground cinnamon).*

Salt to taste

RAVISHING ROSEWATER

This exotically fragrant decoction was distilled at least as early as the ninth century, when Al-Kindi, Baghdad philosopher and scientist in the Caliph's House of Wisdom, wrote about it in his *Kitab Kimya' al-'ltr wa al-Tas'idat* (Book of Perfume Chemistry and Distillation). To this day, blooming damask roses are harvested at dawn, some ten thousand blossoms are slowly simmered with about thirteen gallons of water, and the steam is condensed in a cooling tank, collected, and bottled as a clear elixir. Its uses? They are legion. A medicine that benefits the heart and stomach. A delicate food flavoring splashed into elegant dishes, into tea, into soups. And a mark of hospitality, light-heartedly welcoming or sending off guests by misting them with essence of rose from exquisitely wrought silver sprinklers—really, when you think about it, so generous, so poetic, such a rare and intimate gift.

THE DANGERS OF SPICE

Baharat—literally "spice" in Arabic—is an all-purpose spice mix that varies from region to region, usually including pepper, cinnamon, cloves, cumin, and coriander, and sometimes including rose petals or hot peppers or dried citrus peel. Always, though, it is heady, fabulous, bringing zest and excitement to plain, everyday dishes. The following story of *baharat* is adapted from Pinhas Sadeh's *Jewish Folktales* (1989).

Consider the story of the poor Jewish peasant who came to Baghdad and found himself in a spice bazaar with its barrels of cinnamon and cloves, pepper and ginger, coriander and mint, and all kinds of other good scents. Suddenly he fainted dead away. Nothing could revive him, not smelling salts, not cinnamon, not anything. Just as it looked as if he would never recover, a quick witted man seized a shovel, scooped up some donkey dung, and brought it right under the peasant's nose. Instantly the peasant opened his eyes, sneezed twice, and got to his feet. "A miracle!" the spice merchant exclaims. "By no means," replies the hero, "it was the spices that made him swoon; the familiar scent of manure brought him back to earth."

FOR THE *KIBBE* SHELL

1 pound lean boneless beef, with no fat, finely minced (again, freeze the meat and let thaw just enough to cut into cubes for processing)

2 cups ground rice (available in specialty markets; or see below)

Salt and pepper to taste

Ice water

FOR THE SOUP

2 tablespoons olive oil

6 garlic cloves, chopped

4 ripe tomatoes, peeled and chopped, or 6 canned tomatoes

4 tablespoons tomato paste

8 cups (2 quarts) Beef Stock (page 26)

Salt and pepper to taste

1 cucumber, peeled and cut into thin finger shapes

2 to 3 lemons, juiced

2 tablespoons finely minced fresh mint or ½ teaspoon dried, for garnish

TO PREPARE

1. If you are unable to find ground rice, soak 2 cups long-grain rice in water overnight. Drain the rice, rinse it well, then scrape it into a blender and start blending on high speed, slowly pouring in just enough water to allow the blades to easily grind it. Drain it in a strainer and rinse one last time.

2. Prep the remaining ingredients as directed in the recipe list.

3. Make the *kibbe* filling: Mix the minced lamb with the onion

in a food processor, then add the saffron liquid, rosewater, spices, and salt. Set aside.

4. Make the *kibbe* shell: Mix the beef with the ground rice, salt, and pepper and process in the food processor. Add ice water (as much as ¼ cup), pulsing, to get a very smooth and workable paste.

5. Dip your hands in ice water, then take a round tablespoon of the beef-rice paste, hold it in your left hand (if you're right-handed) and stick your right index finger into the center of it, working the paste to make a little mini-vase shaped like a torpedo. If the paste cracks, dip your finger in the ice water and smear it over the crack to seal. Fill the torpedo with a tablespoon of the lamb-onion filling and close the opening by pinching the edges together and smearing them with ice water to seal. Set the *kibbes* side by side on a plate and refrigerate until you are ready to cook them in the soup. There will be about 40 of them. (You may freeze them if you're not using them until the next day or later.)

To Cook

1. Heat the oil in a large soup pot with a wide bottom over medium heat and fry the garlic and tomatoes until soft and concentrated. Stir in the tomato paste and cook for 1 more minute. Pour in the stock and bring to a boil. Reduce the heat to medium-low. Season with salt and pepper.

2. Carefully add the *kibbes,* one by one, in different parts of the pot so they aren't touching, cover, and let them cook for 15 minutes.

3. Add the cucumber fingers and cook for another 15 minutes, until the cucumber is cooked but still firm and the *kibbes* are cooked inside. Test one to make sure — you don't want them under-cooked.

To Serve

Stir in the lemon juice, check for seasoning, and sprinkle with the mint. Carry the soup to the table and ladle it into bowls, evenly distributing the *kibbes* among them.

MOROCCO

SPICY PUMPKIN AND SPLIT PEA SOUP
L'HAMAAK DIL GAR'A
Serves 6 to 8

THIS IS SUCH a pretty soup; all earth tones with chunks of bright pumpkin or winter squash jostling each other, sprinkled generously with parsley. And how about the aroma and taste? Exotically fragrant and sweetly spicy. Serve in thick pottery bowls, if you have them — Morocco is famous for its ceramics. In the souks of Fez you can see men spinning their potter wheels at all times.

10 cups (2½ quarts) Chicken Stock (page 24)
1¼ cups dried yellow split peas
1 large onion, chopped
¼ cup olive oil
1 teaspoon ground cinnamon
¼ teaspoon ground ginger
¼ teaspoon saffron threads, heated and crumbled
*6 cups peeled, seeded, and cubed pumpkin (from a 3- to
    4-pound pumpkin; you can substitute butternut or another
    winter squash)*
Salt and pepper to taste
Minced fresh parsley, for garnish

TO PREPARE

Prep the ingredients as directed in the recipe list.

TO COOK

   1. Bring the stock, split peas, and onion to a boil in a large soup pot over high heat. Reduce the heat to low and simmer, partially covered, for 30 to 40 minutes.

   2. Stir in the oil, cinnamon, ginger, saffron, and pumpkin. Bring to a boil again over high heat,

then reduce it to low and simmer, partially covered, for about 1 hour, stirring occasionally. The pumpkin will be beginning to fall apart and the peas will be tender.

3. Season with salt and pepper.

TO SERVE

Ladle the soup into bowls and garnish each portion with generous amounts of parsley.

PUMPKIN IN MOROCCO

Once, during my sojourn in Morocco, it was getting close to Halloween and suddenly every American in Casablanca wanted perfect pumpkins to carve into jack o'lanterns. My friend Sandy resolutely set off to her favorite and reliably cheapest *marché*, putting up with its limited selection in the interest of bargains. She went to the first dealer, with his produce in boxes on the ground. *"Un potiron, s'il vous plaît,"* she said. A pumpkin, please. When he showed her a dish of pumpkin pieces, she shook her head. *"Non, pas pour le tagine. Je veux un grand potiron, complet."* No, not to make stew. I want a whole big pumpkin, uncut. His eyes widened. *"Un moment, madame."* After a whispered conference with his son, the boy dashed off and returned shortly with a whole pumpkin and a lot of interested onlookers. *"C'est parfait,"* said Sandy. *"Combien?"* Perfect. How much? He quoted her a price so high, she just stared at him in disbelief before stalking to another dealer. And thus began a grim march around the market, soliciting a whole pumpkin, having to wait while each merchant sent away for one that wasn't cut, then unsuccessfully trying to bargain down the price. All at once, she told me later, laughing at her herself, she realized that there was only one whole pumpkin in the entire market, and it was following her from merchant to merchant—the same one!—with the crowd of interested onlookers growing ever larger and more hilarious. "Well, did you buy it in the end?" I asked. "Heavens no," she said, "too expensive!"

YOM KIPPUR

The sunset-to-sunset day of Yom Kippur itself is a fast, but chicken is traditionally the number one item on the menu before and after because of an ancient ritual called *kapparoth*. Imagine this: for every woman in your family you take a chicken, and for every man you take a rooster, and on the eve of Yom Kippur you whirl the birds over each family member's head, saying "May this sacrificed bird serve as a substitute for [Sarah, or Zaki, or whomever]," then quickly have its throat slit and prepare it for eating. Depending on your family size, you can end up with a lot of chickens this way, and chicken soup is definitely on the menu. Egyptians and Lebanese eat a lemony egg soup, *Beid ab lamouna* (page 275), right before the fast; Greeks eat the same soup—*Avgolemono* (page 315)—to break the fast. And don't forget chicken soup with *kreplach* (page 262), where the dough covers the filling as we all hope kindness will cover our sins on this Day of Atonement.

"A YOM KIPPUR SCANDAL"

In this charming story of a Ukrainian shtetl, 1,800 rubles are stolen from the synagogue of Kasrilevka during the Yom Kippur service. What a scandal! Rabbi Yozifel locks everyone in and orders a thorough search, beginning with his own pockets. When he comes to Lazer Yossel—a "jewel of a young man," the smartest and most admired young man in town—Yossel turns white and refuses. Tension mounts. Has he stolen the money? Hands are laid on him; he's turned upside down; his pockets are turned inside out. What's shaken out? "A couple of well-gnawed chicken bones and a few dozen plum pits still moist from chewing. You can imagine what an impression this made—to discover food in the pockets of our prodigy on this holiest of fast days." The 1,800 rubles are never found, but no one cares—it's this scandal that will live to the end of Lazer Yossel's days.

—SHOLEM ALEICHEM, *nineteenth-century Yiddish writer*

LEBANON

LEMONY EGG SOUP WITH CHICKEN
BEID AB LAMOUNA
Serves 6 to 8

THIS MARVELOUS, COMPLEX soup is quite different from its pure Greek cousin, *Avgolemono*. This version is provocatively lemon, chunky with chicken, redolent with herbs, and lapped in a milky white, savory broth. Good enough to eat, one bowl after another after another.

> *8 cups (2 quarts) Chicken Stock (page 24)*
> *1 raw chicken breast, boned, skinned, and halved*
> *Zest of 1 lemon, grated*
> *⅔ cup long-grain rice*
> *¼ cup lemon juice*
> *3 raw egg yolks*
> *1 tablespoon chopped fresh mint, or 1 teaspoon dried*
> *1 teaspoon dried oregano, rubbed into the soup between your*
> *   palms*
> *1 tablespoon chopped fresh parsley*
> *1 teaspoon grated black pepper*
> *Salt to taste*

TO PREPARE
Prep the ingredients as directed in the recipe list.

TO COOK
1. Bring the stock to a boil in a large soup pot over high heat, then reduce it to low and add the chicken breast and half the lemon zest. Cover and simmer for 15 minutes. Remove the chicken, let cool, then cut into small bite-size pieces and set aside.

2. Bring the stock to a boil again, add the rice, and reduce the heat to a simmer. Cook, covered, for 20 minutes. Add the cooked chicken to the soup and let simmer while preparing the sauce.

3. In a small bowl, whisk the lemon juice, remaining zest, and the egg yolks. Lighten the mixture with ½ cup hot stock, then stir the sauce into the simmering soup until it clouds and thickens a bit. Do not let the soup boil, or it will curdle.

TO SERVE

Stir in the mint, oregano, parsley, and pepper. Season with salt, then ladle the soup into bowls and serve immediately.

LUSCIOUS LEMONS

Lemons likely began life as a "citron" some 8,000 years ago in India or in the fertile crescent between the Tigris and Euphrates rivers in what is now Iraq. Ancient Mesopotamians raised them for their beauty and aroma—they were large, 4 to 8 inches across, and flowered throughout the year. Egyptians loved them for their aid in embalming. Jews brought them to Israel from their captivity in Babylon some 2,500 years ago. Romans used them as mothballs until Persian slaves taught them to put them to better use in their kitchens. At various places and times, citrus fruits have been identified as aphrodisiacs, as cures for fever and colic, and as protection against poisons. Europeans in the Dark Ages, however, were sure that lemons were poisonous themselves—even when crusaders brought them back from Palestine with rave reviews.

The original variety—the fragrant citron *Citrus medica* Linn—is one of the Four Species used in the synagogue service on the Feast of Tabernacles. In ancient times, it was a popular Jewish symbol on coins, graves, and synagogues—called *etrog*, a word of Indian origin—and was used ritually, especially as a handle for the circumcision knife. It was so popular, in fact, that it was proposed as a standard of measure. And when, following the Jewish rebellion against Rome in A.D. 66, Jews were dispersed throughout the Roman Empire, they took their citron with them, planting trees across the Mediterranean in Spain, Italy, Sicily, Tunisia, Algeria, and Turkey. Its scarcity in northern Europe during the Middle Ages caused much anguish for the many Jews who had migrated there.

SUKKOT

This "gathering in" or "season of joy" festival comes on the heels of Yom Kippur, and it celebrates for eight days the end of the judgment period, the bounty of the harvest, and new beginnings — all at once. The traditional celebration takes place in a *sukkah*. What is a *sukkah*? In Leviticus 23:42, the Lord says that after the harvest, "you shall dwell in booths for seven days . . . that your generations may know that I made the people of Israel dwell in booths [in the wilderness] when I brought them out of the land of Egypt." Thus small temporary booths are built outside, with fronds, light planks, or tree boughs; people sit in them and welcome friends; lots of eating goes on — it's a lovely festival. The focus is on fruit and vegetables, thus the lovely fruit soups like the Polish spiced plum soup on the next page, but the Ashkenazis still favor chicken soup with dumplings for this holiday, and many Sephardis favor fresh fava bean soup or spicy lentil stews.

MARC CHAGALL'S *FEAST OF THE TABERNACLES*

Two men sit at a table in a traditional *sukkah,* one eating soup with a big spoon, while a woman passes more food through a window in the side of the *sukkah;* a boy plays on the ground with a chicken; and another man carries the four species (the citron etrog, palm shoot, myrtle, and willow branches) to the synagogue. It's a gorgeous goache painting, painted in 1916 and originally commissioned as a mural for a secondary school outside St. Petersburg, then called Petrograd. Chagall was born in Vitebsk in 1887; he studied art in St. Petersburg and Paris in his twenties, then returned for a visit home to Vitebsk in 1914 and got stuck there when World War I broke loose. So he just settled right in, married his childhood sweetheart, became director of the local academy of arts, and began painting these gorgeous village paintings. His daughter, Ida, was born just as he was painting *Feast of the Tabernacles.*

POLAND

SPICED PLUM SOUP

ZUPA ŚLIWKOWA

Serves 6 to 8

THIS IS A strongly flavored, sweet-tart appetizer soup to a vegetarian meal, redolent of fragrant harvests and autumn weather. The sour cream stirred in at the end creates a wonderful contrast of color and flavor. Of course, if you plan to serve meat in the main course, you should omit the sour cream and garnish the soup with toasted croutons. This soup is excellent piping hot — and also chilled.

> 2 pounds ripe purple plums, washed, cut in half, and pitted
> 6 cups water
> 1 teaspoon cornstarch dissolved in 1 tablespoon cold water
> 1 6-inch thin strip of orange zest (scrape away any bitter white pith)
> 1½ cups orange juice, or more as needed
> ¼ teaspoon ground cinnamon
> ⅛ teaspoon ground cloves
> ½ cup honey
> ½ cup plain sour cream, whipped (optional)
> 2 teaspoons balsamic vinegar
> Sour cream or croutons, for garnish

TO PREPARE

Prep the ingredients as directed in the recipe list, to include toasting the croutons if you plan to garnish the soup with them.

TO COOK

1. Mix the plums, water, cornstarch, orange zest, orange juice, cinnamon, cloves, and honey in a saucepan. Bring to a boil over high heat, then reduce the heat to low, cover, and simmer for about 30 minutes, until the fruit is very soft.

2. Puree the mixture in a blender, skins and all. Optionally, stir in the sour cream. If you plan to serve the soup cold, chill it in the refrigerator for several hours.

To Serve

Whether you are serving the soup hot or cold, add more orange juice, if you like, to get the consistency the way you like it. Stir in the balsamic vinegar, then ladle the soup into small bowls. Swirl a spoonful of sour cream into each portion as a garnish or top with toasted croutons.

Plum Crazy

Plums have been cultivated since the dawn of mankind, their stones showing up even in the detritus of prehistoric Swiss Lake sites. Babylonians grew them in orchards; Assyrian herbalists recommended eating them with honey and butter; and Egyptians doted on them. Alexander the Great himself was said to have introduced them into Greece from Syria or Persia. Plums really came into their own in Renaissance Europe, though, with botanists cultivating exquisite varietals like the Greengage and Mirabelle. But purple *Prunus domestica,* likely a hybrid of *Prunus cerasifera* (the cherry plum) and *Prunus spinosa* (the sloe), was always and continues to be the rage in Poland and all of central Europe, eaten and cooked with pleasure, dried into prunes and pastes, and distilled into the lethal *śliwowica* brandy.

PASSOVER

Passover, or Pesach, commemorates the Jewish exodus from Egypt, when the Hebrews left so suddenly that they only had time to bake and take unleavened bread into the wilderness.

In honor of this "unleavened bread of affliction," as required in the Torah's injunction ("Seven days shall there be no leaven found in your house"), no leavening is used or kept in any house during the eight-day festival. That means no yeast, no baking powder or soda, not even flours that could conceivably get wet and ferment. So how does the unleavened flour of matzo pass muster? It is "guarded"—that is, specially harvested and stored wheat is milled between new, bone-dry millstones to become "Passover flour," mixed with water and immediately cooked—guaranteed never to have gotten damp. Matzo first showed up in Franco-German chicken soups at the seder table to replace forbidden dumplings. Thus were matzo balls born—and in popular folklore their shape is said to represent the round stone thrown by Moses to smash the walls that bound the Jews within Egypt.

Other Passover soups also became traditional in different climes. In Alsatian France, a delicate beef bouillon with delicately spiced matzo balls is favored. In Spain, Jews eat leek soup, or *sopa de prasso.* In Morocco, fava bean soup, *bessara,* is enjoyed to commemorate the fava beans eaten by the Hebrew slaves. In Italy, Jews prepare chicken soup with cinnamon, eggs, and matzo bits cooked to disintegration. In Yemen, Passover is celebrated with chicken soup flavored with the famous *chuwayil* spice, made of black pepper, cardamom, turmeric, saffron, and caraway. In Georgia, there's *khengali,* a chicken soup with walnut balls. Then there's *russel borshch,* an astonishing sour beet soup with brisket and potatoes from Russia.

"PESACH EVE IN OUR LITTLE SHTETL"

Pesach preparations would begin immediately after Purim when we were finished with the tasty hamantashen.... Everyone, who was able, immediately bought wheat meal. Avrum Shebach, the miller, already was concerned that the meal ground in his mill should not become "chometzdick" (impure for Passover use)....

When the matzoh ritual concluded, koshering of the home began.... I also remember the job of beet [preparation]. After the beets were left standing [in water] for three weeks, the water became scummy. The scum was removed; and a good borshch remained for Pesach to have with matzoh.

Wine was made from raisins and water. Honey was cooked with water; hops were added. This was allowed to sit. As dear Pesach arrived, there were resources to treat one's guest. When Seder night arrived, the home was not recognizable. Every house apppeared so pure and holy.

The father of the family donned his kittel [a white linen robe worn on solemn occasions and used as a shroud after death] and sat upon his regal leisure chair like a real king. His wife was the queen, and around them were their children. Wine was poured for everyone at the Seder without forgetting a cup for Elyohu-Hanovi [Elijah the Prophet].

The youngest child asked the Four Questions, and the father had to answer. The door was opened for Elyohu-Hanovi to enter. The mother could hardly sit through the first Seder, so tired was she from the preparations.

On Khalemoyed (the intermediate week-days of the holiday), girls and young men traveled as guests to other shtetls to together with family and, in the meantime, to take advantage of the time to see about a match. Thus, the Jews lived for centuries, worried about livelihoods and were happy with their spiritual life without [the bounties of] wider civilization, without radio and television, without electrical devices—until the coming of Hitler, may his name be blotted out, killed everyone.

The Jews who emigrated to other lands and continents have acclimated themselves to their environments. But, from time to time, they remember and yearn for those times.

—HINDE BINKOVITZ-WIENER, *an oral history as part of the Yizkor Book Project*

RUSSIA

TART BEET SOUP

RUSSEL BORSHCH

Serves 6 to 8

TO GET THIS right, you must mark the calendar and start making the *russel*, or sour beet juice, a month before *Pesach*. It's worth it, though—this soup is a tasty and filling meal during Passover, with the tender brisket of beef and delicate potatoes perfectly set off by the eggy sweet/tart broth.

FOR THE SOUR BEET JUICE *(RUSSEL)*
    8 medium red beets, peeled and cut into eighths
    8 or more cups warm water

FOR THE SOUP
    2-pound piece of beef brisket
    2 medium onions, chopped
    2 bay leaves
    4 cups cold water
    Salt, pepper, and sugar to taste
    1 egg, beaten

GARNISH
    6 to 8 boiled waxy potatoes (1 per person)
    Chopped hard-boiled eggs
    Chopped cucumber
    Chopped fresh parsley

TO PREPARE

1. One month ahead, put the beets in a large glass or ceramic bowl, cover with warm water, then cover loosely with plastic wrap, leaving space for air to get through, and top with a clean cloth. Let stand in a warm spot to ferment for about a week. Remove the white scum that has formed on the top, stir, then re-cover. At the

end of the month, strain the juice through moistened cheesecloth, reserving the beets and the juice separately.

2. Prep the remaining ingredients as directed in the recipe list.

3. Prepare the garnishes. Boil the potatoes until tender, then drain, peel, and keep them warm; hard-boil the eggs, cool, peel, and chop; peel and chop the cucumbers; and chop the parsley.

To Cook

1. Place the brisket, reserved beets, onions, bay leaves, and cold water in a large soup pot and slowly bring to a boil over medium heat. Reduce the heat to low, cover, and let cook for 2 to 3 hours, until the brisket is tender.

2. Remove the brisket to the side and discard the bay leaves. Pour 4 cups of the reserved *russel* into the soup and bring to a boil. Reduce the heat and season with salt, pepper, and sugar. This is a matter of individual taste, but you want to achieve a sweet-tart effect. Let the soup simmer for 15 minutes and taste again.

To Serve

1. When the soup is seasoned to your liking, stir in the beaten egg and keep stirring as it thickens a bit.

2. Cut the brisket into six or eight serving pieces, one piece per guest. Ladle the soup into bowls, then place a piece of meat and a potato in each and garnish with the egg, cucumber, and parsley.

YEMEN

CHICKEN SOUP WITH *CHAWAYIL* SPICE
FTUT
Serves 6 to 8

THIS WONDERFULLY AROMATIC soup has come to be regarded as
Israeli, it is so popular in restaurants there, but in fact it was
brought there by Yemeni Jews as part of their ancient cuisine only
in the 1950s, as part of Operation Magic Carpet, which airlifted
them away from a hostile government. Its distinguishing mark is
the use of *chawayil*, the all-purpose Yemeni spice made of black
pepper, turmeric, cardamom, saffron, and caraway seed. It may *look*
like plain old chicken vegetable soup, but stand back for a soup that
is uniquely and superbly spiced. *Ftut* can also be made with beef or
lamb for festive occasions such as a wedding.

>1 tablespoon chawayil, *or to taste (see sidebar)*
>4 pounds chicken pieces
>2 tablespoons oil or rendered chicken fat
>2 ripe tomatoes, peeled and chopped, or 4 canned tomatoes,
>   juice reserved
>2 medium onions, finely chopped
>Up to 10 cups (2½ quarts) cold water
>2 carrots, peeled and cubed
>1 cup cooked chickpeas (canned are fine, but drain and rinse
>   them)
>2 medium potatoes, peeled and cubed
>1 medium-large zucchini, washed and cubed
>Salt *and* chawayil *to taste*

To Prepare

1. Rub the *chawayil* into the chicken pieces and let marinate at least 2 hours.

2. Prep the remaining ingredients as directed in the recipe list.

To Cook

1. Heat the oil or chicken fat in a large soup pot over medium heat, then add the spiced chicken pieces and let them cook gently, turning once, for about 10 minutes. Stir in the tomatoes and onions, mixing them well with the spiced chicken pieces, and let them cook down for about 10 minutes, stirring from time to time. Pour in the water and reserved tomato juice to equal 10 cups and bring to a boil over high heat. Reduce the heat to low, cover, and simmer for 30 minutes.

2. Add the carrots, chickpeas, and potatoes to the pot and cook, uncovered, for 15 minutes. Remove the chicken pieces from the soup and let cool. (You may either serve the chicken separately, one piece to a bowl, or you may cut it off the bone and add it back to the soup before serving, discarding the bones and skin.)

3. Add the zucchini and cook, uncovered, for 8 to 10 more minutes, until the zucchini is just tender.

4. Season with salt and *chawayil* (adding as much as another tablespoon of *chawayil*) and, if you like, add the chicken pieces back into the soup.

To Serve

Skim the soup of all surface fat and ladle it into bowls. If you have left the chicken pieces separate, add one piece to each bowl.

The Romance of *Chawayil*

I love this unusual spice, not just for its distinctive flavor but also because it reflects the distinctive history of Yemeni Jews, the protectors of King Solomon's spice caravans. I can imagine the soldiers coming home at the end of a long trek, saying "Sarah, I've brought you some pepper all the way from the Malabar coast of India; turmeric from southwest Asia; caraway from the Mediterranean; cardamom from Sri Lanka; saffron from Persia—all here to our little village in Sheba. God is great!"

Chawayil

1 tablespoon freshly ground black peppercorns
1 teaspoon turmeric
1 teaspoon caraway seeds
1/2 teaspoon ground cardamom
1/4 teaspoon saffron threads, heated and crushed

Grind all the spices to a powder. Makes about 2 tablespoons.

THE ASTONISHING HISTORY OF YEMENI JEWS

How on earth did Jews come to Yemen in the first place, and how did they stay isolated and unknown for some 3,000 years? The story goes that it all started with the Queen of Sheba's clever businessmen. These Sabaean (or Sheban) traders specialized in precious spices, growing and harvesting frankincense and myrrh in their own backyards and augmenting their inventory by sailing up the Persian Gulf to pick up the last leg of the cassia and cinnamon trade from Asia. When the Queen of Sheba said about King Solomon circa 950 B.C.E. that he was to her "a bag of myrrh, that lies between my breasts" (Song of Solomon 1:13) he was likely thinking the same thing about her, and not necessarily in symbolic terms. He wanted and needed those precious Sabaean goods, so he could burn that sweet myrrh in his new temple and use those spices for the good life that God had promised him: "I will also give you riches, possessions, and honor, such as none of the kings had who were before you, and none after you shall have the like" (2nd Chronicles 1:12).

But trading routes were treacherous. How to protect the rich spice caravans in Sheba (present-day Yemen) trekking north along the Red Sea coast through desert and wilderness, easy prey for desert tribes? Soldiers, of course. And the soldiers he sent from Jerusalem, seeing the writing on the wall about how long they'd be pulling this duty, set off with their wives and children. They settled in what is now Yemen, convoying shipments from the southern tip of the Arabian peninsula all the way to Jerusalem and back again. When trade with Jerusalem dried up, following the death of Solomon, they remained in their new home, zealously guarding their cultural and religious traditions and raising generations of children, but completely losing contact with their original homeland.

18
ISLAMIC FESTIVALS

"The most delicious dish is — 'fast and then eat.' "

ONCE UPON A time, I took my children to Casablanca to live. Everything was new and strange, and it was Ramadan. Six days into the venture, here's what I wrote home:

> I should mention that we are in the third week of the holy season of Ramadan. Mohammed decreed that for one month out of every year, all Moslems would show their respect to Allah and the poor of the world by fasting every day for twelve hours during the main part of the day. This means that from about 8 A.M. to 8 P.M., no matter what the heat (and it's hot!), *nothing* shall pass the lips of a Moslem — not a morsel of food, not a sip of water. If you smoke as a rule, you give that up. Alcohol is totally forbidden for the duration. And you have never seen so many stressed faces. The construction workers across from our apartment drag themselves along with their cinderblocks. You can see the men on the street dying for a cigarette. Women out with children clearly find their tempers growing short. And I especially feel sorry for the food merchants — out in the hot sun with water, water everywhere and nary a drop to drink.

Well, it was a pretty superficial impression, all things considered, but still a powerful one for someone new to the concept.

Houston Rockets basketball superstar Hakeem Olajuwon is reported to pick up an order of "soup to go" during Ramadan at a Houston Anthony's Restaurant, so it's at the ready to eat after sunset.

ISLAMIC FESTIVALS

As laid down in the Qur'an, festivals focus on the precepts of Islam, not on historic events, per se. Because the Islamic calendar is based on a 354-day year, all festivals are "movable" and cycle through the seasons, thus Muharram, the beginning of the new year, has nothing at all to do with the end of winter and the beginning of spring. And there are no official harvest festivals, likely because Islam was born in arid Arabian deserts, Mohammed himself beginning life as a young shepherd with a desert tribe. Instead, festivals have everything to do with fasting, alms giving, and pilgrimage/sacrifice, three of Islam's five Pillars. Traditional foods associated with the holidays of course conform to the Qur'an's dietary laws, which proscribe pork, blood, and alcohol and require meat to be slaughtered freshly and with a prayer ("In the name of God, God is most great").

- *Muharram*, the first month of the Islamic year, is tied to the Pillar of fasting, but of a voluntary nature—in honor of Mohammed joining the Jews in Medina on the tenth of the month in their fast for Passover. Foods are not part of the observance.

- *Ramadan*, the ninth month of the calendar, is the obligatory twenty-nine-day month of fasting. Muslims break each daylong fast at sunset, then sit down to dinner *(iftar)* after the sunset prayer is offered and eat one last meal *(suhur)* just before dawn.

- *Eid al-Fitr*, the Feast of Fast Breaking, celebrates the end of Ramadan for three days and focuses on sharing meals with the poor. Various soups are eaten as part of celebrations across the world, but usually not as a matter of tradition—except in Pakistan, where the feast is begun with *yakhni*, a rich broth. No, it's a time to feast on the best one can afford, from exquisite sweets to lavish entrees.

- *Eid al-Adha*, the Feast of Sacrifice, on the tenth day of the twelfth month, both commemorates the end of the pilgrimage season (when those who can afford it, return from their *hajj* to Mecca) and celebrates the great sacrifice of Abraham (who was ready to offer up his son Isaac for the love of God) by families sacrificing an animal, often a lamb, and distributing its meat to the poor.

RAMADAN

Ramadan was decreed by Mohammed after the archangel Gabriel revealed God's word to him: "O ye who believe! Fasting is prescribed to you as it was prescribed to those before you, that ye may learn self-restraint" (Qur'an 2:183). It is a monthlong movable fast, based on the lunar calendar, one of the five Pillars of Islam, a holy time when people must feel the pangs of hunger and thirst to understand how it feels to be needy and without food, a time when, purified of food, one should strive for spirituality and closeness to God.

At sunset in Casablanca, people avidly wait for the evening siren to sweep the city, announcing the end of the fast and signaling that it's okay to dip their ladles into a pot of very special soup — fragrant, bubbling *harira*, the spicy-lemony lamb and vegetable soup that traditionally breaks the fast in Morocco.

Why soup? For a lot of very good reasons.

First, it is recorded in the Traditions that Mohammed ended his own daily prescribed fast with soup — specifically with dates, water, and often a barley broth called *talbina* or *tirbiyali*.

Second, it's hugely refreshing and nutritious — a powerful shot of thirst-slaking liquid with hunger-relieving solid nutrition that prepares the body and soul for the prayers that follow, before the proper evening meal is taken.

Then, too, soup is no quick, solitary nibble out in the kitchen. It is necessarily formal, communal, and profound. You've got to put it in a bowl, sit down with it, and eat it with a spoon. Night after night, for some thirty straight days, family members — all hungry, thirsty, and excited — sit down together, lift their spoons together, smile at one another, and shovel in that first mouthful of sustaining soup.

Since those years in Morocco, *harira* has been one of my all-time favorite soups. One taste and I am unfailingly transported back to that home away from home — its brilliant souks and earthy smells; the haunting sunsets over Fez and bad-tempered camels in Marrakech; Massa'oud and Medea, Farida and Mustapha; back to spices and leather and carpets and Ramadan.

RUMI ON RAMADAN, PART 1

The month of fasting has come, the emperor's banner has arrived; withhold your hand from food, the spirit's table has arrived.

The soul has escaped from separation and bound nature's hands; the heart of error is defeated, the army of faith has arrived.

Fasting is our sacrifice, it is the life of our soul; let us sacrifice all our body, since the soul has arrived as guest.

—JALAL AL-DIN RUMI, *thirteenth-century Sufi poet*

ALGERIA

TANGY WHEAT AND HERB SOUP
JARY

Serves 6 to 8

THICK, LEMONY, AND bristling with green herbs and mint, this wheat soup traditionally breaks the fast in Algeria during the month of Ramadan and is a vegetarian delight year-round.

4 tablespoons olive oil
2 medium onions, chopped
8 garlic cloves, chopped
2 teaspoons paprika
¼ teaspoon cayenne pepper
½ cup tomato puree
8 cups (2 quarts) Vegetable Stock (page 23)
½ cup bulgur (cracked wheat)
1 cup chopped fresh parsley
½ cup chopped fresh cilantro
½ cup chopped fresh mint
1 cup cooked chickpeas (canned are fine, drained and rinsed)
Salt and pepper to taste

GARNISH
2 to 4 tablespoons lemon juice
Finely minced fresh parsley, cilantro, and mint
Lemon wedges (optional)

TO PREPARE
Prep the ingredients as directed in the recipe list, including the garnish.

To Cook

1. Heat the oil in a large soup pot over medium heat. Sauté the onions until tender, about 5 minutes, then stir in the garlic, paprika, and cayenne. Cook, stirring, for a minute or two, then stir in the tomato puree and stock.

2. Bring to a simmer over medium-high heat, then stir in the bulgur. Reduce the heat to low, cover, and simmer for 30 minutes, stirring occasionally, until the bulgur is tender.

3. Puree the soup, solids first, then add the parsley, cilantro, and mint, and puree until the soup is almost smooth. Return the soup to the pot. Stir in the chickpeas and heat through. Season with salt and pepper.

To Serve

Ladle the soup into bowls and stir a few spoonfuls of lemon juice into each one. Sprinkle each portion with the minced herbs and serve immediately. You may serve extra lemon wedges on the side.

Claire Denis's 1999 film *Beau Travail* studies anachronistic, self-absorbed French Legionnaire society in Djibouti. Christian officers enthusiastically set out a great feast, oblivious of three Muslim legionnaires sitting outside the inner circle during Ramadan, enduring their fast and expressionlessly watching their comrades chow down.

INDONESIA

SOUP PORRIDGE WITH VEGETABLE SPICE

BABUR ANYANG

Serves 6 to 8

"The man who is not hungry says the coconut has a hard shell."

LET THERE BE no doubt that this soup will still the most urgent hunger pangs after a day of fasting. It's filling and soothing — like a very thick potato soup — but at the same time bristling with flavor, color, and texture. Then — oh, those toppings! Imagine spooning fresh bean sprouts, chopped herbs, crispy fried shallots, coconut, and hot pepper sauce onto the surface of this thick soup. You're an artist; the soup, your creation.

FOR THE SOUP
1 cup long-grain rice (preferably jasmine)
½ pound boneless beef, cut into small pieces
10 cups (2½ quarts) cold water
1 teaspoon salt
1 cup peeled and diced carrots
2 cups peeled and diced potatoes
Salt and pepper to taste

FOR THE SPICE PASTE
3 shallots
2 garlic cloves
1 tablespoon peeled and chopped fresh ginger
6 raw almonds
2 hot chile peppers, or to taste, seeded
1 tablespoon soy sauce
2 tablespoons peanut oil
½ teaspoon turmeric
¼ cup hot water

ANYANG TOPPINGS

1 cup bean sprouts

¼ cup chopped fresh parsley

¼ cup chopped green onion

¼ cup sliced shallots fried in hot peanut oil until crispy and
*   drained on paper towels (goreng bawang)*

¼ cup dried unsweetened coconut

Hot chile peppers finely chopped with shallots, garlic, lemon
*   juice, peanut oil, and soy sauce (sambal kecap)*

TO PREPARE

1. Soak the rice overnight in plenty of water.
2. Prep the remaining ingredients as directed in the recipe list.
3. Prepare the spice paste.
4. Prepare the toppings.

SULTAN MAKMOUD AR-RASYID CREATES A RAMADAN SOUP TRADITION

Soup porridge—a traditional Indonesian breakfast dish—was adapted for Ramadan by the Great Mosque in Medan and passed on as a tradition by Sultan Makmoud Ar-Rasyid, the ninth sultan of Deli in Medan, northern Sumatra, in 1906. Today, hundreds of the faithful camp outside the Mosque in tents, waiting for the big drum to be struck, signaling the end of the fast and the beginning of prayers. The Mosque chefs, proud of the tradition, have not changed the menu for nearly a thousand years. In a large cauldron, they start the meat boiling in water early in the afternoon. After about an hour, they toss in the rice, to cook for 30 minutes into a thick porridge. Then they add vegetables and the spice paste. Before afternoon prayers, some seventy "take-out" bags are distributed, for those who want to go home and break the fast with their families, but these faithful take only the soup, without any toppings. Another 200 portions are served when the sunset drum is beaten—these with all the marvelous condiments.

Interesting to me is that this soup porridge is remarkably similar to *hareesa*, the ancient Arabic wheat or barley porridge that Mohammed called "the Lord of dishes." Rice is substituted for wheat, beef for mutton, but the preparation is the same and both are garnished with spicy toppings. To this day, *hareesa* (or variants like *al-harees, jary, haleem, haleeme gusht, and keshkek*) break the Ramadan fast throughout the Islamic world, and there's even an Indian variation that features chicken smothered in dal that's at least a second cousin twice removed.

To Cook

1. Place the meat in a large soup pot with the cold water and 1 teaspoon salt, and slowly bring to a boil over medium heat. Reduce the heat to low, cover the pot, and simmer for 1 hour.

2. Drain the rice, rinse it well, and scrape it into the soup pot. Let it simmer for 30 to 40 minutes, until the rice is just tender.

3. Stir in the spice paste, then the carrots and potatoes. Bring to a boil over high heat, then reduce the heat to low, partially cover the pot, and let simmer for another 30 minutes, or until the potatoes and carrots are tender.

4. Put the toppings into separate bowls.

To Serve

Taste the soup and season with salt and pepper. Whisk it hard for a minute or two, then ladle it into bowls and serve immediately, with the toppings on the side for your family and guests to help themselves.

LEBANON

CLASSIC RED LENTIL SOUP
SHORABIT ADAS
Serves 6 to 8

THIS CREAMY, DELICATE, but substantial soup is traditionally served in Syria, Lebanon, Saudi Arabia, and other Arab countries — simple but thirst-quenching and full of protein for those who have refrained from all food and liquid from sunrise to sunset.

> *8 cups (2 quarts) cold water*
> *2 pounds lamb with bones (shank is excellent)*
> *2 medium onions, finely chopped*
> *1½ cups red lentils, rinsed and picked through for stones*
> *Salt and pepper to taste*
> *Spices and finely cut vegetables that you have on hand (any*
>   *combination of tomato, garlic, carrot, celery, potato, rice,*
>   *chickpeas, chile peppers, leeks, cumin, paprika, saffron,*
>   *cardamom, turmeric, cinnamon, or mint)*
> *Lemon wedges and finely minced fresh cilantro or parsley, for*
>   *garnish*

To Prepare
Prep the ingredients as directed in the recipe list.

To Cook
1. Put the water, lamb, onions, lentils, salt, and pepper in a large soup pot and bring to a boil over medium heat, then reduce it to low, cover, and simmer for 2 hours. Stir from time to time so the lentils don't stick to the bottom of the pot.

2. Remove the lamb and add any vegetables, herbs, and spices you like. Cut the lamb into small pieces, discarding the bones, and stir them back into the soup. Season to taste.

RUMI ON RAMADAN, PART 2

Fortitude is as a sweet cloud, wisdom rains from it, because it was in such a month of fortitude that the Koran arrived.

. . . Wash your hands and your mouth, neither eat nor speak; seek that speech and that morsel which has come to the silent ones.

—JALAL AL-DIN RUMI,
thirteenth-century Sufi poet

TO SERVE

Ladle the soup into bowls. Squeeze the lemon juice directly into each portion, then sprinkle with parsley and/or cilantro. (You may also serve wedges of lemon on the side.)

RED LENTILS IN ANCIENT HISTORY

This little legume, packed with protein, goes all the way back to 8000 to 7000 B.C.E., in southwestern Asia on the fertile lands that now border the Indus River. From there it spread all over the Mideast and to northeast Africa, then to Europe and throughout Asia.

Most famously, it figures in the Biblical story of Isaac's boys, when Jacob extorts the birthright of his starving brother Esau in exchange for a mess of pottage, meaning red lentils. To this day the term *Esau* means "lentil" in many cuisines.

> And Esau said to Jacob, feed me, I pray thee, with that same
>   red pottage; for I am faint . . .
> And Jacob said, Sell me this day thy birthright.
> And Esau said, Behold, I am at the point to die: and what
>   profit shall this birthright do to me?
> And Jacob said, Swear to me this day; and he sware unto
>   him: and he sold his birthright unto Jacob.
> Then Jacob gave Esau bread and pottage of lentils.
>
> —GENESIS 25:30–34

MOROCCO

LEMONY LAMB AND CHICKPEA SOUP
HARIRA
Serves 6 to 8

HARIRA IS FULL of lamb, lentils, chickpeas, vegetables, herbs, and spices, all stirred up with lemon and egg strands. Pardon my prejudice, but this is quite possibly the best soup in the world. If your guests *really* like the tang of lemon, serve traditional little bowls of freshly squeezed lemon juice with demitasse spoons on the side. One thing is sure: this is a lovely way to break a day of fasting in the loving company of your family.

>   1 cup cooked chickpeas (canned are fine), drained and rinsed
>   2 tablespoons butter
>   1 pound boneless lamb, cut into small cubes
>   1 teaspoon turmeric
>   1 teaspoon black pepper
>   1 teaspoon ground cinnamon
>   ¼ teaspoon ground ginger
>   ¾ cup chopped celery with leaves
>   2 medium onions, chopped
>   ½ cup chopped fresh parsley and cilantro
>   2 pounds ripe tomatoes, peeled and chopped, or canned
>   tomatoes with juice
>   Salt to taste
>   8 cups (2 quarts) water
>   ¾ cup lentils, rinsed and picked through for stones
>   ¼ cup thin soup noodles
>   2 eggs, beaten with the juice of ½ lemon
>   Pepper to taste
>   Ground cinnamon and thick lemon wedges, for garnish

TO PREPARE

1. If you are using dried chickpeas, soak them overnight in plenty of water.

2. Prep the remaining ingredients as directed in the recipe list.

TO COOK

1. Put the butter, lamb, spices, celery, onions, and herbs in a large soup pot and stir over low heat for 5 minutes. Add the tomato pieces and continue cooking for 10 to 15 minutes. Salt lightly.

2. Pour in the water (or tomato juice and water to equal 10 cups liquid) and the lentils. If you soaked the chickpeas, drain them, rinse them, and add them at this point; if you are using canned, wait to add them. Bring the soup to a boil over medium-high heat, then reduce to low, partially cover, and simmer for 2 hours.

ARMIES TRAVEL TO MOROCCO ON THEIR CHICKPEAS

Chickpeas graced the tables of Egypt and the Levant from earliest antiquity, then spread across the Mediterranean. They were popularized in Rome as poor people's food, thus the Roman poet Horace, tired of power games in the Imperial City, tells Senator Maecenas in *Satire 1.6* that he's gone back to his humble roots, eating dinners of leeks and chickpeas and crackers.

Above all, chickpeas were the staple of Rome's conquering legions, traveling with them throughout the Roman Empire and taking root when climate permitted. That's how they ended up in Volubilis, the third-century B.C.E. capital of Rome's Mauritanian province in present-day Morocco. A thousand years later, in the eighth century, Arab armies brought them there again, conquering North Africa and Spain on the strength of their chickpea rations.

Where did chickpeas get their name? From the Romans—*Cicer arietinum*—who peered at the sculptured legume and saw *Aries*, a ram's head, there. Take a look. You will see the curling horns.

3. Add the canned chickpeas, if using, and the noodles and cook for 5 minutes. Then, with the soup cooking at a steady simmer, stir the lemony eggs into the stock with a long wooden spoon. Continue stirring slowly to create long egg strands and to thicken the soup. Season with salt and pepper.

To Serve

Ladle the soup into bowls and dust with cinnamon. If you have inveterate sourpusses in the crowd, serve with extra lemon wedges or pass around little bowls of extra lemon juice with tiny spoons.

SAUDI ARABIA (AND SYRIA)

BARLEY BROTH
TIRBIYALI
Serves 6 to 8

THIS SOUP PACKS an unexpected punch. Not only is it traditional for breaking the fast during Ramadan in both Saudi Arabia and Syria, but its very tradition stems from the fact that Mohammed himself ended his daily prescribed fast in Ramadan with dates, water, and often this kind of barley broth, called *talbina* or *tirbiyali*. It's smooth, tangy, thick, and rich—just the thing to slake one's thirst and settle the stomach for the prayers ahead.

> *8 cups (2 quarts) rich Beef Stock (page 26) or lamb broth*
> *½ cup barley flour*
> *2 tablespoons fresh lemon juice*
> *2 eggs*
> *Salt and pepper to taste*

TO COOK

1. In a large soup pot, bring the meat broth to warm over medium heat.

2. Mix the barley flour, lemon juice, and eggs, and whisk into the lukewarm meat broth. Turn up the heat to medium-high and whisk constantly, while bringing it to a boil, to thicken the soup.

3. Season with salt and pepper.

TO SERVE

When you hear the siren signaling the end of the fast, ladle the soup into bowls and serve immediately.

"BENEFICENCE"

*Who for the hungry spreads a
bounteous board,
Of worldly fame lays up a
gen'rous hoard.
In active goodness unremit-
ting prove,
And imitate below your God
above.*

—SAADI, *thirteenth-century
Persian poet*

TURKEY

DILLED YOGURT-RICE SOUP
YAYLA ÇORBASI
Serves 6 to 8

TALK ABOUT AN awfully interesting soup — tangy and buttery yogurt deeply flavored with dill and made substantial with rice. Traditional, and obviously perfect, to break the fast at Ramadan or to start the main meal after evening prayers, because it is stimulating, thirst quenching, and satisfying. It's good hot; it's also good cold. You can count on it to refresh and stimulate the spirits of your family and guests.

> 1 cup raw rice
> 3 cups water
> 4 tablespoons (¹/₂ stick) butter
> 3 cups plain whole-milk yogurt
> 1 cup Chicken Stock (page 24)
> 1 large garlic clove, pressed
> Salt to taste
> 1 tablespoon chopped fresh dill, or 1 teaspoon dried, crushed
>   between your palms
> Sprinklings of fresh dill, for garnish

TO PREPARE

1. Cook the rice in 2 cups of the water and set aside.
2. Prep the remaining ingredients as directed in the recipe list.

TO COOK

1. Melt the butter in a large soup pot over medium heat and cook until it is just golden brown.
2. Reduce the heat to a simmer and carefully whisk in the yogurt, beating until it has incorporated the butter. Pour in the stock and the remaining 1 cup of water, the garlic, and salt. Whisk con-

MILK IN ISLAM

Milk, yogurt, and all other dairy products are not only permitted foods under Islamic dietary laws, they are recommended. "And verily in cattle will you find an instructive sign. From what is within their bodies, between excretions and blood, we produce, for your drink, milk, pure and agreeable to those who drink it" (Qur'an 16:66).

THE FRAGILITY OF YOGURT

Treat yogurt carefully around heat and never bring it to a boil or it will curdle. Low-fat or nonfat yogurt is the worst, so you can be either completely safe by stabilizing the yogurt with a slurry of flour, cornstarch, or beaten eggs, or if you can handle the strength of it, use goat yogurt, which doesn't curdle when you boil it — it just gets stronger. Unexpectedly, Romanian playwright of the absurd Eugene Ionesco has a character in *The Bald Soprano* catalog the benefits of yogurt: "very good for the stomach, the lumbar regions, appendicitis and apotheosis."

stantly until it is perfectly smooth. Stir in the rice and dill and let simmer to heat through.

TO SERVE

You may serve the soup immediately, ladling it into bowls and topping with a little fresh dill, or you may let it cool to serve at room temperature or refrigerate to serve it cooler.

CHILDREN SING "THE FIVE PRINCIPLES"

All Muslims have to say
The shahaadah *once a day*
All Muslims have to say the salaah
And that they say five times a day
Muslims say salaah *five times a day*

All Muslims have to pay
The zakaat *once a year*
Zakaat is for the poor once a year
And that they pay once a year
Muslims pay zakaat *once a year*

All Muslims have to fast
Ramadhaan once a year
All Muslims have to fast Ramadhaan
And that they fast 30 days in a year
Muslims fast thirty days for Allah

All Muslims go to hajj
Once in a lifetime
All Muslims would go to the hajj
And that they'd do if that they can do
Muslims go to hajj *if they can do so*

—F. S. A. MAJEED

EID AL FITR

At last! The long month of fasting is over. Eid al Fitr is the feast that marks the end of Ramadan and begins three days of celebration and sharing food with the poor.

PAKISTAN

CHICKEN BROTH
YAKHNI
Serves 6 to 8

TRADITIONALLY THIS SOUP is made out of the bones and vegetable scraps that are left over from preparing the main courses of the feast. It can be made from chicken bones or beef bones, potato and carrot peelings, and the trimmings and skins of onions, garlic, and celery. It can also be made from whole chicken pieces, with the chicken stewed until it is just done, then removed and saved for frying as a main dish with rice. It's the seasonings that make the soup special, though, steeped as they are in the broth like some exotic tea. In the end, it's a steaming broth whose fragrance wafts you out of the kitchen and into the spice bazaar   earthy and aromatic, exciting your nose as well as your palate. Serve it in pretty cups or glasses and invite your guests to drink up.

> 10 cups (2½ quarts) rich Chicken Broth (page 24)
> 1 large onion, coarsely chopped
> 6 garlic cloves, coarsely chopped
> Vegetable kitchen scraps
> 3 cinnamon sticks, or ½ teaspoon ground cinnamon
> 2 teaspoons cumin seed, or ½ teaspoon ground cumin
> 1 teaspoon whole cloves
> 1 teaspoon cracked black peppercorns
> 1 teaspoon cardamom pods, or ¼ teaspoon ground cardamom
> Crumbled dried mint, for garnish

RIDDLE ME THIS

QUESTION: What is it that leaves its house only after breaking down the door?

ANSWER: A chicken

Yakhni as Medicine

In a 2001 Gallup poll conducted in the urban and rural areas of Pakistan's four provinces, 7 percent of all respondents said they relied exclusively on *yakhni* to cure them of the flu. The rest? Thirty-three percent said they took Joshanda, a popular herbal medicine; 13 percent went to the doctor; and 12 percent just let it run its course.

To Prepare

Prep the ingredients as directed in the recipe list.

To Cook

1. Put all the ingredients in a large soup pot and slowly bring the broth to a boil over medium heat. Reduce the heat to low, cover, and let the spices steep for 30 minutes.

2. Strain the soup through several layers of moistened cheesecloth or through coffee filters if you have used mostly ground spices. Don't press on the solids; you want the broth as clear as it is fragrant. Return to the pot for the final reheating.

To Serve

Bring the broth to a boil, ladle it into pretty cups or glasses, and garnish each portion with a very fine pinch of mint.

19
CHRISTMAS

ONCE UPON A time, some two thousand years ago, a baby was born in Bethlehem who was destined to change the history of the world and the hearts and souls of millions of people across the world.

I've always liked the fact that apostles Luke and Matthew, and everyone else since then, have made so much of this birth. They didn't have to. Most other religions don't dwell on births. And, certainly, other events in Christ's life—his crucifixion and resurrection—are far more central to Christian doctrine and mysteries, and far more revelatory.

But there you are: they and we *do* make much of it. We love it. We love the concept. We spiritually mill around his little manger, grinning from ear to ear, amazed at the miracle of babies in general and of Christ's life in particular. We don't much think about the passion to come. These days we don't much fast or tuck ourselves away in solitary prayer and reflection. Nope, it's a community thing. Imagine: a serious holiday, anchored in a profound mystery, that absolutely requires unbridled smiling, generosity, and "good will towards men."

So we go to church and festivals together. Sing carols together, even just walking down the street. Exchange Christmas cards. Give gifts to one another, often going overboard in the spirit of the Wise Men. We party, eat, and drink with abandon when we can, and we sit down to traditional meals on Christmas Eve or Christmas Day—and we eat soup.

BOLIVIA

CHRISTMAS CHICKEN SOUP
PICANA DE POLLO PARA NAVIDAD
Serves 6 to 8

TASTY AND FILLING, this traditional soup is just the thing to pump you up after the traditional fasting on Christmas Eve, and to fuel hours of dancing into the night to celebrate the birth of Jesus — and life and love in general.

> *1 bay leaf*
> *1 (3-pound) chicken, cut into 8 pieces*
> *1 cup shelled fresh or frozen green peas*
> *1 cup finely chopped onion*
> *1 cup peeled and minced ripe or canned tomatoes*
> *3 carrots, peeled and chopped*
> *2 celery stalks with leaves, minced*
> *½ cup raisins, plumped in hot water for 5 minutes, then drained*
> *1 hot chile pepper, seeded and chopped*
> *¼ cup finely minced fresh parsley*
> *6 to 8 whole potatoes, peeled (1 per person)*
> *12 to 16 (1-inch-thick) slices fresh corn on the cob (2 per person)*
> *2 cups water*
> *2 cups dry white wine*
> *1 teaspoon dried thyme, crumbled between your palms*
> *1 teaspoon cracked black peppercorns*
> *2 teaspoons salt*

TO PREPARE
    1. Prep the ingredients as directed in the recipe list.

TO COOK
    1. In a large, heavy Dutch oven, layer the ingredients, beginning with the bay leaf, then the chicken on the bottom, then the

peas, onion, tomatoes, carrots, celery, raisins, chile, and parsley. Put the whole potatoes on top, then the slices of corn. Mix the water, wine, herbs, and seasonings, and pour over the ingredients.

2. Place the Dutch oven on a burner and bring the soup to a boil over high heat. Reduce the heat to the lowest heat, seal the pot with aluminum foil, and top with the cover. Simmer for 2 to 3 hours.

To Serve

Pluck the corn and potatoes off the top of the casserole and reserve. Ladle a chicken piece into each soup bowl with a generous ladleful of vegetables and broth. Then top each portion with one whole potato and two pieces of corn. Finally, evenly distribute the remaining soup among the bowls. Discard the bay leaf. Serve immediately.

RIDDLE ME THIS

QUESTION: What am I?
You throw away the outside and cook the inside. Then you eat the outside and throw away the inside.

ANSWER: *Corn on the cob*

CHRISTMAS SOUP AT THE BEAUTY SHOP

There I was, fingers dipped in a manicure bowl in Falls Church, Virginia, when Christina, originally from Oruru, Bolivia, told me all about this rich and chunky soup. A petite and dramatically beautiful woman with sharp features and honey-colored eyes, a stylish dresser with brilliant clothes and small, rich jewelry, she came to the United States when she was twenty years old with her six-year-old daughter. A perfectionist, she loves to cook, especially breads and pastry, everything from scratch. Now married to a man originally from Mexico, she still likes to cook the traditional Bolivian soups, *chanko* best of all—a heavy meat and potato soup. "In Bolivia," she says, "we like meat the best. Meat and potatoes."

But she has a special spot in her heart for Bolivia's traditional Christmas soup, for sentimental reasons. "You go to midnight mass on Christmas Eve, then come home, open Champagne, hug all the little children and open presents, then sit down to a big bowl of *picana* to eat while you drink the Champagne. Then the best part—turning on the music and dancing." "You start dancing at 2 o'clock in the morning on Christmas?" I ask in disbelief. She shrugs. "Dancing, always, always—we love to dance. Dancing until dawn, so many times."

CHILE

CONGER EEL (OR FISH) CHOWDER
CALDILLO DE CONGRIO (PESCADO)
Serves 6 to 8

The cars ran fast. The trains, all crowded and with people standing over the platforms, looked like serpent's light rings. From all of the City's streets there came rivers of people. And because in Chile Christmas meets with the end of spring and the beginning of summer, there were streams of warm air under the exuberant green of the trees.

—LUIS ORREGO LUCO, *nineteenth-century Chilean novelist, from* CASA GRANDE

IMMORTALIZED BY PABLO Neruda in his *Elementos Odas'* "Oda al Caldillo de Congrio" (page 310), this classic fish soup of the Chilean coast is simple, tasty, and filling. Inspired by Neruda's poem, you will surely cook it up in a haze of pleasure and dine on it as if you were in heaven. If you want to add potatoes for heartiness, cook them, diced, in a little fish stock until tender and add with the fish.

4 tablespoons olive oil
8 garlic cloves, chopped
2 large onions, chopped
2 jalapeño peppers, seeded and finely chopped
8 ripe or canned tomatoes, peeled and chopped, juices reserved
2 pounds conger eel, skinned but still on the bone, or other saltwater fish fillets
1 pound raw large shrimp, peeled and deveined
4 cups Fish Stock (page 22)
3 medium potatoes, diced and cooked until tender in a little fish stock (optional)
2 cups heavy cream

Salt and pepper to taste
Minced fresh parsley or green onions, for garnish

TO PREPARE

Prep the ingredients as directed in the recipe list, to include cooking the potatoes if you plan to add them to the soup.

TO COOK

1. Heat the oil in a large soup pot over medium-high heat and stir in the garlic, onions, and jalapeño peppers. Sauté until soft.

2. Add the tomatoes and cook down over medium heat for about 8 minutes. Toss in the eel and shrimp, cover the pot, and steam the seafood for about 2 minutes. Remove the cover and let stew gently for 5 more minutes, until the eel is just done and a little shrunk.

3. Pour in the reserved tomato juices and the stock and bring to a boil. Stir in the potatoes, if using, and return to a simmer. Stir in the cream. Season with salt and pepper and allow the soup to return to a simmer.

TO SERVE

Fork the eel off the bone into the soup, discarding the bone. Ladle the soup into bowls and garnish with minced parsley or green onion.

CHILEAN CUISINE . . . AND CHRISTMAS

Chile's *cocina criolla chilena* combines food traditions of its native Mapuches, Pehuelches, and Tehuelches peoples with those especially of the Spanish who came to conquer and stay in the sixteenth century. Castilians, Andalusians, and Basque came to the New World bearing strange new gifts of food—rice, fruits, new meats, and dairy products—that transformed the food culture. With a coastline (2,650 miles long) ten times longer than its width, though, Chile has always been anchored in the bounty of the sea—abalone, eel, scallop, turbot, large barnacle, king crab, and salmon—and people love nothing better than to take these out of the sea and put them straight into their soup kettles for *caldillos*.

At Christmas time—the middle of the summer season—Catholics observe the *novena*, nine days of prayer and fasting before December 25. Children keep a watch for *Viejo Pascuero*, or Old Man Christmas, who climbs through the windows of this nation of small chimneys. Christmas Eve dinner is usually eaten after Midnight Mass, *Misa del Gallo*—the fish soup followed by turkey and salads washed down with local Chilean wine.

"ODE TO CONGER CHOWDER"

In the storm-tossed
Chilean
Sea
lives the rosy conger,
giant eel
of snowy flesh.
And in Chilean
stewpots,
along the coast,
was born the chowder,
thick and succulent,
a boon to man.
You bring the Conger, skinned,
to the kitchen
(its mottled skin slips off
like a glove,
leaving the
grape of the sea
exposed to the world),
naked,
the tender eel
glistens,
prepared
to serve our appetites.
Now
you take
garlic,
first, caress
that precious
ivory,
smell
its irate fragrance,
then
blend the minced garlic
with onion
and tomato
until the onion
is the color of gold.

Meanwhile
Steam
our regal
ocean prawns,
and when
they are
tender,
when the savor is
set in a sauce
combining the liquors
of the ocean
and the clear water
released from the light of the
    onion,
then
you add the eel
that it may be immersed in
    glory,
that it may steep in the oils
of the pot,
shrink and be saturated.
Now all that remains is to
drop a dollop of cream
into the concoction,
a heavy rose,
then slowly
deliver
the treasure to the flame,
until in the chowder
are warmed
the essences of Chile,
and to the table
come, newly wed
the savors
of land and sea,
that in this dish
you may know heaven.

—PABLO NERUDA, 1990

CZECH REPUBLIC

CHRISTMAS FISH SOUP
VÁNOCNÍ RYBÍ POLÉVKA
Serves 6 to 8

ALTHOUGH TRADITIONALLY SERVED in Czech homes at 6 o'clock in the evening on Christmas Eve, this heady soup is now just as traditionally doled out to the needy (and tourists!) by the mayor of Prague at Old Town Square on Christmas Eve afternoon. It's a marvelous concoction: delicate chunks of sweet carp made sweeter by gently sweating root vegetables in butter, and very pretty with the buttery croutons and parsley on top. It's the first course to a meal of fried carp and potato salad. And when did Christmas Eve carp become such an entrenched tradition? In the eighteenth century, when the poor couldn't afford the venison or turkey that was served on the tables of the rich, but could reliably catch this freshwater fish to put on the family table.

FOR THE BROTH
  8 cups (2 quarts) Fish Stock (page 22), ideally made of the head and tail pieces of a hen carp
  2 pounds freshwater fish fillets, preferably carp, but catfish is just fine
  1 medium onion, sliced

FOR THE SOUP
  4 tablespoons (1/2 stick) butter
  2 parsnips, peeled and diced
  1 turnip, peeled and diced
  2 carrots, peeled and diced
  1 medium onion, diced
  1 fish roe (if available)
  2 tablespoons flour
  Dash of grated nutmeg

CZECH CARP

Carp, the Christmas fish of choice, has been famous in Czech Bohemia since the sixteenth century. Now these sweet-faced fish are "grown" in special ponds and "harvested" right before Christmas. Their "farmers" catch them by draining the ponds and scooping them up to ship to Prague, live, in baskets. They're not tiny: most weigh in at 4 pounds.

CHRISTMAS CZECH: NAUGHTY OR NICE?

Czech Christmas begins on December 5 with *Mikulas,* when a Saint Nicholas figure, dressed in a long robe and holding a staff, walks around town in the company of a Devil and an Angel. Saint Nicholas visits children and gives them gifts, but first asks them if they've been good or not—with the Devil and Angel paying close attention to the answers. By the next week, houses are being cleaned top to bottom and decorated. Special cakes and sweets are made from "risen" dough. And by December 20, tubs of carp appear for sale on the streets, in preparation for Christmas Eve dinner.

In the old days, of course, the celebration was more austere, as Christmas Eve was a Catholic fast, but people also were more superstitious. Dinner then was usually pea or lentil soup followed by barley and mushrooms, only an even number of people would be seated around the table, and fortunes were told when dessert apples were handed out and cut in half. If you saw a cross, you could be sure of sickness and even death; if you saw a star, good luck and riches.

Salt and pepper to taste
Chopped fresh parsley and buttered croutons, for garnish

TO PREPARE

1. If you make the fish stock from carp, place the fish head and tail pieces in 8 cups of salted water in a large soup pot. Add the fillets and onion and bring to a boil over medium-high heat. Reduce the heat to low, cover partially, and simmer until the onion is soft, about 20 minutes. If you are starting with basic fish stock, bring the stock to a boil over medium-high heat, reduce to low, and simmer the onion and fillets in the stock for 20 minutes. Strain, setting aside the fish fillets and discarding other solids.

2. Prep the remaining ingredients as directed in the recipe list, including the parsley and croutons (cut cubes of bread, then toss them in a skillet with a tablespoon of butter until they are nicely toasted).

TO COOK

1. Melt 2 tablespoons of the butter in a large saucepan over medium-low heat, stir in the parsnips, turnip, carrots, onion, and fish roe (if using), and gently sweat, partially covered, until soft, about 10 minutes. Scrape the vegetables into the broth, washing out the pan with a cup of broth to get every scrap of flavor.

2. In that same saucepan, melt the remaining 2 tablespoons of butter, whisk in the flour, and stir until the roux has browned (see page 337 for roux shortcuts). Pour a cup of the simmering stock into the roux and whisk to thicken, then stir the roux into the soup.

3. Bring the soup to a boil over medium-high heat, then reduce the heat to low and simmer, partially covered, for 30 minutes.

4. Add the reserved fish, broken into bite-size pieces. Add the nutmeg and season with salt and pepper.

TO SERVE

Ladle the soup into bowls, top with the parsley and croutons, and carry it steaming to the table.

FINLAND

CHRISTMAS DRIED FRUIT SOUP
SEKAHEDELMÄKEITTO
Serves 6 to 8

THIS TRADITIONAL DISH of dessert soup is a lovely way to finish Christmas dinner. It's *so* pretty with all the different color fruits in a crystal broth, sweet and thick, mounded with whipped cream and sparkling with sugar. But the proof is in the tasting — creamy, sweet-tart, and crunching sugar in every mouthful. Hard to beat.

FATHER CHRISTMAS IN FINLAND

Joulupukki lives in a fell in eastern Lapland, far, far away in Korvatunturi (apparently the Finnish Broadcasting Company placed him there in 1927 and he's been headquartered there ever since). Some say the mountain has three ears, which is how Father Christmas knows what you'd like for Christmas. On Christmas Eve, he comes to your door with his helpers, he knocks, and he enters your house bellowing, "Are there any good children here?" When he gets the right answer, he is jolly and asks for a song. Then he hands his basket full of presents to his helpers to hand out to you and he leaves. After all, he's got a lot of other homes to visit before the night is done. Only after the presents have been handed out may you sit down at table to enjoy the Christmas Eve meal.

Joulupukki, which means "Yule Buck," actually started out life in pagan times as a ferocious, demanding goatlike creature. In December, when days were shortest, pagans in Finland would hold festivals to ward off evil spirits, certain members of the tribe putting on goatskins and horns and scaring all the children with their dancing and their demands. Only with the arrival of Christianity and over many, many years did this loathsome creature soften into a loving Father Christmas.

1 pound dried mixed fruits
8 cups (2 quarts) water
¾ cup sugar
2 cinnamon sticks
Dash of salt
3 tablespoons potato starch
4 tablespoons cold water
Whipped cream and sugar sprinkles, for garnish

To Prepare

1. The night before, rinse the mixed fruit in cold water and leave to soak overnight in the water.

2. Prep the remaining ingredients as directed in the recipe list, to include whipping the cream for the garnish.

To Cook

1. Strain the fruit, reserving the soaking liquid, then pour this liquid into a large soup pot and bring to a boil over medium-high heat. Stir in the sugar to dissolve, then add the soaked fruit, cinnamon sticks, and salt. Reduce the heat to low, cover, and simmer until done, 15 to 20 minutes. (At this point you can take the soup off the heat and hold until you are ready to serve dessert.)

To Serve

1. Reheat the soup over medium-high heat, then reduce the heat to medium-low and transfer the solid fruit pieces to a tureen or distribute evenly among small dessert soup bowls, removing and discarding the cinnamon sticks.

2. Dissolve the potato starch in the cold water and slowly pour into the bubbling fruit juice, stirring constantly. Then let the juice thicken to a boil without stirring.

3. Remove the soup from the heat immediately and pour over the fruit. Garnish with great dollops of whipped cream and sprinkle sugar on top.

GREECE

LEMON SOUP
SOUPA AVGOLEMONO
Serves 6 to 8

AN EXQUISITE AND provocative soup for lemon lovers. Nothing's prettier than a paper-thin lemon slice sprinkled with minced fresh parsley floating in an egg-thickened milky broth, but one spoonful of its savory tartness and your appetite is raging. Of cultural interest: this soup is very pure and simple compared to its Lebanese cousin (see page 275).

8 cups (2 quarts) Chicken Stock (page 24)
1 teaspoon grated lemon zest
2/3 cup raw long-grain rice
1/4 cup lemon juice
3 raw egg yolks
Salt and white pepper to taste
Paper-thin slices of lemon and minced fresh parsley, for garnish

TO PREPARE
Prep the ingredients as directed in the recipe list.

TO COOK
1. Bring the stock to a boil in a large soup pot over medium-high heat and add the lemon zest and rice, then reduce the heat to a simmer. Cook for 20 minutes.

2. Whisk the lemon juice and the egg yolks in a small bowl.

3. Stir the lemon sauce into the simmering soup until it clouds and thickens a bit. Season with salt and pepper.

TO SERVE
Ladle the soup into bowls and float a round of lemon on each portion, then top with parsley. Serve immediately.

ANCIENT GREEK SOUP BOASTINGS

But what I have accomplished in this [cooking] art of mine, no play-actor has ever accomplished at all. This art of mine was an empire of smoke. I was a sour-sauce maker at the Court of Seleucus. . . .

—DEMETRIUS in Areopagile, quoted in Athanaeus' DEIPNOSOPHISTAE, A.D. 200

JUDAS REFLECTS ON THE FIRST CHRISTMAS . . . ALREADY IN A.D. 32

Jostling in [Judas's] mind were the signs and prodigies which had surrounded this youth from his birth, and even before: how, when the marriage candidates were assembled, the staff of Joseph—among so many others—was the only one to blossom. Because of this the rabbi awarded him to Mary, exquisite Mary, who was consecrated to God. And then how a thunderbolt struck and paralyzed the bridegroom on his marriage day, before he could touch the bride. And how, later, it was said, the bride smelled a white lily and conceived a son in her womb. And how the night before his birth she dreamed that the heavens opened, angels descended, lined up like birds on the humble roof of her house, built nests and began to sing; and some guarded her threshold, some entered her room, lighted a fire and heated water to bathe the expected infant, and some boiled broth for the confined woman to drink. . . .

—NIKOS KAZANTZAKIS, *twentieth-century Greek novelist, from* THE LAST TEMPTATION OF CHRIST

HUNGARY

CHRISTMAS WINE SOUP
BORLEVES
Serves 6 to 8

A SUPERB CHRISTMAS Eve dinner tradition, this elegant soup is nicely dry, light, and lightly spiced, just heady and festive enough to lead off a holiday dinner and spark the appetite for good food and good conversation.

> 7 cups good-quality dry white wine (*Hungarian* Hárslevelü
>   *is traditional*)
> 1½ cups water
> 1 cup granulated sugar
> 8 whole cloves
> 2 small cinnamon sticks
> 8 egg yolks

TO PREPARE

Prep the ingredients as directed in the recipe list.

TO COOK

1. Pour 6 cups of the wine and the water into a large soup pot with the sugar, cloves, and cinnamon and bring to a boil over medium-high heat.

2. While the soup is heating, beat the egg yolks with the remaining 1 cup wine in a medium bowl until they are creamy. When the broth is at a boil, drizzle 1 cup of it, little by little, into the egg-yolk mixture, beating constantly so the egg yolks don't curdle.

3. Incorporate a second cup of the hot broth into the eggs, then beat the egg-yolk mixture into the remaining broth. Whisk constantly while reheating and let the soup thicken a bit.

HECTOR BERLIOZ AND THE *RÁKÓCZI MARCH*

George Lang, in his *Cuisine of Hungary*, repeats a favorite local story about this French composer visiting Somló and sampling the wines. In a state of intoxication, Berlioz heard a gypsy girl, also fired by the local wine, play an impassioned air on her violin. Inspired by it, he later developed it into his famous March. No surprise about all that inspiration. The 1802 vintage of Somló wine was said to be so potent that it could be lit with a match and burn like brandy.

TO SERVE

Strain the soup, then ladle it into small elegant bowls or cups. Serve immediately with your best silver spoons.

HUNGARIAN WINE

Hungarian wine is possibly the best kept secret in the world. Hungary's vines have been under cultivation in Hungary for thousands of years—Roman emperor Marcus Aurelius directed his legions to plant them throughout "Pannonia" in the third century A.D.—and Hungary's wine is planted just as firmly in the national character. Consider, for example, that its national anthem thanks God for Hungarian wines, from the poet Ferenc Kölcsey's "Hymn":

Ears of ripe corn wave to us
Across Cumanian meadows,
Tokay grapes extend to us
Honey dripping shadows

Likewise, an old Hungarian proverb says that a man needs only four things to be happy in this world: wine, wheat, peace, and a beautiful wife . . . with wine in first place.

IRELAND

BEEF CONSOMMÉ WITH IRISH WHISKEY

"DESSICATED" SOUP
Serves 6 to 8

IT'S A FINE soup, and that's the truth: sophisticated in its clarity, and teasing both the nose and the palate with its sweet-savory kick. This is a classic stimulus to the appetite and to conversation. Portions should be small and in exquisite cups, with small silver teaspoons on the side.

> *3 pounds cracked beef bones*
> *2 pounds soup bones with meat*
> *Any leftover meat or meat fat that could strengthen the broth*
> *2 carrots, scrubbed and trimmed*
> *2 medium onions, quartered*
> *Handful of fresh parsley, chopped*
> *2 parsnips, scrubbed and trimmed*
> *3 garlic cloves, crushed*
> *2 bay leaves*
> *2 teaspoons salt*
> *2 teaspoons black peppercorns*
> *12 cups (3 quarts) cold water*
> *Fine Irish whiskey, for garnish*

TO PREPARE

1. An hour before you start the soup, roast the bones and meat in a large roasting pan in a 450°F. oven for 1 hour. Put the bones in a large stockpot, then deglaze the roasting pan with a cup of water and pour that water into the stockpot.

2. Prep the remaining ingredients as directed in the recipe list.

TO COOK

1. Add the remaining ingredients, including the cold water, to

your stockpot full of roasted bones. Bring to a boil slowly over medium heat, then reduce the heat to low and simmer, covered, for 2 hours.

2. Remove the cover and simmer for at least another hour. You want to reduce the soup to about 6 to 8 cups of broth, strongly flavored. Strain and pour into a clean pot. If you are making the soup ahead, let it cool, uncovered, to room temperature and only then refrigerate, otherwise it will cloud. Do not remove the fat until you are ready to use the broth.

TO SERVE

Completely remove the fat from the soup's surface, heat the broth to a boil over high heat, then ladle it into small cups. Stir a teaspoon of Irish whiskey into each one just as you're taking them to the table. Really a lovely start to Christmas — or any — dinner.

PORTRAIT OF AN IRISH CHRISTMAS AS A YOUNG MAN

A great fire, banked high and red, flamed in the grate and under the ivy-twined branches of the chandelier the Christmas table was spread. They had come home a little late and still dinner was not ready: but it would be ready in a jiffy his mother had said, They were waiting for the door to open and for the servants to come in, holding the big dishes covered with their heavy metal covers.

. . . Mr. Dedalus dropped his coat-tails and went over to the sideboard. He brought forth a great stone jar of whisky from the locker and filled the decanter slowly, bending now and then to see how much he had poured in. Then replacing the jar in the locker he poured a little of the whisky into two glasses, added a little water and came back with them to the fireplace.

—A thimbleful, John, he said, just to whet your appetite.

—From the famous Christmas dinner opening of James Joyce's
PORTRAIT OF THE ARTIST AS A YOUNG MAN, 1916

ITALY

CHICKEN ESCAROLE SOUP
MINESTRA DI NATALE
Serves 6 to 8

THIS RECIPE IS traditional to the Isle of Capri, across the bay from Naples. It is such a snap, you can make it in twenty minutes if you have the ingredients on hand. Of course, it's nice and traditional to make the stock from scratch, too, especially for *i primi* of Christmas dinner. The soup is hugely bright green and fresh tasting, fragrant with lemon and Parmesan cheese, delicate in taste.

> *8 cups (2 quarts) Chicken Stock (page 24)*
> *1 teaspoon grated lemon peel*
> *2 bay leaves*
> *1 tablespoon grated onion*
> *1 whole chicken breast, boned, skined, and cut in half*
> *1 head escarole (about 1 pound), carefully washed and cut into*
> *   1-inch squares*
> *Salt and pepper to taste*
> *Freshly grated Parmesan cheese, for garnish*

TO PREPARE
Prep the ingredients as directed in the recipe list.

TO COOK
1. Bring the stock to a boil in a large soup pot over medium-high heat, then stir in the lemon peel, bay leaves, and grated onion. Add the chicken, reduce the heat to low, and let simmer for 10 minutes.

2. Remove the chicken and let cool for a minute before cutting into bite-size pieces. Bring the soup back to a boil, then stir in the escarole and chicken pieces. Reduce the heat and let simmer, covered, for another 5 minutes. Season with salt and pepper.

ESCAROLE? WHAT'S THAT?

Though a staple of Italian cuisine, escarole is confusing. Is it a chickory? An endive? Most grocery stores get it mixed up, too. In fact, it's *Cichorium endivia,* the broad-leaved or Batavian side of the family, closely related to chickory, but different. In its wild state—and it's abundantly wild in Italy—it is common to Europe, Africa, India, and Asia. But it has been cultivated for millennia by ancient Egyptians, Greeks, and Romans, which last particularly preferred it to the more bitter chickory and knew how to blanch its remaining bitterness away. To shop for escarole, look for a head that looks like a curly green lettuce—the leaves will be broad and slightly curled.

TO SERVE

Ladle the soup into bowls and sprinkle each portion with Parmesan cheese, which will melt beautifully into the soup. Serve immediately and pass extra Parmesan cheese, if you like.

CINEMATIC CHRISTMAS IN CAPRI

Director Michael Radford's exquisite 1994 film *Il Postino*, about Pablo Neruda's inspiring exile on Capri, celebrates Christmas 1953 with a village procession from Our Lady of Sorrows to the shore that ends by launching a candle-lit wooden effigy of the Madonna into the sea. It's a serious moment. The children of Cala di Sotto are dressed as angels, the postman Mario (Massimo Troisi) as the Holy Ghost, and his communist employer as a saint. Nothing is more important than good catches for the subsistence fishermen of the village, and the bright blue Madonna is pasted all over with lira to attract good fortune and lots of fish. On an island run by corrupt absentee politicians and with no running water, even soup is hard to come by when the water cisterns run dry, as they routinely do. Early in the film, Mario and his father dine on milk soup, eating it out of deep bowls with large spoons. Imagine the extravagance, then, of *Minestra di Natale*—so rich with chicken, broth, and cheese.

NEW ZEALAND

GREEN CLAM SOUP
TOHEROA CHOWDER
Serves 6 to 8

THIS SOUP IS a wonderfully delicate and sophisticated—and a lovely shade of green for Christmas dinner. It's especially nice served cold in December, in the heat of a New Zealand summer, but is equally delicious served hot. It features the delicate and distinctly green surf clam Toheroa *(Paphies ventricosa)*, native to northern and southern beaches in New Zealand and much beloved and fished by the Maori. Alas, they were overfished for the cannery industry and now are carefully protected by law. For fun, you can serve this soup cold and in punch cups: with that sprinkling of nutmeg, they'll look like Dr. Seussian green eggnog.

> *12 large fresh Toheroa clams or 24 ounces canned Toheroas (4*
> *   small cans) (See Note)*
> *2 large onions, chopped coarsely*
> *6 cups Fish Stock (page 22), clam juice, or a combination of the*
> *   two*
> *Salt and pepper to taste*
> *4 egg yolks*
> *1 cup heavy cream*
> *Grated nutmeg, for garnish*

NOTE: If you are forced by necessity to substitute other clams, as most of us are, you may puree a little cooked spinach with the onion and clams to get the distinctive green color.

TO PREPARE

1. Mince, then puree the clams with their liquid in a blender. Toss in the onions and blend until pureed.

2. Prep the remaining ingredients as directed in the recipe list.

HOW DID THESE LITTLE CRITTERS GET THEIR NAME?

There are a couple of different stories: (1) from a powerful historic Maori chief by the name of Tohe; (2) from a benign spirit who directed starving Maoris to them, urging them to dig deep, or *toheroa*, because these agile clams can burrow 10 inches down in the sand in no time at all.

A last note: Heard the one about the American who doted on these clams so much that he tried to buy New Zealand just so he'd have exclusive rights to the soup? There's that ugly American again.

MISS PIGGY ON CLAMS

"I simply cannot imagine why anyone would eat something slimy served in an ashtray."

TO COOK

1. Pour the clam mixture into a large soup pot, then add the stock and season to taste. Bring to a simmer over medium heat, stirring well, then reduce the heat to low and simmer gently, partially covered, for 30 to 40 minutes.

2. Beat the egg yolks, then whisk a cup of simmering soup into them. Pour the egg-yolk mixture into the saucepan, stirring constantly until the soup has thickened.

TO SERVE

Stir in the cream and reheat to a simmer. Season with salt and pepper. Ladle the soup into delicate cups, sprinkle with a little nutmeg, and serve immediately.

POLAND

MUSHROOM SOUP
ZUPA GRZYBOWA
Serves 6 to 8

THERE ARE many versions of this soup—some very chunky with vegetables and barley, some thickened with sour cream at the end, some with square pasta bits, called *lazankami.* I especially love this variation, though. It's light and pure, intensely mushroom, a simple but elegant beginning to your Christmas Eve meal.

> *1 cup dried bolete* (porcini) *mushrooms*
> *4 cups warm water*
> *6 cups Vegetable Stock (page 23)*
> *2 cups chopped fresh mushrooms*
> *Salt and pepper to taste*
> *½ cup square pasta* (lazankami; *optional)*
> *Minced fresh dill or parsley, for garnish*

TO PREPARE

1. Soak the dried mushrooms overnight in the warm water. Drain the soaked mushrooms, reserving the liquid.

2. Prep the remaining ingredients as directed in the recipe list.

TO COOK

Bring the combined stock and reserved mushroom liquid to a boil in a large soup pot over medium-high heat. Chop the rehydrated mushrooms into bite-size pieces and add them to the pot along with the fresh mushrooms, salt, and pepper. Reduce the heat to low, partially cover, and simmer the soup for 1 hour. If you wish to add the pasta, cook it in a separate pot while the soup is simmering and add it just as you're ready to serve the soup.

QUESTION: What am I?
With quite a big head, I
stand easily on one foot.
I'm quite small, but can
knock down the strongest.
I can't walk a single step,
but I arrive each day with
great speed—even so, any-
one who wants me has to
come find me. To those
who love me, I will sacrifice myself. If you've
guessed my riddle and
come looking for me, don't
mistake me for my bastard
brothers, for they'll kill
you.

ANSWER: A mushroom

TO SERVE

Ladle the soup into delicate bowls and garnish with minced dill or parsley.

POLISH *WIGILIA*

Zupa gryzbowa traditionally begins the Christmas celebration at *Wigilia* (Latin *vigiliare*, the last day of fasting), but rarely today includes all the superstitions of the olden days. This last meal of the fast never began until the first star appeared in the sky on Christmas Eve. Families were careful to seat an even number of people around the table, and that included a "traveler" who would otherwise be alone—an orphan, a stranger, a widow, or other single person. The meal began with the ritual breaking and sharing of *oplatek,* a wafer, then the soup was served—the start of an uneven total number of dishes, which were thought to bring good luck and a bountiful harvest in the next year.

PUERTO RICO

CHRISTMAS CHICKEN SOUP
ASOPAO DE POLLO
Serves 6 to 8

ASOPAO IS HUGELY festive and Christmassy, with its bright green peas and ribbons of pimiento. Thick with chicken and rice, the soup is both warming and filling. It's traditional to start from scratch with a whole chicken, but this variation is so easy to prepare — once you make or get hold of the traditional seasonings — and so elegant to serve and eat without all those chicken bones, that, well, I just can't resist.

2 pounds boneless chicken breasts, cut into bite-size pieces
2 to 4 teaspoons adobo *seasoning (page 46), or to taste*
3 tablespoons annatto oil (page 166)
4 ounces smoked ham, diced
½ cup recaíto (page 46)
1 cup finely chopped ripe or canned tomatoes
½ cup alcaparrado (page 166)
6 cups water or Chicken Stock (page 24)
1 cup raw short-grain rice
Salt and pepper to taste

GARNISH
½ cup cooked petite green peas
½ cup julienned pimiento

TO PREPARE
1. Season the chicken pieces with *adobo* and briefly marinate.
2. Prep the ingredients as directed in the recipe list, including making the annatto oil, the *recaíto*, and the *alcaparrado*.
3. Prepare the peas and pimiento for the garnish.

WHAT ON EARTH IS ANNATTO?

Basically a color. And a huge color, at that. The seeds of tropical New World tree *Bixa orellana* are sealed in a hard red pulp that is practically tasteless, but can it ever turn things orangey-red! Ever wonder about the origin of the term "redskin" for Native American? Likely it began with Spanish explorers who were amazed by the Carib tribes who dyed their skin with a liquid made from these seeds. In Mexico, Aztecs used to infuse their chocolate drinks with it, likely for its high fat content. The seeds are harvested from the brilliant red spiny pods of this evergreen tree and can be used whole to color cooking oil or lard, or ground into a paste. Because it has no real flavor, only a little aroma, it has been a popular additive in butter, margarines, cheeses, and lipstick.

To Cook

1. Heat the annatto oil in a large soup pot over medium heat, then sauté the ham pieces for a few minutes. Stir in the *recaíto*, tomatoes, and *alcaparrado,* cover, and cook for 5 minutes.

2. Toss in the chicken, stirring to cover the pieces completely with the sauce, and cook, covered, for 5 minutes.

3. Pour the water or stock into the soup pot and bring it to a boil over medium-high heat. Add the rice, season with salt and pepper, then reduce the heat to low. Cover and simmer for 30 minutes.

To Serve

Ladle the soup into festive bowls and garnish with the peas and ribbons of pimiento.

RUSSIA

CHRISTMAS BEET SOUP
BORSHCH
Serves 6 to 8

THIS FABULOUS, MANY layered, complex borshch is compliments of Sándor Fenyvesi, an air traffic controller in Budapest, Hungary, who was educated at a special school for navigating officers and air traffic controllers in Riga, Latvia, when he was eighteen years old and learned this soup while there. Start it the day before you are planning to serve it, then ladle up this Ukrainian-style soup, specially loved by Russians, for Christmas lunch or to start off a wonderful Christmas dinner.

FOR THE BROTH
8 cups (2 quarts) Beef Stock (page 26)
½ medium head green cabbage, finely shredded
3 medium potatoes, peeled and cut into 1-inch cubes

FOR THE RED VEGETABLES
1 teaspoon bacon fat
1 large red beet, peeled and shredded
1 tablespoon red wine vinegar
2 teaspoons sugar
2 ripe tomatoes, peeled and chopped, or 4 canned tomatoes, chopped

FOR THE MIREPOIX
2 tablespoons butter
2 medium onions, diced
1 carrot, peeled and diced
1 parsley root or ½ parsnip, peeled and diced

ANTON CHEKHOV WAXES RHAPSODIC

But even better is a borshch, prepared with beets, Ukrainian style, you know the way, my friend, with ham and country sausages. It should be served with sour cream, of course, and a sprinkling of fresh parsley and dill.

FOR THE SEASONING

6 peppercorns

3 allspice berries

3 bay leaves

1 whole head of garlic, cloves chopped

2 tablespoons bacon fat

½ cup chopped fresh parsley

Sour cream and minced fresh dill and parsley, for garnish

TO PREPARE

1. Start the soup at least one day ahead so it has time to ripen.

2. Prep the ingredients as directed in the recipe list.

3. Put the peppercorns and allspice berries into a small tea ball or cheesecloth bag for easy removal at the end.

RUSSIAN TESTIMONIALS

Scratch a Russian and inevitably he or she will bleed borshch—"Oh yes, my favorite soup!" Those on record include rulers (Catherine the Great, who ate it from handmade silver plates given to her by *Zaporozhye* Cossacks; Alexander II, who ate it from Saxony porcelain; Nicholas I, who actually preferred the simpler cabbage soup *shchii*, but declared for borshch to please his subjects; and Nikita Khrushchev); poets (Alexander Pushkin); novelists (Nikolai Gogol, and a vegetarian version for Leo Tolstoy); dancers (Rudolf Nureyev and Natalya Krassovska); musicians (Isaac Stern); singers (Maria Guleghina); artists (Boris Zaborov); and even tennis players (Marat Safin). It was Khrushchev who popularized the soup in the twentieth century, ordering Kremlin chefs to serve hot borshch with cold sour cream and inadvertently starting a trend in Western spy movies. Which reminds me: borshch was the hands-down fave of the infamous East German spymaster Marcus Wolf, who outspokenly adores all things Russian.

TO COOK

1. Bring the stock to a boil in a large soup pot over medium-high heat, add the cabbage and potatoes, reduce the heat to low, and simmer for 15 minutes.

2. In a saucepan, heat the bacon fat over medium heat, then add the beet, vinegar, sugar, and tomatoes, stirring, and cook gently over low heat, covered, for about 5 minutes. Set aside.

3. In another small pan, heat the butter over low heat, mix in the onions, carrot, and parsley root (or parsnip), cover, and sweat for 5 minutes.

4. When the cabbage and potatoes are finished simmering, add the beet mixture, the onion mixture, the peppercorns and allspice berries in a spice sack, and the bay leaves to the soup and cook another 10 minutes.

5. Stir in the garlic, bacon fat, and parsley. Then turn the heat down to a very low simmer, lightly cover the pot, and simmer very slowly for about 4½ hours. Turn off the heat, let cool, and allow to ripen for 12 to 18 hours.

TO SERVE

Reheat the soup gently, remove the bay leaves and spice sack, and ladle the soup into bowls. Top each portion with a teaspoonful of sour cream and a sprinkling of dill and parsley and serve with a slice of dark rye or pumpernickel bread.

SLOVAKIA

SOUR CABBAGE AND MUSHROOM SOUP

Kapustnica

Serves 6 to 8

TALK ABOUT A fitting soup for Christmas! It is tart to recall the bitterness of life before the birth of Jesus, with a little undertone of plum sweetness to come. It's a creamy apricot color from the paprika and sour cream, chunky, many textured and layered, and lush with meat — better, of course, to serve on Christmas Day if you're still observing the fast the night before. Some families serve it by ladling it into soup bowls over thick noodles. Your choice.

1 cup dried bolete (porcini) *mushrooms*
2 cups warm water
2 pounds smoked kielbasa sausage
8 cups (2 quarts) water
2 pounds sauerkraut with juice (Slovakians prefer homemade, of course: sliced cabbage pressed into a small keg with apples, beets, salt, pepper, and other spices, then left to ferment for a month)
2 medium onions, roughly chopped
6 pitted prunes, chopped
Zaprazka thickener: 2 tablespoons oil or lard, 2 tablespoons flour, 1 tablespoon paprika, 2 cups sour cream
Salt and pepper to taste
Minced fresh parsley, for garnish

TO PREPARE
1. Soak the mushrooms in the warm water for 20 minutes. Remove the mushrooms and strain the liquid.
2. Prep the remaining ingredients as directed in the recipe list.

TO COOK

1. Place the sausage and water in a large soup pot and bring to a boil over medium-high heat. Reduce the heat to low and simmer, covered, for 15 minutes.

2. Add the mushrooms with their liquid to the soup, cover, and cook for 15 minutes.

3. Add the sauerkraut with its juice, the onions, and prunes. Return to a boil over medium-high heat, then reduce the heat again to low and simmer, covered, for 1 hour.

4. When the sausage is about to burst its skin, remove the sausage and let it cool.

5. Prepare the *zaprazka:* heat the oil or lard in a skillet over medium heat, then whisk in the flour and cook for 1 to 2 minutes. Take off the heat, stir in the paprika, continuing to stir for a minute, then whisk in the sour cream until it is smooth.

6. Whisk in as much as a cup of the soup broth into the *zaprazka,* then stir the *zaprazka* into the soup and let it thicken, uncovered, over a very low simmer for 5 to 10 minutes.

7. Slice the sausage into bite-size pieces. (If you wish to serve the soup over thick noodles, begin boiling the noodles at this point.)

8. Add the sausage slices to the pot, and season the soup with salt and pepper.

TO SERVE

Ladle the soup into large bowls (over thick noodles or not), garnish each portion with minced parsley, and serve with sliced bread.

SLOVAKIAN CHRISTMAS

In Catholic Slovakia, as in Poland, families begin their joyful celebration at *Stedry Vecer* or *Vilija,* the Bountiful Christmas Eve supper, when the first star appears in the sky on Christmas Eve. The traditional family celebration is deeply ritualized and very beautiful. First, the father and mother carry a lighted candle, representing Christ, to the table. Mom sprinkles holy water on the table. Dad serves a special wafer *oplatka* to everyone, mom first, and kisses and hugs are exchanged in a ritual of reconciliation. Dad then makes a sign of the cross on everyone's forehead with honey, to keep thoughts of Christ's sweetness uppermost. Why the *oplatka*? Because in the old days people couldn't get through the high snows to attend the Christmas church service. Understanding priests blessed the wafers well beforehand and gave them to families so they would be reminded of the Eucharist during the celebration. Following the *oplatka* and the honeyed baptism, the feasting would begin.

THE BAD NEWS ABOUT
AJOBLANCO

According to recipe contrib-
utor José Luis Vivas,
Ajoblanco is a dieter's worst
nightmare. Thanks to the
high energy contents of the
almonds and bread, it is a
caloric bomb. In fact, he
says, these soups were usually consumed by country
laborers in Andalusia during
the harvest months as a mid-
morning snack. They would
have breakfast very early
(5 A.M.), then about 11 o'clock
would stop to prepare the
soup (or have someone bring
it from the house) and eat it
to brace themselves for temperatures above 95°F. from
noon onward. Of course
they'd stop about 2 P.M. and
have a light lunch and a
siesta, unless they were picking cotton and a storm was
on the way.

SPAIN

ICED WHITE ALMOND SOUP
ANDALUSIAN *Ajoblanco*
Serves 6 to 8

THIS COLD SOUP is wonderful—refreshing and very "drinkable"
in texture, with unexpected richness, depth of flavor, and true sa-
voriness. It's hard to believe it's so bad for you. Today in Andalusia
it has its own special fiesta day on September 7, and it is traditional
to take a bowl on Christmas Day. In Málaga, it is customary to
serve *Ajoblanco* with peeled and seeded grapes or with apple slices.
Melon, small shrimps, or sliced, toasted almonds also go very well
with this soup.

> *½ pound crusty white bread, with the crusts cut off*
> *1 cup raw (not toasted) peeled almonds (to peel, dip them for a*
> *   few seconds in boiling water, then pop the skins off with a*
> *   squeeze of your fingers)*
> *2 garlic cloves*
> *¼ teaspoon salt*
> *1 generous cup olive oil*
> *Vinegar, preferably red wine or sherry vinegar*
> *7 cups cold water*
> *Fruit, shrimp, or toasted almonds, for garnish*

TO PREPARE

1. An hour ahead, soak the bread in plenty of water, pouring
off what it doesn't absorb.

2. With a powerful blender, grind the almonds, garlic, and a
little salt as fine as you can (the finer the almonds are ground, the
creamier the soup will be).

3. Add the soaked bread to the blender and process until you
get a white homogeneous paste. Still blending, add the oil in a
thread, as you would for a mayonnaise, and then the vinegar (for
the quantity, follow your taste, but just a teaspoon or so is

sufficient — otherwise you will mask the flavor) and the cold water. You must add the oil and water slowly: you want a smooth emulsion, not a curd! That's it, you're done. Just refrigerate.

TO SERVE

Serve the soup very cold. When you're ready to take it to the table, mix it one last time, then pour it into cups and garnish each portion with your choice of fruit, such as sliced and seeded grapes, apple slices, or melon balls, or small shrimps or slivered toasted almonds.

SANCHO PANZA ON SOUP AND LIFE

Ajoblanco was, of course, the original *gazpacho*, long before the days when tomatoes and peppers made it to Spain from the New World. The original gazpacho/*ajoblanco* was introduced into Andalusian Spain by the Moors sometime after A.D. 800—made with bread, garlic, olive oil, vinegar, salt, and water, all packed into unglazed earthenware pots to keep it cool. On a good day, it might include almonds and almond milk. Anyway, it was white, it was thick, it filled the belly and cooled the brow of laborers during the heat of the day. It was this "gazpacho" that Miguel Cervantes's beloved Sancho Panza knew and loved, saying in *Don Quixote*, at the end of his days as governor, "A Spade does better in my Hand than a Governor's Truncheon; and I had rather fill my Belly with Gazpacho, than lie at the Mercy of a Coxcombly Physick-monger that starves me to Death."

CAJUN NIGHT BEFORE
CHRISTMAS

Twas de night before
*   Christmas*
An' all t'ru de house
Dey don't a t'ing pass
Not even a mouse.
De chirren been nezzle
Good snug on de flo'
An' Mama pass de pepper
T'ru de crack on de do'.
Den Mama in de fireplace
Done roas' up de ham
Stir up de gumbo
An' make bake de yam

—TROSCLAIR

UNITED STATES

NEW ORLEANS SEAFOOD GUMBO
CREOLE/CAJUN GUMBO
Serves 6 to 8

ALTHOUGH GUMBO TRADITIONS in New Orleans are most strongly and longly associated with Lent's *gumbo z'herbes* (see page 240), rich seafood gumbo is extraordinarily popular at Christmas along the Cajun Louisiana coast. It's said that the original French settlers from Acadia—they were driven out of that Canadian colony by British troops in the 1750s during the so-called French and Indian War—were adapting their native French fish stews to local ingredients that often had come by way of Africa. The word *gumbo*? Bantu for "okra."

This recipe is literally groaning with seafood—a richness appropriate for such a high holiday. It's a heavenly combination of textures and flavors. And it's a beautiful dish, earthy colored like the bayous but punctuated with the traditional red and green colors of Christmas.

FOR THE BROTH
    ½ cup peanut oil
    ½ cup all-purpose flour
    1 large onion, chopped
    1 large red bell pepper, seeded and chopped
    4 celery stalks with leaves, chopped
    4 garlic cloves, chopped
    8 cups (2 quarts) Fish Stock, heated (page 22)
    1 teaspoon dried thyme, rubbed between your palms
    Salt and pepper to taste
    ¼ teaspoon cayenne pepper, or more to taste

FOR THE RICE
    4 cups water
    2 cups raw white rice

FOR THE SOUP

1 pound fresh or frozen okra, trimmed and sliced (about 5 cups)

2 pounds raw shrimp, peeled and deveined

1 pound lump crabmeat, with any shells picked out

2 pints (4 cups) shucked oysters, with their liquor

Minced fresh parsley, for garnish

TO PREPARE

Prep the ingredients as directed in the recipe list.

TO COOK

1. Heat the oil over medium-high heat in a heavy pot (ideally iron), then sprinkle the flour on it, whisking like crazy as it cooks to a dark milk-chocolate color.

2. As the roux approaches this color, reduce the heat to medium and start adding the vegetables, stirring hard with a wooden spoon. Let cook, stirring, for about 10 minutes, until the vegetables are tender, then pour in the stock, season with the thyme, salt, pepper, and cayenne, and stir until the roux is dissolved. Reduce the heat to low, cover, and let simmer for 1 hour.

3. In a separate saucepan, bring the water to a boil over high heat, stir in the rice, reduce the heat to low, and simmer, covered, for 20 minutes. Remove from the heat and set the rice aside. It will hold until the final assembly.

4. Stir the okra into the broth. Re-cover the pot and let cook for about 10 minutes. Then add the shrimp and cook for a few minutes, until they turn pink, then toss in the crab by handfuls. When the crab is warmed through, pour in the oysters with their liquor and cook just until their edges curl. Remove from the heat immediately.

TO SERVE

Spoon ½ cup of the cooked rice into each bowl and ladle the gumbo on top. Garnish each portion with a little parsley. Serve immediately.

MAKING THE ROUX

Cooks tear their hair to get the Cajun version right without burning it. In older, slower days, you might not mind standing and stirring the flour in hot fat over a low heat for some 30 minutes, greatly reducing the chances of burning it. In today's world, that's a little *too* slow. One technique is to add a smidge of sugar with the flour—its caramelizing action darkens and sweetens the mix. And if you're a lover of gumbo and make lots of roux, chef Art Meyer suggests baking just the flour in an iron skillet in a 350°F. oven until it's evenly brown, then storing it, ready-made, in a jar for future use. At that point, you just toss the dark flour into hot fat and go to the next step. The flour is already cooked *au point*.

20

KWANZAA

ONCE UPON A TIME, Professor Maulana Karenga, then chairman of California State University's black studies program, had a dream. It was 1966 and Karenga wanted to find a way to unite African Americans in a powerful way—to connect this diverse group with a common identity, common values, and common culture.

This was not an easy thing to do. African Americans came to America as slaves and, later, by choice—from Africa, from the Caribbean, from places all over the globe. Very specific and diverse cultural traditions were brought into the mix or lost altogether. New traditions have been created, totally unconnected to the past, mostly on regional levels. Old tribal religions have been largely replaced with Christianity and Islam. How on earth to reconcile all the differences? How to find a common culture that all would embrace?

Dr. Karenga reached into the heart of humanity to bring forth Kwanzaa, all the way back to the earliest rhythms of civilization, when all peoples set their clocks to nature's cycles and the harvest.

Kwanzaa means "first fruits of the harvest" in the East African dialect Kiswahili. There is no festival by that name in any African country, but the features of Kwanzaa would be very familiar to people who celebrate harvest festivals across that continent.

Celebrated from December 26 through January 1, the seven days of Kwanzaa are a time of feasting and gift giving, but they are

most especially a time to reflect on family and community values —
seven of them, one for each day of celebration.

On the first day of Kwanzaa, families put the *kinara*, or seven-
branched wooden candleholder, in an honored spot. Seven
candles — *mishumaa saba* — are placed in it: three red candles on the
left, in memory of the blood shed by so many over so many years;
three green candles on the right, in hopes for the future; and one
black candle in the center, symbolizing unity and pride. Each night,
families gather to light the candles and discuss the meaning of the
day, and then begins a feast of traditional dishes, often beginning
with an African soup.

THE SEVEN PRINCIPLES OF KWANZAA

1. *Umoja,* or unity
2. *Kujichagulia,* or self deter-
   mination
3. *Ujima,* or working together
   for the happiness of all
4. *Ujamaa,* or working together for the prosperity
   of all
5. *Nia,* or working together
   for the glory of all
6. *Kuumba,* or creating
   beauty in the world
7. *Imani,* or faith in the future
   of our community

HOSPITALITY

Okonkwo's first wife soon finished her cooking and set before their guests a big meal of pounded yams and bitter-leaf soup. Okonkwo's son, Nwoye, brought in a pot of sweet wine tapped from the raffia palm.

—CHINUA ACHEBE, twentieth-century Nigerian novelist, in THINGS FALL APART, 1958

CAMEROON

BITTER-LEAF SOUP
NDOLÉ
Serves 6 to 8

THIS NATIONAL DISH of Cameroon originated with the Douala people along the Atlantic coast and spread throughout the region. It started out as a simple soup with the bitter leaf known as *ndolé (Vernonia amygdalina)*, which was used medicinally both to stimulate the digestive system and to reduce fevers. Then, as a taste for the leaf developed, it became the soup of choice for marriages and baptisms, but a soup also stuffed with the most precious meats and fish in honor of the occasion. The simple recipe below, popular for everyday meals, is common to Nigeria and Cameroon, and still serves to stimulate the appetite, though it substitutes other greens for the nearly unobtainable *ndolé* leaf. It's a rich and pretty soup with its generous garnish of crushed peanuts contrasting with the dark green leaf and bright red tomato bits.

> *4 tablespoons vegetable oil (palm oil, if you can get it)*
> *2 medium onions, minced*
> *1 to 2 hot chile peppers, seeded and minced*
> *2 cups ripe or canned peeled and chopped tomatoes, reserving the juice*
> *3 pounds fresh greens (any combination of kale, collards, spinach, mustard, and beet greens), washed, tough stems removed, then stacked, thinly sliced, and finely minced*
> *8 cups (2 quarts) Chicken Stock (page 24)*
> *¼ cup raw white rice*
> *Salt and black pepper to taste*
> *Finely crushed roasted peanuts, for garnish*

TO PREPARE
Prep the ingredients as directed in the recipe list, including the garnish.

To Cook

1. Heat the oil in a large soup pot over medium-low heat, add the onions, and cook, stirring, until the onions are transparent, about 5 minutes. Add the chiles and tomatoes, and continue cooking for 5 to 10 minutes, until the tomatoes are thick and concentrated. Stir in the greens, turn the heat to medium-high, then cover and cook until the greens are limp, about 5 minutes.

2. Pour in the stock and any reserved tomato juice, bring to a boil over medium-high heat, and add the rice. Reduce the heat to low, cover, and simmer until the rice is very tender, about 45 minutes. Season with salt and pepper.

To Serve

Ladle the soup into festive bowls and sprinkle with roasted peanuts.

"Self-Reliance"

I love the man whose lofty mind
  On God and its own strength relies;
Who seeks the welfare of his kind,
  And dare be honest though he dies;
Who cares not for the world's applause,
  But, to his own fixed purpose true,
The path which God and nature's laws
  Point out, doth earnestly pursue. . . .

—JAMES M. WHITFIELD,
African-American poet, 1853

GHANA

PEANUT SOUP

NKATE NKWAN

Serves 6 to 8

THIS IS REALLY a pretty first-course soup—juicy and intense, earthy and piquant. It's based on a traditional soup from Ghana but Americanized by adding so many New World ingredients. Also, crushed peanuts are far more traditional than processed peanut butter, but it's precisely the peanut butter that gives the sensationally rich texture, which, after all, speaks on a culinary level to the principles of Kwanzaa.

2 tablespoons oil
2 medium onions, chopped into big pieces
1 large green bell pepper, seeded and chopped into big pieces
1 large red bell pepper, seeded and chopped into big pieces
4 garlic cloves, minced
2 pounds ripe or canned tomatoes, cut into quarters, juice reserved
10 cups (2½ quarts) Chicken Stock (page 24)
½ teaspoon coarsely ground black pepper
½ teaspoon red pepper flakes
½ cup raw brown rice
⅔ cup creamy peanut butter
Crushed peanuts, for garnish

TO PREPARE
Prep the ingredients as directed in the recipe list.

TO COOK
1. In a large soup pot, heat the oil over medium-high heat, then sauté the onions, peppers, and garlic until they begin to brown. Reduce the heat to medium, add the tomatoes, and cook for 5 to 10

minutes, stirring from time to time, until they cook down.

2. Pour in the reserved tomato juice, the stock, black pepper, and red pepper flakes. Bring to a boil over medium-high heat, add the rice, then reduce the heat to low. Simmer, partially covered, for 45 minutes.

TO SERVE

Stir in the peanut butter until it melts and the broth is smooth. Reheat to a simmer, then ladle into festive bowls and sprinkle with crushed peanuts.

"SONGS FOR THE PEOPLE"

Let me make the songs for the people,
Songs for the old and young;
Songs to stir like a battle-cry
Wherever they are sung.

Not for the clashing of sabers,
For carnage nor for strife;
But songs to thrill the hearts of men
With more abundant life.

Let me make the songs for the weary,
Aid life's fever and fret,
Till hearts shall relax their tension,
And careworn brows forget.

Let me sing for little children,
Before their footsteps stray,
Sweet anthems of love and duty,
To float o'er life's highway.

I would sing for the poor and aged,
When shadows dim their sight;
Of the bright and restful mansions,
Where there shall be no night.

Our world, so worn and weary,
Needs music, pure and strong,
To hush the jangle and discords
Of sorrow, pain, and wrong.

Music to soothe all its sorrow,
Till war and crime shall cease;
And the hearts of men grown tender
Girdle the world with peace.

—FRANCES E. W. HARPER, *African-American poet, 1895*

NIGERIA

OKRA SOUP
OBE ILE
Serves 6 to 8

THIS BEAUTIFUL, SPICY soup features big chunks of red, white, and green in a rich, piquant broth. It is lighter than the traditional thick Nigerian soup, and the earthiness of its okra and the fire of its hot peppers stimulate the appetite—and the discussion—for the rest of the Kwanzaa feast to come.

> *4 tablespoons vegetable oil, ideally palm oil*
> *3 medium onions, chopped*
> *4 small hot green chile peppers, seeded and chopped, or 1 habanero, or 1/2 teaspoon dried hot red pepper*
> *4 cups fresh or canned tomatoes, peeled and chopped, juice reserved*
> *10 cups (2 1/2 quarts) Vegetable or Chicken Stock (pages 23 and 24)*
> *1/4 cup raw white rice*
> *5 to 6 cups okra fingers, cut into bite-size triangles, or 1 pound frozen okra*
> *Salt and pepper to taste*

TO PREPARE

Prep the ingredients as directed in the recipe list.

TO COOK

1. Heat the oil over medium heat in a large soup pot, then toss in the onion chunks and sauté until yellow. Add the chile peppers and stir for a minute. Then add the tomatoes and cook them down over medium heat for 5 to 10 minutes.

2. Pour in the stock and any reserved tomato juice, bring to a boil over high heat, sprinkle in the rice, then reduce the heat to low, cover, and cook for 15 minutes.

3. Raise the heat to medium-low, add the okra, and cook for another 15 minutes or so, until the okra is done. Season with salt and pepper.

TO SERVE

Ladle the soup into pretty bowls, and let the feast begin.

TANZANIA

CREAMY COCONUT-BANANA SOUP
M'TORI SUPU
Serves 6 to 8

THIS EAST AFRICAN soup is a rich and filling meal, traditionally made from scratch with stewing beef for the broth, then removing the meat, pureeing the thick soup, and serving the beef on the side. For the purposes of Kwanzaa, though, the soup is more easily made and more attractively served as a first course by forgoing the stock-making steps and serving the soup as a mélange of fruit and vegetable chunks in an earthy, coconutty, and piquant broth, festively topped with crisp plantain chips. It's really scrumptious — such an interesting combination of flavors and textures, sweetness and starch.

3 tablespoons butter
1 small onion, diced
8 cups (2 quarts) rich Beef Stock (page 26)
¼ teaspoon red pepper flakes
½ teaspoon white pepper
3 cups peeled and diced potatoes
2 cups peeled and diced plantains
2 cups peeled and diced bananas
Salt to taste
1 cup coconut milk
Fried plantain chips (ready-made or homemade), for garnish

TO PREPARE

1. Prep the ingredients as directed in the recipe list.

2. If making the fried plantain chips for the garnish, fry thinly cut plantain circles in hot oil until crispy, then drain them completely on paper towels.

To Cook

1. Melt 1 tablespoon of the butter in a large soup pot over low heat, stir in the onion, cover, and sweat for 5 to 10 minutes, until transparent. Pour in the stock, add the red pepper flakes and white pepper, and bring to a boil over high heat.

2. Add the potatoes, plantains, and banana; reduce the heat to low, cover, and let simmer for 30 to 40 minutes, until all the ingredients are very tender. Season with salt.

To Serve

Stir in the coconut milk, then for enrichment, stir in the remaining 2 tablespoons of butter. Allow the soup to reheat at a low temperature (otherwise the coconut flavor will degrade), then ladle it into bowls, garnish with fried plantain chips, and serve immediately.

"Mother to Son"

Well, son, I'll tell you:
Life for me ain't been no
   crystal stair.
It's had tacks in it,
And splinters,
And boards torn up,
And places with no carpet on
   the floor—
Bare,
But all the time
I'se been a-climbin' on,
And reachin' landin's,
And turnin' corners,
And sometimes goin' in the
   dark
Where there ain't been no
   light.
So boy, don't you turn back,
Don't you set down on the
   steps
'Cause you finds it's kinder
   hard.
Don't you fall now—
For I'se still goin', honey,
I'se still climbin',
And life for me ain't been no
   crystal stair.

—Langston Hughes,
African-American poet, 1922

NDEBELE EXPRESSIONS

"If you can walk you can dance. If you can talk you can sing."

"Between true friends even water drunk together is sweet enough."

ZIMBABWE

SPICY VEGETABLE AND PEANUT STEW
HUKU NE DOVI
Serves 6 to 8

THIS CEREMONIAL DISH for special occasions in Zimbabwe villages is a "must-eat" for anyone who loves good food. It's rich and sweet, thick and succulent—not to mention piquant—with an unusual and beautiful combination of vegetables. Chicken is expensive in Zimbabwe and brought out only for feasts, which is to say that vegetarians would not be at all violating the authenticity of the dish by cutting out the chicken and substituting vegetable stock for the chicken stock. But by all means serve this with *sadza*, or fried cornmeal mush. It's traditional to eat the stew with delicate fingertips right out of the pot (or from a big serving dish), a truly wonderful communal meal to serve on one of the nights of Kwanzaa.

> 2 tablespoons olive oil
> 2 medium onions, chopped
> 4 cups (1 quart) Vegetable or Chicken Stock (pages 23 and 24)
> 1 cup creamy peanut butter (more traditionally, finely crushed peanuts)
> 2 cups fresh or canned peeled and chopped tomatoes, juice reserved
> Salt and pepper to taste
> 1/2 teaspoon red pepper flakes, or less—this is pretty spicy
> 2 cups finely chopped cabbage
> 3 sweet potatoes, peeled and chopped
> 4 carrots, peeled and chopped
> 2 turnips, peeled and chopped
> 12 whole okra, fresh or frozen, with stems trimmed
> 2 to 3 cups chopped cooked chicken, in big chunks

To Prepare

Prep the ingredients as directed in the recipe list.

To Cook

1. Heat the oil in a large soup pot over medium-high heat and fry the onions until soft, about 3 minutes. Reduce the heat to medium and stir in 1 cup of the stock. Whisk in the peanut butter, then stir in the rest of the stock, the tomatoes with their juice, salt and pepper, and red pepper flakes. Bring to a boil over high heat, then reduce the heat to low, cover, and let simmer for 30 minutes.

2. Stir in the cabbage, sweet potatoes, carrots, and turnips; bring back to a high boil, then reduce the heat to low again, cover, and cook for 20 more minutes.

3. Stir in the okra and chicken, cover, and let stew over low heat for 30 minutes.

To Serve

Pour the stew into a large serving dish, gather your guests around a table, and invite them to dig in with their fingers. Or, ladle the soup out into individual soup bowls and serve with corn bread or the traditional fried cornmeal mush.

"NIKKI-ROSA"

childhood remembrances are always a drag
if you're Black
you always remember things like living in Woodlawn
with no inside toilet
and if you become famous or something
they never talk about how happy you were to have your mother
all to yourself and
how good the water felt when you got your bath from one of
  those
big tubs that folk in Chicago barbecue in
and somehow when you talk about home
it never gets across how much you
understood their feelings
as the whole family attended meetings about Hollydale
and even though you remember
your biographers never understand
your father's pain as he sells his stock
and another dream goes
and though you're poor it isn't poverty that
concerns you
and though they fought a lot
it isn't your father's drinking that makes any difference
but only that everybody is together and you
and your sister have happy birthdays and very good christ-
  masses
and I really hope no white person ever has cause to write about
  me
because they never understand Black love is Black wealth and
  they'll
probably talk about my hard childhood and never understand
  that
all the while I was quite happy

—NIKKI GIOVANNI, *African-American poet,*
from BLACK FEELING, BLACK TALK, BLACK JUDGMENT, 1968

Pelican Publishing Company, Inc.: Excerpt from *Cajun Night Before Christmas* by Trosclair, illustrated by James Rice. Copyright © 1973, 2001. Reprinted by permission of the licenser, Pelican Publishing Company, Inc.

Peter Pauper Press, Inc: Excerpt from a poem from *Fruits of the Earth* by André Gide, translated by B. A. Lenski. Copyright " 1969 by Peter Pauper Press. "Oblivion" from *Verlaine: Poems by Paul Verlaine*, translated by Jacques Leclerq. Copyright " 1961 Peter Pauper Press. Reprinted by permission of Peter Pauper Press, Inc.

Polish Institute of Arts and Sciences of America: "Pan Tadeusz" from *Polish Institute of Arts and Sciences of America* by Adam Mickiewicz, translated by Watson Kirkconnell. Copyright © 1962, 1981 by the Polish Institute of Arts and Sciences of America. Reprinted by permission of the Polish Institute of Arts and Sciences of America, 208 East 30th Street, New York, NY 10016.

The Prague Post: "Waggismania" by Eva Munk from the *Prague Post* (December 23, 1998). Reprinted by permission of the *Prague Post*.

Princeton University Press: "Mount of Olives" from Selected *Poems of Tudor Arghezi* by Tudor Arghezi. Copyright " 1976 by Princeton University Press. Reprinted by permission of Princeton University Press.

Ronnie Reed: "Starving Artist Soup" by Ronnie Reed. Reprinted by permission of the author.

Alan Rems: "Pesach Eve in Our Little Shtetl" by Hinde Binkovitz-Wiener, translated by Alan Rems. The story originally appeared as part of a collaborative effort with the Yizkor Book Project on the website of Jewish Gen, Inc. Reprinted by permission of the translator.

Hardie St. Martin: "The Meaning of Soup" by Gabriel Celaya, translated by Hardie St. Martin and Robert Mezey. Reprinted by permission of Hardie St. Martin.

Fenyvesi Sandor: "In Praise of Bouillon" by Berda József, translated by Fenyvesi Sandor. Reprinted by permission of the translator.

Scribner and A.P. Watt Ltd.: "A Prayer for My Son" from *The Collected Works of W. B. Yeats, Volume I: The Poems, Revised* by W. B. Yeats, edited by Richard J. Finneran. Copyright © 1928 by The MacMillan Company, copyright renewed © 1956 by Georgie Yeats. Reprinted by permission of Scribner, an imprint of Simon & Schuster Adult Publishing Group and A.P. Watt Ltd. on behalf of Michael B. Yeats.

Shambhala Publications, Inc.: Two haiku poems from *Narrow Road to the Interior* by Matsuo Bashō, translated by Sam Hamill. Copyright © 1998 by Sam Hamill. Reprinted by arrangement with Shambhala Publications, Inc., Boston, www.shambhala.com.

Louis Simpson: "A Story About Chicken Soup" by Louis Simpson. Reprinted by permission of the author.

Henry Taylor: "Canticle of Created Things" by Francis of Assisi, translated by Henry Taylor, from *An Afternoon of Pocket Billiards* by Henry Taylor. Copyright " 1972 by Henry Taylor. Reprinted by permission of the author.

Thy Tran: Excerpt from "Fish Sauce" by Thy Tran, from the *Washington Post* (January 29, 2003, F01). Reprinted by permission of the author.

University of California Press: "Ode to Conger Chowder" from *Selected Odes of Pablo Neruda*, translated/edited by Peden, Margaret Sayers, one ode, English translation of Conger Chowder. Copyright © 1990 by Regents of the University of California, © Fundación Pablo Neruda. Reprinted by permission of the Regents of the University of California and the University of California Press.

University of Minnesota Press: Slightly adapted version of "Recipe for Meatball and Dumpling Soup" from *Scandinavian Feasts: Celebrating Traditions Throughout the Year* by Beatrice Ojakangas. Copyright " 1992 by Beatrice Ojakangas. (University of Minnesota Press, 2001, pp. 148–49). Reprinted by permission of the University of Minnesota Press.

University of Texas Press: "Death Is Sitting at the Foot of My Bed" by Óscar Hahn, translated by Sandy McKinney, and "Provincial Sundays" by Ramón López Velarde, translated by Julian Manriquez, from *Twentieth-Century Latin American Poetry: A Bilingual Anthology*, edited by Stephen Tapscott. Copyright " 1996. Reprinted by permission of the University of Texas Press.

Tobias Yarmolinsky: "Spring" by Pyotr Vyazemsky from *Two Centuries of Russian Verse,* edited by Avrahm Yarmolinsky and translated by Babette Deutsch. Copyright © 1949 by Random House. Reprinted by permission of Tobias Yarmolinksy.

ACKNOWLEDGMENTS

Behind every book stand many hands, eyes, and, in this case, mouths. Thanks to Dave Bloom, who put me up to it. Thanks to my long-suffering children, Meg and Bill, who ate many bowls of soup along the way and lived to tell about it. Thanks to Art Meyer and Rita Rosenkranz, who saw a book in my website. Thanks to Nancy Manuszak, friend, editor, and cheerleader *extraordinaire*. And thanks to my editor, Carrie Thornton, and designer Lauren Dong, who shaped the final book with intelligence and grace.

Index

CONVERSION CHART

EQUIVALENT IMPERIAL AND METRIC MEASUREMENTS

American cooks use standard containers, the 8-ounce cup and a tablespoon that takes exactly 16 level fillings to fill that cup level. Measuring by cup makes it very difficult to give weight equivalents, as a cup of densely packed butter will weigh considerably more than a cup of flour. The easiest way therefore to deal with cup measurements in recipes is to take the amount by volume rather than by weight. Thus the equation reads:

1 cup = 240 ml = 8 fl. oz.   1/2 cup = 120 ml = 4 fl. oz.

In the States, butter is often measured in sticks. One stick is the equivalent of 8 tablespoons. One tablespoon of butter is therefore the equivalent to 1/2 ounce/15 grams.

SOLID MEASURES

| U.S. AND IMPERIAL MEASURES | | METRIC MEASURES | |
OUNCES	POUNDS	GRAMS	KILOS
1		28	
2		56	
3½		100	
4	¼	112	
5		140	
6		168	
8	½	225	
9		250	¼
12	¾	340	
16	1	450	
18		500	½

LIQUID MEASURES

FLUID OUNCES	U.S.	IMPERIAL	MILLILITERS
	1 teaspoon	1 teaspoon	5
¼	2 teaspoons	1 dessertspoon	10
½	1 tablespoon	1 tablespoon	14
1	2 tablespoons	2 tablespoons	28
2	¼ cup	4 tablespoons	56
4	½ cup		120
5		¼ pint or 1 gill	140
6	¾ cup		170
8	1 cup		240
9			250, ¼ liter
10	1¼ cups	½ pint	280
12	1½ cups		340
15		¾ pint	420
16	2 cups		450

OVEN TEMPERATURE EQUIVALENTS

FAHRENHEIT	CELSIUS	GAS MARK	DESCRIPTION
225	110	¼	Cool
250	130	½	
275	140	1	Very Slow
300	150	2	
325	170	3	Slow
350	180	4	Moderate
375	190	5	
400	200	6	Moderately Hot
425	220	7	Fairly Hot
450	230	8	Hot
475	240	9	Very Hot
500	250	10	Extremely Hot

Any broiling recipes can be used with the grill of the oven, but beware of high-temperature grills.

EQUIVALENTS FOR INGREDIENTS AND TOOLS

all-purpose flour—plain flour
baking sheet—oven tray
buttermilk—ordinary milk
cheesecloth—muslin
coarse salt—kitchen salt
cornstarch—cornflour
eggplant—aubergine

granulated sugar—caster sugar
half and half—12% fat milk
heavy cream—double cream
light cream—single cream
lima beans—broad beans
parchment paper—greaseproof paper
plastic wrap—cling film

scallion—spring onion
shortening—white fat
unbleached flour—strong, white flour
vanilla bean—vanilla pod
zest—rind
zucchini—courgettes or marrow